St. Peter's Sq.,

One of the main aims of the Education Reform Act has been to give parents more say in their children's education. But the school scene now is very different from twenty-five years ago, when today's parents were at school. And the new bill has changed the situation still more. So before they can take these new opportunities, parents need information.

What will be in the National Curriculum? What is the thinking behind the new exams? What are the advantages and disadvantages of opting out? How does the new situation affect children, parents, teachers, local authorities?

This book gives information and guidance on this and other questions. It is written for ordinary, non-specialist parents, who want to understand what is happening in their children's schools, and propose to get involved in supporting them.

Charles Martin has had thirty years' experience of teaching, and was Principal of Bilborough Sixth-Form College, Nottingham, from 1975 to 1987. He has written several books on educational subjects, including a series on moral education.

SCHOOLS NOW

A PARENTS' GUIDE

Charles Martin

A LION PAPERBACK
Tring • Batavia • Sydney

Copyright © 1988 Charles Martin

Published by
Lion Publishing plc
Icknield Way, Tring, Herts, England
ISBN 0 7459 1546 9

First edition 1988

British Library Cataloguing in Publication Data
  Martin, Charles
  Schools now.
  1. England. Schools
  I. Title
  371'.00942

  ISBN 0-7459-1546-9

Printed and bound in Great Britain by
Cox & Wyman, Reading

CONTENTS

Introduction — From the Butler to the Baker 7

1 The Education System — who's in charge? 11

2 Schools — how are they managed? 31

3 Children — and how to educate them 59

4 Parents — and their choices 74

5 A National Curriculum — for all? 97

6 Religious and Moral Education — the debate 126

7 Assessment — tests and grades 148

8 Standards — and how to raise them 173

9 Life after School — careers 188

10 Teachers — and how to make the best of them 205

11 Governors — and their task 224

Books and Reports 238

Abbreviations often used in Education 240

Addresses 242

School Expenditure 244

It is impossible to acknowledge individually all those who have contributed to this book. The friendships, conversations and arguments in several staff rooms; conferences and seminars galore; the many books, reports and articles — not least the weekly ministrations of the *Times Educational Supplement* — have taught me my trade. Many students have added their pennyworth. I should perhaps pay special acknowledgment to the National Association of Headteachers. Their local branch taught me what little I know of the real education that goes on in primary schools, and their Secondary Advisory Council, on which I was privileged to serve, was a revelation of information, sound sense and practical wisdom.

INTRODUCTION

From the Butler to the Baker

The new Education Reform Act 1988 is with us. After months spent winding its controversial way through Parliament and after millions of words in press and TV comment, it will come into force progressively over the next few years. Parents may well wonder what difference it will make and what these new opportunities are that they keep hearing about. This book will try to tell you, and much more.

There have been Education Acts — plenty of them — since the trend started in 1870. The most famous, in 1944, set the scene for the education of most of today's parents. The 1988 Act hit the headlines partly because it first made its appearance leading up to an election. For the first time, education was a major election issue. It also came after a long period of unrest and conflict in schools and followed a pay-and-conditions settlement imposed by the Secretary of State on battling teachers and local authorities — who both claimed it was his fault for not giving them enough cash. It was also hailed as being new and radical, making great changes. Some of its proposals were fiercely contested. The media enjoy controversy, so the areas of dispute were well and truly aired.

By way of introduction we might look at three things: what the Secretary of State hopes to achieve by this Act; a summary of what the Act says; and how it can be dealt with in a short book.

MR BAKER'S DREAM
According to the Secretary of State, the Act has three main aims:

- to improve the quality of education in our schools, colleges, polytechnics and universities;
- to raise the standards achieved by our pupils and students;
- to extend freedom of choice in education.

The Secretary of State acknowledges that much good work goes on in many schools and colleges. His predecessor said the same and even told us that he had come to realize that the teacher's task is a difficult one. But all schools and teachers are not as good as the best. Also, by comparison with other nations — especially competitors such as Germany and Japan — our pupils do not leave school with the same level of attainment. 'We have been letting too many of our children down. The brightest tend to pull through. But not all of them are fully challenged. And too many of the average and below-average are not engaged.' The Act is intended to provide a framework in which things can improve. Whatever his critics say, that's his story and he's stuck to it well enough to get the Act on the statute book.

WHAT THE ACT SAYS

l. A basic curriculum. This includes provision for religious education for all registered pupils, and a curriculum for all registered pupils of compulsory school age at the school (to be known as 'The National Curriculum') comprising core and foundation subjects. There will be tests of core and foundation subjects at age 7, 11 and 14. A National Curriculum Council and a School Examination and Assessment Council are being set up to supervise this.

This major topic is dealt with in chapters 5, 6 and 7.

2. Changes in the way admission to schools is controlled. The power of LEAs to fix limits in order to spread children among schools gives way to parents' ability to choose any school that is not 'full' to its actual capacity.

See chapters 4 and 11.

3. Local Financial Management. Instead of LEAs controlling almost all the schools' expenditure, a large part of this will be transferred to the control of the Governing Bodies of the schools. This will also include wider control over appointment and dismissal of staff.

See chapters 2 and 11, and chapter 10 as regards teacher appointment.

4. Changes in the daily 'act of worship'. Laid down by the 1944 Act, this need no longer be the whole school, but can be smaller groups. It need not be at the beginning of the day, but must still be every day. It must 'reflect the broad tradition of Christian belief' and be appropriate to pupils' age and aptitude, family background and religion.

See chapter 6.

5. The establishment of Grant Maintained Schools. The press have called this 'opting out'. Parents can vote to 'go it alone' with DES grant instead of LEA support and control.

See references in chapters 1, 4, 10 and 11.

6. The establishment of City Technology Colleges. These are being set up by individuals or corporate bodies in urban centres for pupils wishing to specialize in technology. There will only be twenty of them initially.

See mentions in chapters 1 and 4.

7. Control and funding of colleges of further and higher education, polytechnics and universities. Polytechnics to be controlled by a new Higher Education Corporation (not LEAs). Further education college governors are to have financial delegation and powers similar to those referred to above (3) for schools.

See mention in chapter 9, in relation to careers of pupils at school.

8. The Inner London Education Authority is to be disbanded. Its duties will be spread among the constituent boroughs.

9. The limitation of academic tenure by university staff.

WHAT DOES IT MEAN?

It is impossible to look at the 1988 Act in isolation. Many of its ideas have been discussed among teachers for ten years or more. The Inspectors of schools (HMI) published a document about curriculum in 1977; the Taylor Commission published a report about governors in the same year. Both contain many of the ideas behind the Act. The political drive behind the Act is part of a policy developing since 1979, when the Conservative Government came into power.

In January 1984 the seeds were watered by Sir Keith Joseph, then Secretary of State, in his 'Sheffield speech'. Working parties, papers and conferences have gone on ever since. Education Acts in 1980 and 1981 had made some changes. The 1986 Act made a major change in the importance of governing bodies and the involvement of parents. The 1988 Act completes the picture.

In discussing the 1988 Act I have therefore had to refer to a lot of the earlier discussion. I hope it is not too full of history and jargon. I have dealt with it on a topic basis — the idea of a national curriculum, assessment, and so on — rather than following the order in the Act. This has allowed more room for comment and to give the reader a clearer perspective on it all.

The content of the 1988 Act has been under discussion for a long time. Teachers and others have produced masses of information and good advice over this time, but not much agreement. Now that the Secretary of State has acted, firmly and clearly in one direction, a great deal of time and energy has gone into opposing his 'reform' and explaining why he has got it wrong. But now that it is law, the job is to understand it and live within it for the greatest good of the greatest number of children.

The last comparable — or even greater — change was the 1944 Act of Mr R.A. Butler. He has passed into honoured memory as the architect of our post-war education system, and much of his Act remains untouched and valuable.

A wag reminds us of the butler and baker in Pharaoh's prison, whose dreams were interpreted by Joseph (of Technicolour Dreamcoat fame). The butler was restored in honour to the court; the baker was executed. Our Baker has survived so far. We shall see how his dream works out.

A more hopeful parallel might come from Mr Butler's speech introducing his 1944 Act. Seeing the Roman Catholic Archbishop (who didn't like the Act) coming into the distinguished strangers' gallery, he quoted the hymn:

> Ye fearful saints, fresh courage take,
> The clouds you so much dread
> Are big with mercy and shall break
> in blessing on your head.

The opposition to Mr Baker has come only partly from the church, more from teachers. He hasn't quoted any hymns to them, though he has, incidentally, published an anthology of poetry while edging his Bill on its way.

CHAPTER 1

The Education System

who's in charge?

State education is relatively new in Britain — not quite 120 years old, in fact. Before 1870 schools were run by private individuals (good and bad) and a variety of voluntary bodies mostly connected with the church. From 1833 — when Parliament gave them £20,000 between them — the schools got some aid from public funds. Official opinion can be gauged from the Newcastle Commission set up in 1858 to propose measures for 'sound and cheap' education. The Commission came up with a 'payment by results' scheme (based on attendance plus three R's — a scheme which proved disastrous) and also said that compulsory attendance was 'neither attainable nor desirable'. Not a promising start, you may think.

However, a few years later, after a change of government, the Elementary Education Act 1870 was passed. It was heralded as a great step forward, providing 'elementary education for all' — i.e. up to 10 years old. By 1876 attendance was compulsory for all children aged 5 to 10 who lived within 2 miles' walking distance of school. These schools had sprouted up all over the country by the energetic efforts of the new schools boards, and you can still see the proud inscription 'Blogsburgh Board School' on some school buildings today. In 1899 the school-leaving age was raised to 12 and since then there's been no stopping it.

Diagram 1 shows that before 1962 you left on your 15th birthday (as many of today's parents remember). After that, the leaving date depends on your birthday. Those born between 1 September and 31 January leave at the end of the Easter term. Those born on other dates leave, in the official jargon, 'the Friday before the last Monday in May'. So children born in June and July actually get let off a few days' school. In 1972 the school-leaving age was raised to 16.

A DUAL SYSTEM: CHURCH AND STATE SCHOOLS

In 1870 the church was very possessive about education; after all, religious trusts and churches had provided most of the

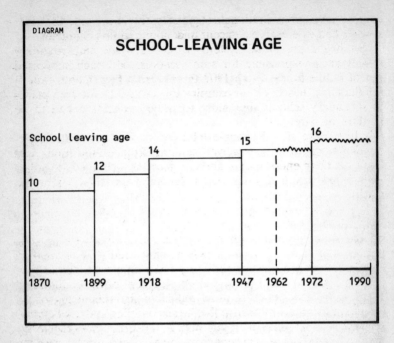

DIAGRAM 1

SCHOOL-LEAVING AGE

School leaving age

10 | 12 | 14 | 15 | 16

1870   1899   1918   1947   1962   1972   1990

nation's education for centuries. They could not possibly provide the greatly expanded service required, so some compromise was essential. The Act tried to acknowledge this religious heritage, without supporting any one denomination and it laid down that religious instruction in the new board schools must not include 'particular denominational catechisms or formularies'. So the Act 'annoyed the Church without satisfying the Non-conformists'. Mr Baker may be cheered to know he is not the first politician to disappoint everybody.

A major change came with the 1902 Education Act which abolished the school boards and put borough or county councils in charge of State education. They were the 'local education authorities' (LEAs) and were responsible for free elementary and paid secondary education. In addition, voluntary schools (those run by churches and a few other groups) got aid from the rates, amid great political uproar, including cries of 'Rome on the rates!' Rates were paid by everybody. Most of the voluntary schools were Church of England, with a few Roman Catholic. Non-conformists were not happy to think of their rates going to Anglicans or Roman Catholics, who could, of course, have denominational religious instruction, while the State schools had to preserve a decent undenominational character.

So began the 'dual system' with the State and voluntary bodies each responsible for some schools, and each supported out of public funds. From 1907 there were a few (means-tested) scholarships, based on an examination at age 11 for free places in secondary schools, but most secondary education had to be paid for by parents.

There were also the long-established public (now called independent) schools who received nothing from public funds and lived on their endowments and the fees they charged, together with a few tax and rates perks derived from their charitable status.

THE LEAs

So the local education authorities became a key factor in education — 'a national system locally administered'. There are now 104 LEAs with the responsibility to 'contribute towards the spiritual, moral, mental and physical development of the community' by making 'efficient education' available for the needs of all people in its area. In practice this means building and maintaining schools, setting up governing bodies, ensuring attendance by children, employing teachers, providing school meals, clothing grants, transport and other minor duties. Since 1944 all compulsory education in LEA schools has been free. LEAs are responsible in different ways for 'maintained' and 'voluntary' schools as will be explained later. They are not responsible for independent schools nor for the Grant Maintained Schools that may be set up under the 1988 Act nor for the City Technology Colleges (also set up under the Act) which started in 1988. The largest Authority, so large as to be in a class of its own, was the Inner London Education Authority (ILEA). Under the new Act this is to be disbanded and its duties given to individual inner London boroughs.

THE SECRETARY OF STATE AND HIS DEPARTMENT

Officials keep changing their titles. Up to 1964 we had a Minister of Education, now we have a Secretary of State for Education and Science who must 'secure the effective execution by LEAs of the national policy providing a varied and comprehensive education service in every area'. This is for England and Wales. Scotland and Northern Ireland each have their own departments.

13

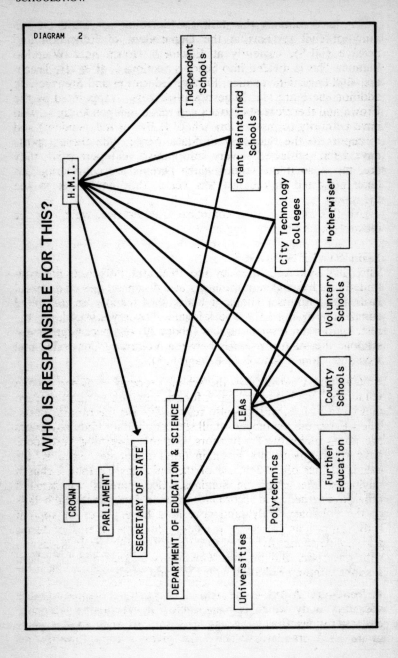

DIAGRAM 2

WHO IS RESPONSIBLE FOR THIS?

Independent Schools

Grant Maintained Schools

City Technology Colleges

"otherwise"

Voluntary Schools

County Schools

Further Education

H.M.I.

LEAs

Polytechnics

Universities

CROWN

PARLIAMENT

SECRETARY OF STATE

DEPARTMENT OF EDUCATION & SCIENCE

To assist him in this task the Secretary of State has an army of civil servants at the Department of Education and Science (DES), currently at Elizabeth House near Waterloo Station. This is divided into Schools Sections I, II & III, Teachers, Buildings, Universities, Further Education and Statistics. In addition there are Her Majesty's Inspectors — appointed by the Crown and therefore able to act and speak independently — who have authority to inspect *any* school (LEA or independent) and to report to the Secretary of State. Since 1982 these reports have been published — very informative and perceptive they are, too — so if the school which parents are considering has been inspected in the last few years, they could ask to see the report.

All this amounts to a complicated enterprise, which can be illustrated, roughly, by diagram 2.

VOLUNTARY SCHOOLS

The 'dual system' started by the 1870 and 1902 Acts has continued and has all the advantages and disadvantages of a typical British compromise. The large majority of schools are controlled completely by the LEA and known as 'county schools'. Of the rest, apart from a small number (about 20) of 'special-agreement schools' the main division is between Voluntary Controlled and Voluntary Aided Schools (see diagram 3).

● **Voluntary Controlled** — the school property is owned by the voluntary body but all expenses for maintenance or alteration are met by the LEA, which is also responsible for the running costs. The LEA is the 'employer' of all staff. Voluntary body governors are not a majority of governors, but the governing body does have some powers not given in other maintained schools; for example, 'out of school' use of the buildings, so that a church might use the school on Sundays. Also, parents can demand religious instruction in accordance with the denominational beliefs of the voluntary body, and governors have power to appoint staff (known as 'reserved teachers') for this. Dates of terms and holidays are fixed by the LEA (usually after discussion with governors and unions). Governors fix the times of school sessions (after consultation with LEA and headteacher).

● **Voluntary Aided** — the school property is owned by the voluntary body which is responsible for external maintenance and alterations (including any necessary to keep the property up to LEA standards). The LEA gives a grant towards this

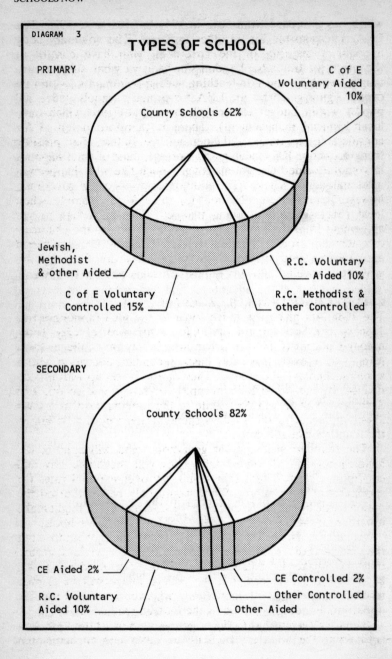

DIAGRAM 3

TYPES OF SCHOOL

PRIMARY

County Schools 62%

C of E
Voluntary Aided
10%

Jewish,
Methodist
& other Aided

C of E Voluntary
Controlled 15%

R.C. Voluntary
Aided 10%

R.C. Methodist &
other Controlled

SECONDARY

County Schools 82%

CE Aided 2%

R.C. Voluntary
Aided 10%

CE Controlled 2%

Other Controlled

Other Aided

which has increased from 50% in 1944 to 85% since 1975. The LEA is responsible for all other expenses. The voluntary body appoints a majority of the governors, who have control of the ethos of the school, admission policy, what subjects are taught, teaching and non-teaching staff appointments (within an overall figure given by the LEA for primary schools under 200 pupils; within budget for schools over that figure which have local financial management). There is therefore potential for considerable experiment and independence. In fact, apart possibly from distinctive RE teaching and worship, most of what happens in voluntary-aided classrooms is very much like what happens in most maintained schools. The additional powers of the governors, however, can raise complications for an LEA, for example, when local reorganization is being planned. The LEA has to get agreement from the governors for any alteration to the character or catchment area of a Voluntary Aided School. Dates of terms and holidays and times of the school day are fixed by the governors, usually following the pattern suggested by the LEA.

CITY TECHNOLOGY COLLEGES

The 1988 Act gives legislative force to the idea (announced in 1986 by the Secretary of State) for a 'network of City Technology Colleges (CTCs) in urban areas' — twenty colleges for a start — to 'provide a broadly based secondary education with a strong technological element'. These are to be set up with private finance, by individual philanthropists, industry, and so on. The Secretary of State will contribute to the running costs at a level about the same as the LEA is spending per pupil. It is hoped the founders will also chip in.

The founders will appoint governors, who will appoint the headteacher and all other staff. They will 'negotiate pay and conditions' which means they could pay over national rates for specialists in short supply. They would only be reimbursed the national rate by the LEA, and clearly LEAs fear CTCs might make it harder for them to get necessary staff for their own schools.

Admission is to be in the hands of the governors, but they must take from a specified catchment area and ensure that the intake is 'balanced' in ability. The curriculum will be 'broad and balanced' but the college image will be slanted towards technology with increased work experience and training opportunities being provided by the founding industries.

The City Technology Colleges get one section of the 1988 Act, authorizing the Secretary of State to 'enter into an agreement with any person who undertakes to establish and maintain' one. The section specifies that the school must be situated in an urban area and recruit pupils 'wholly or mainly . . . from the area in which the school is situated'. This will partly ease the anxiety that City Technology Colleges would become magnets pulling able technologists from miles around. Much depends on how 'wholly or mainly' is interpreted.

'OPTING OUT'

The new Act offers an opportunity of 'grant-maintained' (or 'opting out') status to all county and voluntary secondary schools, and all county and voluntary primary schools (but not Special Schools) with more than 300 pupils. This limits the opportunity for Grant Maintained School status to about one-quarter of schools. The 18,000 schools with less than 300 pupils will have to wait until the 'success' of the present limited opportunity is known. The Act gives the Secretary of State power to remove or modify the 300 limit if he thinks it right to do so. Governors may resolve to hold a ballot, or 20% of parents may request a ballot. If more than half the parents voting in a secret postal ballot agree, the governors must make a proposal to the Secretary of State asking for the status of Grant Maintained School (GMS). If the total number voting is less than half of all parents, a second ballot must be held. This time a simple majority is sufficient whatever the number voting. There are provisions for local people to object, but if the Secretary of State approves the application — by reference to criteria laid down — then the school becomes grant-maintained, and the new governing body is set up.

When a school becomes grant-maintained:

● Parents have a large say, with at least seven of the governors being parents. This will not be a majority. The majority of governors will be 'members of the local community, committed to the good government and continuing viability of the school'.

● The property is transferred to the new governors.

● Staff contracts, with all previous rights and duties, will be transferred to the new governors, who become the 'employer' and have to provide all necessary administration.

● The school is funded direct by the DES on a formula which gives about the same as other local schools get from the LEA per pupil.

● The school must follow the National Curriculum and teach

RE (former county schools according to the LEA agreed syllabus; former controlled or aided schools in accordance with previous practice).

• Admissions are at the discretion of the governors, but they cannot reduce this below the number in their original application.

• Governors must provide all administration, and also staff training, welfare services, or buy these in from the LEA.

• Changes in size or character of school can only be made with the further approval of the Secretary of State. In response to a Parliamentary question about the possibility of society being 'fragmented' by schools changing to control by a sect (Scientology was mentioned) he agreed that 'a proposal to change the religious ethos of a school is regarded as a significant change of character.'

• In certain cases the Secretary of State can close the school but only after five years' notice (i.e. after at least one General Election).

TYPES OF SCHOOL
In addition to all these different ways of control, there are also several ways of allocating pupils to the various schools.

Before considering the majority, it is fitting to consider the minority for whom life is specially hard, children with 'special needs'. For many years Special Schools — about 1,500 of them — catered for those with physical, emotional or mental handicap. Most were run by LEAs and some by voluntary agencies, providing outstanding care and education for 120,000 disadvantaged young people. The Warnock Committee of 1978 expressed concern that, even so, society was pushing these children to the sidelines. By keeping them in relatively few places, we were robbing them of normal social experience — and also robbing 'normal' children of the chance to meet those less physically fortunate. So there has been a bold attempt to include as many children as possible in 'normal' schools, providing specialist help where needed. A 'statement of needs' is prepared for each child in consultation with educational psychologist and medical or social worker reports. This states the nature of the handicap and the special help needed, such as individual or small group teaching. The more seriously handicapped will still need special schools. Some teachers doubt if 'normal' schools will be able to cope properly, especially where only two or three children are involved and the receiving school does not have the skills or ethos to accommodate them.

The most successful arrangement appears to be for one school to cater for all transfers in a neighbourhood. One such school in Northampton, specializing in speech-needs, has 100 'normal' children aged 5 to 9 with thirty special-needs children. There is also a nursery unit which contains a few special-needs children. The headteacher is enthusiastic — 'we have built up the right ethos, and there is a high standard of care among the children' — and so are parents, both of 'special-needs' and 'normal' children. Staffing ratio in special education is one teacher to seven children, more than twice the 'normal' so the cost per pupil is correspondingly high. The readiness to invest extra resources for the less fortunate is one mark of a humane society and the aim of integration, for all its difficulty, is a worthy ideal.

> 'Respect for human worth and dignity persists however disabled or deviant the individual . . . Special needs make acceptance by others an even more important part of personal security.'

Those working in this area feel that there is still more to be done. They fear that children may be recommended ('statemented') on grounds of what space is available, rather than making space expand to meet the need.

At secondary level, there are also LEA boarding schools where some places are available for those with special learning needs or particular family or personal difficulties who cannot be adequately dealt with in day schools. More is said about this in chapter 4.

For the rest, the vast majority, sound in mind and body, the 1944 Act laid down a selective system:

- 5-11 infant and junior schools;

- 11+ selection, based on school report and examination;

- 11-14/15/16 secondary modern schools; OR

- 11-18 grammar schools (or a few technical schools).

Gradually in the 1950s comprehensive reorganization began and gathered momentum so that by 1975 80% of secondary schools were comprehensive.

The Government circular of 1965 gave a variety of acceptable comprehensive schemes:

● 5-11 infant and junior followed by 11-18 comprehensive secondary;

● 5-11 infant and junior followed by 11-16 comprehensive secondary followed by 16+ sixth-form college, or further education college or tertiary college:

● 5-11 infant and junior followed by 11-14 junior comprehensive followed by 14-18 senior comprehensive;

● 5-8/9 first school followed by 8/9-12/13 middle school followed by 12/13-18 comprehensive secondary.

In practice 'comprehensive' has not always been truly comprehensive. Partly because a 'neighbourhood' school will take its character from the locality, which may be a one-class housing estate. Even when the intake has been more balanced, school management (see next chapter) has merely put selection *inside* the school. The change, apart from giving us the gruesome word 'comprehensivization' gave rise to heated argument, some of which will be looked at later under 'standards'. It has been defended and attacked on political, social and religious grounds — Jesus' parable of the talents has actually been pressed into service to support academic selection. The press find it all good copy, but only reflect deeply divided public opinion, shown for example by two letters from the very many trawled in by *The Sunday Times* in a 1977 series:

> 'My children's experience has proved to me that what seems fine in theory does not work in practice and I am now bitterly opposed to comprehensives, and am prepared to vote Conservative, much as it goes against the grain, to save the remaining grammar schools.'

> 'My two daughters go to a comprehensive school and — unfashionable little beasts that they are — they haven't been beaten up nor, as far as I know, have they done any beating up. Indeed they seem to be happy in a well-ordered atmosphere where they are being made to work hard by teachers who care very much that they should. It seems to me that all this agonising over comprehensives does not take into account areas where — as in ours — the schools went comprehensive early and a lot of money was spent on them.'

PARENTS

Parents now come on the scene. It seems as if they have plenty of choice. We shall see later how far this is true.

Section 36 of the 1944 Education Act lays down: ' . . . the duty of the parent of every child of compulsory school age to cause him to receive efficient full-time education suitable to his age, ability and aptitude either by regular attendance at school or otherwise.' 'Otherwise' includes an independent school not registered with DES, or educating at home. In these cases the LEA must be satisfied with the 'otherwise'. In 1977 an organization 'Education Otherwise' was founded to advise parents in such cases. A well-known system is provided by the Parents' National Educational Union (PNEU, Murray House, Vandon Street, SW1) which uses the individual-learning methods of education pioneer Charlotte Mason and 'provides guidance for parents living in remote places who accept the responsibility for teaching their own children.'

The 'compulsory school age' is 5 to 16, but many parents are anxious to have pre-school or nursery-school places for their children. This may be so that both parents can work, or to give children a better start to school. Teachers urge that such experience is good for intellectual, emotional, social and language development. LEAs are not obliged to provide this, though increasingly they do, often with nursery units attached to infant schools. Between 1960 and 1985 the proportion of children aged 3 or 4 in maintained nursery schools (part-time or full-time) rose from 14% to 43% of the age group, so it is rapidly becoming common practice. The National Association of Headteachers' policy is that LEAs should provide nursery education for all who request it, but that it should not be compulsory.

CENTRAL CONTROL

So the Secretary of State beams over his empire. Apart from the 7% of children in independent schools and the very few 'otherwise' — and even these have to be approved — he is responsible for all compulsory education in England and Wales, all non-advanced further education (FE Colleges) and has considerable powers over polytechnics and universities.

Centralization was a fear in 1944, but the Minister's power was limited by Section 112 which said that all regulations which he made under the Act must be laid before Parliament which had forty days in which to annul them if it wished. The new Act has similar provisions for some of the major Orders the Secretary of State can make, though many minor matters are left to him, sometimes 'after consultation'. Nobody is satisfied with 'consultation' — unless it provides the desired result — and in any case consultation always yields a mass of contrary opinion. This does not excuse high-handed lack of consultation, but it does take the shine off sweetly reasonable pleas that consultation (to quote one) 'could have indicated more fruitful lines for much needed investment in education'. Perhaps so, but there might have been ten different fruitful lines, and in fact the body that passed that resolution had voted 52 to 53 on the motion before it.

Local authorities have loudly complained that their power has been unwisely eroded. They are, they say, more able to listen to local opinion and take local facts into account. Their track record in this has not been uniformly good, and possibly part of the reason for the recent legislation has been Government determination to limit what they see as 'excesses' of a tiny minority of LEAs. In 1969 the Trades Union Congress said LEAs were 'too powerful'. Perhaps it depends upon whether LEAs are doing what you want them to do at the moment.

Power in a democracy is a tricky subject. In theory local or central government is responsive to the electors' wishes. But education is only one of the major factors in citizens' lives. Even if a teachers' or parents' lobby were to campaign on educational issues it is not clear they would influence votes more than other lobbies shouting about unemployment or tax or the Health Service. Of course, people who work in the system are not convinced that all electors understand it well enough to make a 'correct' judgment, anyway.

THE PROBLEMS FACING LEAs

Quite as serious is the task that the LEAs are left with. They still have to ensure that efficient education is available to everyone in their area. But they have less control and less room for manoeuvre than previously. Education is a lengthy business: quite apart from the possibility of higher education it occupies eleven years of every child's life and thirteen years for some. Changes take a long time to plan and work through. For example, the change to comprehensive schools from a selective school system takes seven years before the last 'selected' entry of 11-year-olds leave the sixth forms at 18. The changes due to falling rolls (fewer pupils due to lower birth rates in the 70s) could be foreseen and plans were made. Some schools had to close to keep viable numbers in others. These decisions have never been popular, but at least the decisions and appeals took place against firm knowledge of the facts. Now a school threatened with closure or change of status (from grammar to comprehensive, for example) might 'opt out' and become grant-maintained so altering the situation in which the LEA has to act. The decision to opt out might be pushed through by parents who had only two or three years more interest in the school. The LEA has to plan for much longer ahead. The new City Technology Colleges also affect the scene. They may take 200 children per year out of an LEA's responsibility — if parents get less excited by CTCs the LEA has to have reserve capacity available to absorb those returning to its fold.

There is also the danger that it will be the more able children with more powerful parents who will be sent to Grant Maintained Schools and City Technology Colleges, leaving the LEA with a far from normal cross-section of children. This will mean the LEA will be dealing always with schools that have been 'creamed' and will almost certainly not be able to support normal sixth-form courses.

The political justification for this is 'let a thousand flowers bloom'. Competition will improve everything. If the Grant Maintained Schools and CTCs do a good job, the LEAs will be jerked into action to improve their schools. But if the powerful parents and able children have opted out with Grant Maintained Schools and the vocationally aspiring go to CTCs, then the LEA is left with the least manageable schools, probably in the most under-privileged areas — and then told to 'compete'. It is true that hints have been given that Grant Maintained Schools and CTCs must take a balanced intake, but the LEAs' anxiety is understandable.

POLITICAL FOOTBALL
It is a tragedy that education has become a political football. Local and central government can change every four or five years which is far too short a time to implement and assess any change. This is a classic problem of power in a democracy: we can't trust those we elect for long enough to leave them in charge long enough to get their plans completed.

For example, following a House of Commons motion in January 1965 to abolish selection at 11+, Circular 10/65 told LEAs to submit plans for reorganizing their areas on comprehensive lines if they hadn't already done so. In 1970 a Conservative Government was returned and LEAs slowly got on with the request. In 1976 the Labour Government passed the Education Act of 1976 making comprehensive reorganization compulsory. In 1979 the Conservative Government repealed this.

When changes in local and central government interact, the

result can be even worse. An example: in 1976, the Labour authority in Tameside set up a plan to make Tameside schools comprehensive. In May they were replaced by Conservatives who cancelled the plan. The Labour Government tried to make the LEA continue with the plan but in August the Law Lords by a three-to-two majority upheld the LEA. By then it was too late to alter the arrangements for September, so one year of all-ability pupils entered the secondary schools that were neither staffed nor prepared to deal with them. A teacher wrote 'the whole show is a farce in educational terms . . . we watch the alien wedge gradually gouging its way through the school to its release. It would have been better for them had the system changed as it was intended . . . But don't go away folks. Our political masters are staging a re-run of the old '76 performance. This time the fight will take place with the Council in the Red corner and the Government in the Blue corner.' Worthy of Gilbert and Sullivan if it were not so serious.

When views of what should be done are so polarized, a sensible and balanced outcome is difficult to achieve. LEAs may be cast in the role of 'baddies' with Mr Baker and the parental cavalry coming over the hill to rescue the beleaguered schools. Or LEAs may be seen as knights in shining armour defending educational damsels from dragons or wicked political uncles. Neither view helps discussion or long-term planning. There are, and have been over the years, many people of ability and goodwill in the community, people of all parties who have worked together to establish the best system they could for the locality. In some areas this still goes on but increasingly it is made harder by two factors.

First, education is being asked to do more and more for society. As other agencies, such as family or church, have become weaker, schools have been set the task of inducting children into the ways and values of society. People with strong views of how society should be changed see the schools as the place to get their message across. So, for example, the newspaper headline 'Swann Report asks schools to help change attitudes' (on racism). This may show a pathetic trust in the power of schools (after all, children spend longer in front of a TV set than they spend in front of a teacher), but it does raise fears of 'social engineering'.

Second, education is a big spender. Education Committees do have considerable power. Put cynically, some people could be more anxious to get the committee experience and political limelight than to devote many years to steadily co-operating with all concerned to improve the system. Less cynically, it still must be faced that chairmen of committees like to have 'sound' people with them. This forces people to 'take a stand', rather than be open to argument and looking for consensus. In many Education Committees, the 'party groups' meet before the actual Committee meeting to 'go over the agenda'.

A BIG BUSINESS

Nationally education is a major undertaking. In purely administrative terms, LEAs are looking after more than seven million children in over 25,000 schools. Diagram 4 shows the size of the enterprise.

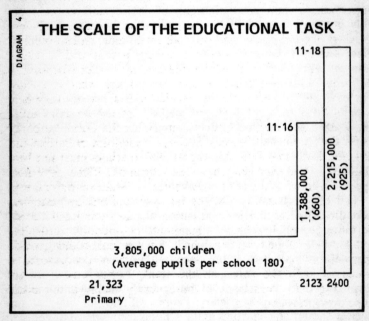

THE SCALE OF THE EDUCATIONAL TASK

DIAGRAM 4

11-18

11-16

2,215,000 (925)

1,388,000 (660)

3,805,000 children
(Average pupils per school 180)

21,323
Primary

2123 2400

In addition there are colleges of further education catering for two million students over 16. The whole programme takes about half a million teachers, 150,000 ancillary staff and 20,000 or so for administration. Independent schools cater for about half a million children, but of course the LEA and DES have no responsibility for them.

This makes education one of the largest public undertakings in terms of the number of customers. As an employer, it is second only to the Health Service. It is certainly the biggest compulsory happening in the country. There are few other things you *must* do with children once you have registered their birth. It is a remarkable instance of what can be done by legislation where there is wide consensus. The docility with which millions of Mums and Dads pack their children off to school every morning would astound the Newcastle Commission with its belief that 'compulsory attendance is neither attainable nor desirable'.

For the majority of families, school is necessary for child-minding while both parents are at work. Most parents also hope schools are doing for the children what they cannot do themselves. But the situation is an ironic example of the complex relationships in a modern society. The State pays great lip service to the importance of parents, their rights of choice, and so on — but only in the context of this massive exercise in coercion. Before the days of compulsion (and still today with independent schools) there was a contract between a willing parent and a willing teacher. The teacher acted for the parent. *In loco parentis* is the legal term and there is case law to say what it means. For example, a colourful case decided that a teacher may beat a pupil 'as a reasonable parent might', but not so as to cause his death. Now the teacher acts as much for the Local Authority as for the (compelled) parent. Society, in the form of Parliament, has laid down that from 15 August 1987 teachers must not beat children — but may give them sex education, if the governors approve, 'in the context of family values' — whatever parents say.

It is big business. Too big by far to let ten million customers have anything like individual attention. On the other hand it could be more charitably seen as a mammoth co-operative, providing a highly developed service which few parents could provide themselves, and also giving society the trained workforce it needs to keep the show on the road. Either way it is not surprising that accusations of bureaucracy, delay and muddle arise every now and then.

THE EXPENSE OF THE SYSTEM

State education accounts for about 11.5% of all UK government expenditure, that is about 5% of the national income (GDP). A lot more is provided by local authorities from the rates. Education is by far the largest spender in local government finance. A typical County Council budget might look like diagram 5.

Within the education section the budget looks like diagram 6. (The 1988 Act takes away the polytechnic responsibility).

This shows the weight of resources towards secondary school (£1,400 per pupil) against primary school (£930). Primary teachers

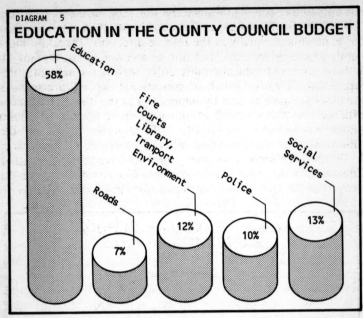

DIAGRAM 5
EDUCATION IN THE COUNTY COUNCIL BUDGET

Education 58%

Roads 7%

Fire Courts Library, Tranport Environment 12%

Police 10%

Social Services 13%

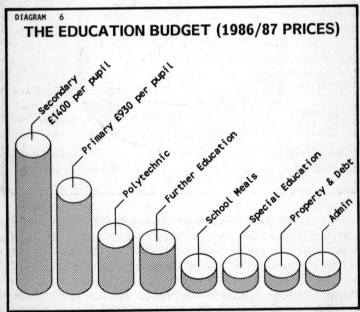

DIAGRAM 6
THE EDUCATION BUDGET (1986/87 PRICES)

Secondary £1400 per pupil

Primary £930 per pupil

Polytechnic

Further Education

School Meals

Special Education

Property & Debt

Admin

not unnaturally complain. Since the war they have dropped from 32% of all educational expenditure to about 21% while secondary has gone almost equally in the reverse direction. There are more pupils in secondary now, but not to account for that swing. It is hard to avoid educationalist John Vaizey's comment: 'this represents a massive switch of educational expenditure towards the older age groups, and by implication in the direction of those with social and educational advantages; that is, favouring Robbins rather than Newsom and Plowden' (the reference is to three educational reports recommending different priorities in education).

Within each section, salaries and wages are the biggest item. Education is the most labour-intensive industry there is, as the analysis of the secondary education budget in diagram 7 shows.

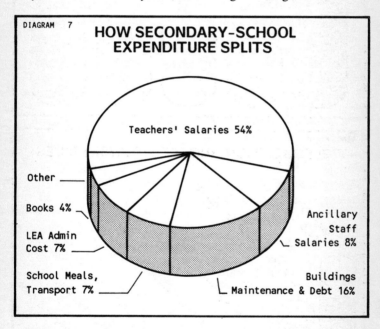

DIAGRAM 7

HOW SECONDARY-SCHOOL EXPENDITURE SPLITS

Teachers' Salaries 54%

Other

Books 4%

LEA Admin Cost 7%

School Meals, Transport 7%

Ancillary Staff Salaries 8%

Buildings Maintenance & Debt 16%

With such a huge demand for resources, it is no wonder that education attracts attention and is asked to account for all the money that is spent on it. It is notoriously difficult to measure 'output'. You can tell if manufacturing industry exports 5% more by volume. But can you talk about schools giving children 5% more knowledge, skill, confidence or charm? Needless to say, those who work in the system say all this money isn't enough. By way of comparison they use the independent sector.

In 1980 the Government began a controversial scheme to fund 6,000 places a year in independent schools. This 'assisted places' scheme was to 'extend choice' especially for poorer families. In fact one independent school headteacher said, 'I've never seen so many people who were so good at falsifying their incomes' — the aspiring working class are under-represented.

However, Michael Pipes, NAHT President, made ingenious use of the arrangement. He showed that the cost to each Authority for an assisted place was almost everywhere more than the authorities spent on their own schools. So he good-naturedly challenged the independent schools — 'Either they are overcharging, or we are underfunded.'

Just to keep the record straight it must be said that another body — the Policy Study Unit plugging Grant Maintained Schools — used the same comparison saying 'some local authorities spend more per pupil than is spent by parents sending a child to a local independent school. Certainly in ILEA . . . ' True for ILEA and two other authorities out of sixty-five for which comparison can be made. You have to be careful with statistics.

The question remains as to how you can assess what education should have. 5% of the national income is twice the proportion it had in 1950, but young people stay far longer in education and far, far more go on to university. Statistics show that the highest spending authorities do not all get the best results (at least in examinations) though, of course, they may have different shares of underprivilege to cope with. Money isn't the only thing, but it is a necessary factor. It needs to be 'targeted', perhaps. At the moment a high priority must be the in-service training of teachers to cope with all the new examinations and courses with which they are being faced.

CHAPTER 2

Schools

how are they managed?

The LEAs and voluntary bodies between them provide more than 25,000 schools. LEAs lay down very broad guidance on how schools should be run, within national Education Acts. The 1988 Act is much more specific than any previous regulation, particularly about what is to be taught, as chapter 5 'A National Curriculum' will explain. But in the UK individual schools still enjoy great freedom, to the envy of many other countries. This chapter looks at the ways in which this freedom is used, and the opportunities it presents.

Each school has a board of governors, and they get a chapter to themselves later on (chapter 11). They, either alone or with the LEA, appoint a headteacher, whose powers and responsibilities are laid down in the Articles of Government. These usually follow the model Articles (1944) which state that the Head 'shall control the internal organization, management and discipline of the school and . . . shall exercise supervision over the teaching and non-teaching staff.'

This gives a very wide scope — how wide can be appreciated when it is spelt out in more detail:

1. **Internal Organization**. Some things are laid down by governors and LEA, such as whether the school is comprehensive or selective, the age range covered, the admission policy and (within limits) the numbers of pupils, whether single sex or mixed, and what sort of buildings. From then on the headteacher can decide the 'internal organization', such things as:

● How pupils are organized for administration and pastoral care:
— in year groups with Year Head and Year Tutors (horizontal);
— in 'houses' spanning all ages, with House Head and House Tutors (vertical);
—arrangements for registration, sick-notes, day-to-day communication, record keeping.

● How pupils are taught:

— in groups of the same age (mixed ability);
— in some primary schools, in groups of different ages (family);
— in groups according to general ability (streamed);
— or according to ability in particular subjects (setting), sometimes with special small group or individual teaching for pupils with particular needs; high ability or learning difficulty in some area.

● How time is spent:
— how much time for form periods or tutor groups;
— how much time for 'subject' teaching;
— how much time for general education, assembly, games, lunch-time arrangements, school meals.

● How resources are allocated:
— by headteacher alone, or a committee of staff;
— whether on large items for whole school (reprographic facilities, audio-visual equipment, computers) or for classroom materials.

● How pupils (and staff and parents) understand the system:
— bulletins, handbook, letters home, reports.

● How parents and outsiders relate to school:
— governors' meetings, parents' meetings, LEA officials, advisors, inspectors, school medical service.

All these represent decisions about how the total resources of the school are to be used. All have been the subject of much debate and some will be dealt with in more detail later. Here we pick on one for comment: consider the grouping of children in classes. Many parents and teachers take it for granted that all pupils will be in classes with those of the same age. Why should this be? Children go to ballet classes, music lessons, swimming instruction at all sorts of ages. They develop physically and emotionally, and probably mentally at different rates. Those who have taught in African schools know it is not unusual to have pupils of 15, 16, up to 25 years of age in one class. Some primary schools in Britain have 'family' groups spanning two or three years, sometimes on grounds of fitting numbers into rooms, sometimes on educational grounds of different development. Unfortunately they all have to move on willy-nilly at 11 or whatever transfer age is fixed by the LEA.

2. **Management.** The headteacher is responsible for the smooth running of the organization. Under the 1988 Act Local Financial Management gives responsibility for a large part of the school's

finance to the governors, who will delegate it to the headteacher. Management involves accountability and delegation. Current jargon talks rather grandly about a 'Senior Management Team', which in a primary school can be headteacher, deputy and one other teacher. In a secondary school, the headteacher and the two or three deputies may meet regularly to consider general policy, monitor day-to-day goings-on and divide regular administration among them, so that, for example, one deputy may be responsible for curriculum, one for pastoral care and one for administration as their first task.

All staff share in this to some extent but a key part is the school office and ancillary services. They do most of the routine work of maintaining records, internal communication, returns to LEA and so on.

In these two areas of organization and management, there are routine 'housekeeping' matters — what happens when windows are broken, or the flat roof leaks; who orders supplies, supervises ancillary staff, sees that health and safety regulations are observed, deals with accidents? Many of these involve routines laid down by LEA. Management structures have to ensure that someone is responsible to see that what is necessary gets done. One school bursar I knew had the splendid, brief (and probably unofficial) job-description 'to do everything necessary to enable the teachers to teach.'

3. **Discipline.** This is not only (or mainly) dealing with naughty children, but with maintaining a firm and reliable framework in which everyone can work. Staff and pupils know what is expected. This includes things like uniform, on which the law has always given governors and headteachers a fairly free hand. Arguments about uniform arise from time to time — very frequently with pupils, as any form tutor or deputy head knows. The main arguments are that it gives pupils an identity with the school, and also stops any ostentatious display by some wealthy child coming in very expensive or way-out gear. Clothing grants are available, so it is said the advantages need not cost any family unduly. Against this is the general disinclination of pupils, certainly of older pupils, who resent being told what to wear and will cheerfully settle for their own 'uniform' of jeans, T-shirt and Parka jacket. A recent law case overturned a headteacher's ruling that a Sikh boy could not wear a turban to school. Most schools now allow Muslim girls to wear their traditional clothing.

Discipline also includes sanctions for those who don't do what they are supposed to. Under the 1986 Act corporal punishment is banned (from 15 August 1987) in State schools. Independent schools are not covered by this, except that they must not beat pupils who are financed by the LEA through the Assisted Places scheme! Corporal punishment was in fact being phased out in the great majority of State schools before this Act came into force, though teachers have complained that it needed to be done very gradually with other sanctions being made available. 'Alternatives' usually involve more personal counselling, and therefore much more staff time. The brunt of discipline is borne by the Year or House Head. Class teachers and form tutors deal with a lot of day-to-day matters, but hardy offenders end up outside the Year Head's door. Sometimes parents will be asked to come and talk matters over with staff and pupil. The Articles of Government give the headteacher 'power of suspending pupils from attendance for any cause which he considers adequate, but . . . he shall forthwith report the case to the governors who shall consult the LEA.' This has to be weighed against the LEA's responsibility to give everyone education in their area. So if Harriet is suspended from school X and the governors don't want to re-admit her, the LEA has to find another school for her. Independent schools can, of course, expel whom they like with no responsibility for their further education. For Grant Maintained Schools there is an appeal committee which parents of expelled pupils can approach, but the governors do not have to ensure continued education elsewhere.

This part of the headteacher's duties absorbs a lot of time, and a lot of time of other staff. It also attracts the most publicity. Pupils regale parents with horror stories, and the media don't line up outside schools where there is no trouble.

4. **Supervision of teaching and non-teaching staff.** Details of appointment procedures are given in chapter 10. Under the 1988 Act (except in primary schools with fewer than 200 pupils) the governors have control of appointment and dismissal of staff.

Except for very small primary schools — those with less than three teachers — every school must have at least one deputy head. Two or three can be appointed in a secondary school. Teaching staff may be given 'incentive allowances' (previously known as 'scale posts') carrying additional salary for particular duties or expertise within the school.

This part of the headteacher's task is perhaps the most important — even unique, as teachers are professionals, with

34

their own skills, enthusiasms and priorities, often individualistic. It is not like an industrial or commercial structure of Chiefs and Indians; all staff are chiefs in their own classrooms or special responsibilities. Headteachers, Heads of Year, Heads of Department are described as 'facilitators' or 'team leaders' rather than 'directors'. The new conditions of service imposed by the Secretary of State after the dispute in 1987 go some way to lay down what teachers should do, and specify five training days and 1,265 hours per year 'directed by the headteacher' apart from marking and preparation that may be done at home. But even this greatly increased power of direction will be used by most Heads with more consultation and consideration than the average shop steward or foreman might think necessary. How staff are deployed will show the priorities and philosophy of governors and headteacher. More will be said about this later.

So the headteacher surveys her corner of the empire. (There are considerably more women than men teachers, and although management by no means reflects this, women do hold far more management positions proportionally than in industry, so I deliberately jolt the reader's stereotype from time to time.) Systems grow slowly, so unless she is starting a new school, there will be many routines that have been going for a long time, and many staff who know 'how we've always done things'. The system has to be kept going. If it were just like painting the Forth Bridge it would be easy. But it is more like painting a train going quickly over the bridge. Society changes, the world into which the children will go changes, new courses are devised, new compromises in the perennial dilemmas are tried out. Change happens when people analyze what the school is doing and compare it with what they hear from inspectors or other teachers on courses, or read about other schools in the teaching periodicals. Individual teachers may change their own teaching styles. Wider change of structure needs consultation and as broad agreement as possible. What follows should help parents get an idea of the complexity of running a school.

WHAT IS THE SCHOOL TRYING TO DO?

Two very basic parts of the plan are:

• Getting pupils in — at 5, 7, 8, ll, 12, 13 or 16;

• Getting pupils out to the next stage — next school, higher education, YTS, employment.

What happens in between usually gets the attention and will be considered later. These two activities take up a great deal of time and resources and so need discussion.

- **Getting pupils in.** A small primary school may admit fifteen to twenty 5-year-olds, some from the nursery section and some who haven't been to school before. A large secondary school may admit 300 pupils from ten primary schools. Either way parents are involved and meetings arranged. Children are taking a new step forward in their career and may be apprehensive. Arrangements are made for them to visit the new school, and in some cases to spend two or three days there in the summer term, to get familiar with the place and the people who will teach them. Teachers know the system and face the annual chore of making new record cards, filling in sheaves of forms, telling all the new pupils the same story of how we do things here. They try hard to remember that for Mary or Tariq it is all very new, rather exciting and a bit frightening.

In the primary section the great resource is time — a lot of time is spent individually, in small groups and also with the whole class to help pupils to feel at home and confident in the school. In secondary schools hours of work goes into 'transfer'. The Head of First Year, or Heads of Houses, will have strong liaison links with the primary schools they take from, arranging visits in the summer term, giving out literature for parents, organizing parents' meetings. All teachers involved with the new intake have to meet and be briefed. The first few days of the new term see forms filled in, regulations explained, questions answered, timetables explained and, in all the new classrooms, books given out, and information on how things will be in this new lesson. Gradually pupils settle and within a week or two feel quite at home, the more adventurous having explored the building and heard from older children a brief outline of what you can get away with. The school office grinds out the paperwork and answers scores of telephone enquiries from parents.

- **Getting pupils out.** For infant and junior pupils moving on to the next school the 'transfer' process works the other way. The teacher responsible for liaison with the new school has to see that documents are up to date and passed on, visits arranged, and individual parent's questions dealt with.

At secondary school the 'getting out' involves a small army. Those going to higher education need to have university (UCCA) or polytechnic (PCAS) forms and references prepared. Those going to further education will need forms and references completed. Those going to YTS or employment will need references. That's only the tip of the iceberg. Pupils need more than paper; they need skills and guidance. So there will be a career specialist co-ordinating a team of tutors and teachers who give individual guidance and some group teaching. Practice interviews, work-experience, a library section on employment and higher education information, it all adds up to a big chunk of resources. What sort of resources and how they are applied will show the school's ethos and priorities. In practice the headteacher has a great influence here. If he is a successful product of the system, and thinks the school's main aim is to get people into higher education, then the careers library will major on university prospectuses and information about the professions. The merits of university and polytechnic courses will be discussed and students coached for interview. Lesser mortals will get a careers interview in spring, with the County Careers Officer.

If, on the other hand, the headteacher values all children and their future occupations, the careers library will start at Abattoir, not Accountancy; all pupils whatever their exit will learn together some of the same basic life skills, employment skills, how to get access to higher education, YTS or employment. Each pupil will get individual counselling. Parents are usually welcome to join in this if they ask, but are *invited* only to a general 'careers' evening. As we shall see in considering curriculum, the school's attitude to 'leavers' will affect what is taught in 14- to 16-year-old classes and in the one-year sixth-form courses. Many courses aim specifically to help the less academically able children move confidently to the next stage of their career.

HELPING PUPILS GROW

In between getting them in and getting them out, what are we doing? The happiest description of schools is 'people-growing places'. Development is the key concept; not filling empty brain-boxes, or programming robots, but helping children grow. They grow all the time, of course, at home, at play and asleep. School helps in ways that can be expressed by looking at two possible diagrams (for a secondary school).

The first model (diagram 8) makes passing exams the main function of the school. You grow by getting knowledge and skills in subject packages that are tested by public examination at the end. The second model (diagram 9) makes personal development the main factor, with provision for getting people through any exams they need. Both models contain important truths.

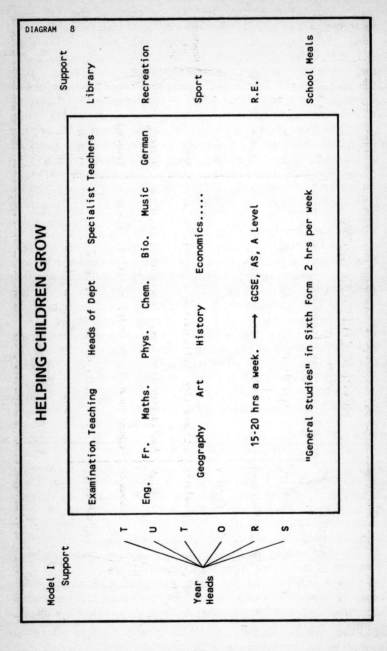

DIAGRAM 8

HELPING CHILDREN GROW

Model I
Support

Year Heads

T
U
T
O
R
S

Examination Teaching   Heads of Dept   Specialist Teachers

Eng.   Fr.   Maths.   Phys.   Chem.   Bio.   Music   German

Geography   Art   History   Economics......

15-20 hrs a week. ⟶ GCSE, AS, A Level

"General Studies" in Sixth Form 2 hrs per week

Support

Library

Recreation

Sport

R.E.

School Meals

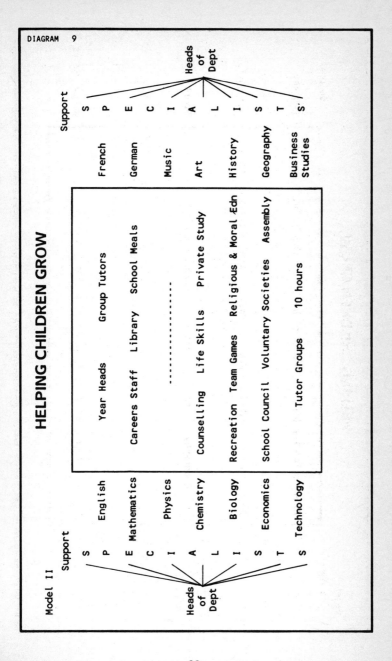

DIAGRAM 9

HELPING CHILDREN GROW

Model II

Support

	Heads of Dept
S	P
P	English
E	Mathematics
C	
I	Physics
A	Chemistry
L	
I	Biology
S	Economics
T	
S	Technology

Year Heads   Group Tutors

Careers Staff   Library   School Meals

- - - - - - -

Counselling   Life Skills   Private Study

Recreation   Team Games   Religious & Moral Edn

School Council   Voluntary Societies   Assembly

Tutor Groups   10 hours

Support

	Heads of Dept
S	French
P	
E	German
C	
I	Music
A	Art
L	
I	History
S	Geography
T	
S	Business Studies

Twenty years ago the first was accepted without question. Staff were appointed by secondary schools for their specialist knowledge and it was assumed they would cope with 'looking after a form' and helping with games. Few schools would accept the second entirely — as any school timetable will show — but increasingly emphasis is being put on 'general education', the parts examinations don't test. Some staff are appointed for skill and experience in administration, counselling, pastoral work and team leadership. They teach a reduced timetable in whatever subject they are trained in, but it is not their principal job. More will be said about this in chapter 5. For the moment, note the management problems raised. The same staff are doing two or more jobs — as specialist teachers of subjects and as part of a general education and pastoral support system. Both functions are equally necessary and should therefore have a share in time and responsibility allowances.

If Mr Smith is a form tutor, he may have to cope at 2 p.m. with George whose bike is missing and Doreen who appears without a note explaining the last two days' absence. He gives George suggestions about who to see immediately, cross-examines Doreen quickly on the unlikely excuse, arranges to see them both at 4 p.m. then dashes off to the lab. to teach the third form Physics. If he is lucky a technician will have set up the equipment. Even so it demands flexibility of mind, and constant judgment about priorities. Meanwhile Mrs Vara (deputy Year Head) is talking to Sandra who, at 15 years of age, has been pushed out of home by an angry Dad. The immediate problem is to find out where she will go this evening from school, while meetings are arranged with parents to try to sort things out. Ringing round friends and calls to Social Services are long drawn out. The time draws on to 3 p.m. when Mrs Vara has to teach second form Geography. She arranges to see Sandra at 4 p.m., leaves some instructions with the office, and hopes she can get through her lesson without interruption.

Unfortunately, teachers' initial training is mainly about teaching their subject in a classroom, and very little about the other things. So it is no wonder that many teachers — especially those trained for a grammar school — should see the general education as less important. In-service training helps bring people up to date, but staff don't readily change the educational philosophy of a lifetime. The 1988 Act says the right things in section 1 — 'spiritual, moral, cultural, mental and physical development' — but then lapses into talk of 'subjects' only.

Headteachers sometimes adopt a so-called 'matrix system' to show how staff are being used (see diagram 10). This will show

DIAGRAM 10

HOW STAFF ARE USED

	Head of Year	Asst Head of Year	Head of Careers	Careers Teacher	I/C Resources	I/C Assembly	Group Tutor	No Pastoral Responsibility
Head of Dept							:·:	·
2nd in Dept			·	··			:·:	
Specialist Teacher	··	···	·	···	·	·	:·:	·
General Teacher	··							
No teaching commitment								

how staff divide their responsibilities, and also how the resources of staff (and incentive allowances) are being used. This is an example of what was said earlier about staff deployment showing the priorities and philosophy of governors and headteacher.

Another diagram can be drawn to show how staff teaching time is spent. Such an analysis usually shows, in secondary schools, that the first three years subsidize the rest. Lower school sets are all fairly large — twenty-five to thirty pupils. When pupils are put into their 'options' in fourth and fifth years, the sets are much smaller, say ten or less for some subjects. In the sixth form still smaller sets appear — half a dozen doing A-level French and even fewer for Music. If the sixth form gets *very* uneconomic, the LEA may try to combine — either by a 'consortium' with, say, three schools making up one sixth form with viable sets staffed by members of all three schools' staff, or by a sixth-form college or tertiary college. Such plans are always fought by parents with 'Save our sixth-form' slogans. The management problem remains — should older children get a bigger chunk of resources?

In primary schools the teaching/care division is less sharp. Pupils spend nearly all their time with one teacher and so a strong relationship is built up in which instruction, teaching, supervision and general guidance go together.

This all adds up to a complicated management exercise. Much depends upon the basic educational philosophy which makes the priorities. Enthusiasts abound for mutually exclusive ideals. A headteacher has to listen, negotiate, encourage, postpone and limit, within the staff resources available. HMI reports consistently say the headteacher is the deciding factor in the school's ethos and style (and often success).

To most parents, however, and to the press, problems come one at a time — 'why don't they do something about X?' — not as part of a total management package. Some of these issues do merit consideration on their own, so we consider size, teaching style, mixed ability, the school and community, multi-cultural education, and the new local financial management.

SIZE — IS SMALL BEAUTIFUL?

Parents and some teachers often complain that schools are too big — not primary schools because they are usually 300 pupils or less, much as parents remember about their own school days. Comprehensive secondary schools get a bad press for being '2,000+ monstrosities'. Two things must be said at once:

● Very few schools are that big. Only half a dozen, at the most, are over 2,000. Most are between 750 and 1,500.

● The schools everyone remembers where 'the Head knew everyone' are usually myths. A distinguished Head in the last century, Dr Thring of Uppingham school, said that 300 was the largest number of pupils one teacher could hope to influence personally, and technology has not done much to extend that. Putting a name to 600 children (and that is quite a feat) is not 'knowing' them. I worked with a headteacher who taught all the first years (11-year-olds) for RE one lesson a week, so at the end of the year he knew all of them by name and more about some of them. So he knew the name of practically all the 700 pupils in the school. But if he was seeing a parent, he would either get briefed by the form teacher or ask the form teacher to be present. What matters is not that someone knows all the children, but that every child is *well* known by at least one teacher — Form Tutor, Year Head or House Head.

Having said that, the management problems of a large school do have to be recognized. The advantages are many:

● Because there are so many children in each year group, there are enough wanting to do all the options on offer. Sensible size sets can then be made. This means that teaching groups in the lower school can be smaller because they don't have to subsidize the richer curriculum in the upper school. One large school will have the same clerical staff as three smaller ones, but they will be concentrated more efficiently, so staff get much better clerical support. A first-class reprographic installation is a luxury only a large school can afford, but adds enormously to teachers' ability to prepare good lesson material.

● Expensive facilities for drama, music, science, engineering, technology and art, which would be beyond the reach of three smaller schools, can be provided in the combined larger school.

● Specialist staff who might be the only ones in their subjects in a small subject, have support from the others needed in the department in a larger school. Teams of staff can work together on curriculum development in ways that would strain the resources of a smaller school.

But there is a price to pay for all this. Staff may feel lost and not very important in a staff room (or staff rooms) of a hundred; they don't even know the names of some staff. Communication lines may be long, so staff can't get things done quickly enough. There may less emotional satisfaction — in a small school it is easy to see when you succeed, and other people see it too. But in a large school who knows, who cares?

A headteacher of a very successful large comprehensive school said, 'It is a general rule of thumb that the advantages of a large school accrue to the children and the disadvantages to the staff.' The job of management is to create a system that keeps the advantages for the children but makes things as easy as possible for the staff. It isn't impossible but it does call for very high management skills.

'FORMAL' AND 'INFORMAL' TEACHING

Parents often comment on how different schools are nowa-days — 'not like in our time, when we sat in rows and listened to teacher. Now they sit round tables or mill about the room. I don't know how they learn anything.' Sometimes primary schools are actually built on 'open plan' which makes impossible the old four-walls-of-the-classroom. Cynics would say this is as much to save money as because of educational ideals. Nevertheless, the question of teaching style has attracted attention.

The trend from class teaching towards individualized learning started in the 1960s and was commended by the Plowden Report (1966). 'We recommend a combination of individual, group and class work, and welcome the trend towards individual learning.'

Dr Neville Bennet of Lancaster University did some research in 1976 into some primary schools in two counties in north-west England — twelve using 'formal' methods and thirteen 'informal'. He found that, in general, 'formal' classrooms showed a slightly higher pupil progress in basic skills than 'informal'. This was in line with similar research in America, but two factors drew special comment. One was that some of the classes were still being taught for the 11+ IQ test. It may be that formal teaching was better at getting all children through that type of examination, though one Chief Education Officer wrote to give a sharp counter-example. More remarkably, the best class by a long way used the 'informal' teaching style. This class was subsequently the subject of a report by E.C. Wragg, a teacher-trainer, who was very impressed with the teacher and also the amount of skill needed in such class management. In an article in the *Times Educational Supplement* he wrote:

'Children around the room are engaged in a variety of tasks, some doing maths, some writing, some doing their topic, others preparing assembly. They are free to talk to each other, move about the room, and have a fair degree of responsibility for their own progress . . . Nevertheless the work rate is high . . . a percentage figure . . . while not perfect, gives a rough-and-ready indication of pupils' application to their task . . . With 81% Margaret Stephens scores higher than anyone we have seen to date, the average being just below 60. Scores as low as 20 or 25 were recorded in classrooms where social chat is not just a lubricant but the principal activity . . . Explanations are crucial in informal teaching; otherwise children have no proper idea of what the task entails. Both subject matter and the way of handling the task are crystal clear after Margaret Stephens has explained them, largely by question and answer and a few intriguing mysteries: "I'm not going to say one word about number seven, but you just think carefully about it." . . . Not every teacher can operate at her energetic level. Her contacts with individual pupils run consistently at the level of about 1,200 to 1,500 per day, her preparation is thorough, and she likes being an informal teacher . . . informal teaching at its best is effective and invigorating.'

The message seems to be that informal methods can be as successful as the formal ones we are more used to, but they make even greater demands on the teacher. Teachers can do well with whatever style suits them if they work at it. Informal teaching in secondary schools shows the same picture — the good is brilliant, but all too often undirected chat just wastes pupils' time.

MIXED ABILITY OR STREAMING?
How should pupils be divided into classes? You could do it alphabetically, A-G with Mr X, H-L with Miss X and so on; or by colour of hair, or favourite TV programme . . . or by reasoning ability.

In the days of selective schools, the division at 11+ was on the basis of verbal-reasoning ability as measured by the IQ test. This was supplemented by the headteacher's report, but the IQ score carried the most weight. Within the grammar schools pupils were soon arranged according to achievement in class tests or examinations so that by the second year 2/1 was established as 'top' set and 2/4 as 'bottom'. Not many moved 'up' or 'down' after that. This had a knock-on effect in primary schools. Certainly by the time a child was 8 or 9, parents wanted him in the A-class because most of the A-class went to grammar school. One pupil later commented, 'We didn't have friends; we had rivals.' In some cases even infant schools were 'streamed'.

When the education system began to 'go comprehensive', two things happened:

• The primary schools did not have an 11+ to coach for, so they could think of different organization, and curriculum.

• The comprehensive secondary schools faced an intake selected only by the neighbourhood of the school.

In many cases the secondary schools settled for divisions within the school. Either by junior school records, or tests at the school, pupils were put in 'bands' or 'streams'. There was some moving 'up' and 'down' but in its cruder versions it resulted in the previous selection system continuing under one roof. Certainly by the time pupils reached the fourth year (aged 14) they would be in GCE or CSE or 'non-exam' streams or sets.

The advantages claimed for 'streaming' were:

• Pupils learn better with those of equal ability;

• Clever children are 'stretched' more;

45

● Less clever children can have easier versions suitable to their ability;

● Class control is easier where all children are paying attention to the teacher all the time, than where groups work on their own.

Disadvantages were listed as:

● 'Streaming' is inefficient. The measuring of ability is uncertain and to change streams part-way through is a great strain on pupils.

● 'Streaming' is self-fulfilling. Several experiments showed that both teaching and learning depended on what stream pupil and teacher thought they were dealing with. A classic case showed a teacher given what he thought was fourth stream, getting the same results as another teacher dealing with what he thought was top stream. In fact the streams had been reversed. Children are 'obliging creatures and very inclined to produce the standard of work that their elders regard as appropriate.'

● Socially, pupils and parents — and some teachers — saw the 'top' stream as 'good' and the 'bottom' stream as 'thick', so children were labelled and did not mix with easy acceptance. The effect was multiplied as the top stream appeared to get the best teachers — they certainly got all the prizes.

The move to 'mixed ability' teaching was strongest in the primary schools and spread to lower forms of comprehensive schools. A few comprehensive schools persisted right through to age 16, but usually examination needs brought back streaming or setting in most subjects by the time pupils were aged 14 or 15. But mixed ability is no panacea. However socially desirable, it won't work unless very well managed and resourced. An HMI report in 1978 criticized the 'level, pace and scope of most unstreamed teaching'. They found class behaviour good, but both the gifted and the least able children getting less attention than they needed. 'Too much emphasis is put on social objectives at the expense of academic development.' The Inspectors commented on some excellent work and added 'Teachers need more training for mixed ability teaching methods . . . at present very few have had any at all.'

The good work showed 'pupils of below average ability did much better in a number of instances because they felt valued and were offered the challenge of work traditionally thought too demanding. They were helped by having more able pupils in the class and there was some evidence that this was especially so in subjects that are less sequential . . . Mixed ability groups were associated with good relationships between pupils and between pupils and teachers, co-operative attitudes on the part of pupils and often a high level of motivation among those of below-average ability. The pride of achievement shown by some of these pupils was greater than that often found in streamed or setted classes.'

Mixed ability teaching clearly involves a lot of individual learning, but this is not self-directed learning. The teacher selects the material, increasing the amount or difficulty for the able pupils. Two key requirements are noted:

● Adequate learning materials — worksheets, information sheets, tape-recordings, videos, books, educational games, science and craft equipment, all with proper storage and access.

● The teacher must be free for as much one-to-one and small group work as possible. So Fatima might get only five minutes actual teacher contact in a lesson but it would be concentrated on her own needs and progress.

The individual teacher-pupil contact is the strength of mixed ability teaching. In the old illustration, you can throw a bucket of water over a lot of bottles and some will go in. Or you can pour from a jug into each bottle. It may take longer, but it is more efficient — and makes the bottles feel better.

SCHOOL AND COMMUNITY

In small rural areas the village school used always to be an important focus of the community. Some of the smaller schools have, sadly, gone; but still there are primary schools which serve the community in many ways. The carol concert and annual pantomime bring parents, staff and most of the village together; the parents waiting for children at 3.30 p.m. are an alternative gossip-centre to the local shop and pub. The children then leave and go to the big school, a three-mile bus ride away. Teachers don't bump into parents in the street — in many cases teachers commute from greater distances than the children. How can such schools serve the community and be accountable to them?

The legal situation has tightened in recent years. Some communication is now compulsory:

● Every maintained school must issue an information booklet giving standard particulars — governors, number of pupils, status (County/Voluntary), type, admission policy, any religious connection, discipline, RE, sex education, and so on. For secondary schools it must also give examination results, showing the numbers of pupils who obtained various grades at GCSE or A-level. Oddly enough, many LEAs interpret this regulation to mean that schools do not have to show the number of failures, so parents cannot calculate a 'pass rate'.

● The 1986 Education Act said schools must have an Annual General Meeting at which governors must present a report on the schools policy, staffing and conduct during the previous year. Parents may attend and make comments or ask questions. Parents representing 20% of pupils may pass resolutions for the attention of LEA, governors or headteacher.

● The 1986 Act also placed upon governors the responsibility for deciding whether sex education should be part of the curriculum and making a written statement of how sex education should be taught. This statement is to be available for inspection at the school.

These are welcome provisions to ensure communication between school, governors and parents. Many schools already do more, with Open Evenings, Parent-Teacher Associations, fuller brochures of their own — to say nothing of the reams of paper that go through the school reprographics department and filter home (through pupil post) on every conceivable aspect of school routine.

The relation between school and community has been a topic of debate and even heated difference:

1. Whose culture? Schools are sometimes seen — often correctly — as agencies of social control. The ethos of the school, its values, order, discipline, ways of getting information across, making decisions, all give the children a firm idea of how life should be lived. This may not be the same as the way home is run. At school you are supposed to put your point of view and make requests quietly and rationally. At home it may be a shouting match. Schools may seem to insist on a way of speech, grammatical correctness, even accent, that is different from home. Critics accuse schools of being run by middle-class teachers imposing their own values on everybody and making working-class children feel inferior. Teachers would respond that, however valuable and colourful different cultural backgrounds may be, children have to make their way in the world. The ability to speak and write intelligibly and accurately, to plan and persevere, and to adopt values of individual responsibility are essential. Colin MacInnes comments in a *Times Educational Supplement* article:

> 'Working-class social relations are less competitive than middle-class; less concerned with status, though not less so with social posture; more tolerant . . . more acceptive, more easy going; less censorious, though not less critical; above all, less fussy, if more nonchalant and lackadaisical . . .
>
> ' . . . if we examine the social mores of the *Daily Express* Giles family, we will find that, though their real income (judging by the luxuries that abound in their household) must be considerable, their social habits remain resolutely proletarian . . .
>
> ' . . . [As far as curriculum is concerned] the reluctance to attend school is due to a genuine belief that much of what is taught is of no practical use within any terms of social reference the pupil can recognize as being relevant to his own life and prospects . . . Its chief obsessions are with any directly provable, practical knowledge and with the acquisition of wealth and status by a collective effort which has the virtue of group loyalty and the defect of contempt for individual initiative . . . In a crisis, the middle-class mind thinks of a committee; the working-class, of a mass meeting.'

At the other extreme are people who feel that the standard of the school collapsed when it 'went comprehensive' and let in all these rough children. They don't even teach them to speak properly now.

But it all depends what you mean by Culture. Is it about how people do live? In a plural society it seems a good idea for children to be aware of a range of speech, attitude, goal and assumption. The next question has to do with evaluation, deciding that one culture is 'better'. For example is 'high' culture 'best'? Ballet and classical music and theatre are minority interests (mostly subsidized, too). They are certainly different from bingo, disco and football terraces, but is it sensible to make judgments of value about them? Wine bars for city stockbrokers are different from the spit and sawdust department of the Rose and Crown or the Working Mens' Club. How does education affect children from these various backgrounds?

Richard Hoggart wrote movingly of the tension felt by a working-class lad who 'goes through the process of further education by scholarship . . . the test of his real education lies in his ability, by about the age of 25, to smile at his father with his whole face and to respect his flighty sister and his slower brother.' Marsden and Jackson researched children of working-class background who were selected for Huddersfield Grammar School:

'Primary school seemed local and familiar in many ways; it was a special continuation of normal neighbourhood life. But grammar school marked, for most children, a sharp break with this former world. Now they spent almost all their time with similarly selected children in a middle-class atmosphere . . . [Years later] almost all are professional-class people . . . Some were doubtful about the society for which they had been trained, and doubtful about the social nature of that training. Others felt the losses in family and neighbourhood life which education had sometimes compelled. But against this, most of the 88 were satisfied with their education and the social rise that had gone with it. Gaps between themselves and their parents had sometimes closed with the birth of grandchildren. On working-class life in general many expressed harsh opinions.'

2. Culture policy. School management has to take account of these tensions. Primary schools are perhaps more successful in making mutual acceptance and joy in diversity a value. The basic discipline may be slack for some by comparison with home and rigorous for others, but children do live together. The quiet and boisterous, loners and mixers, all get attention. At secondary level, the shadow of examination soon falls. The allocation of pupils to roles in society, based on intelligence, grinds on. In comprehensive schools the overt segregation of grammar/secondary modern school may give place to the inner segregation in streams and sets. Various management structures attempt to redress the balance and to acknowledge the worth of all pupils, to give all pupils the tools of living, skills of speech, expression, persuasion, decision and co-operation, but to avoid harsh judgment. People who swear and fight in frustration are difficult to deal with; so are articulate, well-spoken folk who scheme, push and lie to get their own selfish way with courteous singlemindedness. Management means using resources fairly against bullying and blandishment — and being seen to be fair.

3. Community Colleges. One major step in 'contributing to the development of the community' has been the establishment of

Community Colleges. Such colleges have operated in a relatively small way in some LEAs for a long time, but recently much larger units have been developed. Comprehensive schools have been expanded to cater for the whole neighbourhood, so that young people of school age, their parents, other adults and young people over compulsory age, all join with teachers to form a learning and living community. Some will be full-time pupils, others will be part-time, day or evening. Adults join in with GCSE or A-level classes and learn along with their children. The education of the rising generation is the responsibility of everyone, led by professional teachers. Parents and other adults take an interest in and influence the curriculum. They also contribute to the programme whatever skills they have. One by-product has been a drop in vandalism. The property becomes a community asset shared by many people. Members of the wider community work alongside professionals in community projects, often playing a leading part. This is a way forward in meeting the criticism of culture conflict, and providing a healing influence in a divided society.

SCHOOLS IN A MULTI-CULTURAL SOCIETY

A sharp challenge to school management in recent years has been the growing number of pupils from non-white ethnic groups. Their parents were lured to the UK when it needed labour to run the hospitals and buses and the increasingly prosperous heavy industry. People of Indian descent came with roughly the same proportion of professional and managerial occupations as the previous UK population (34%); those of Pakistani (14%), and West Indian (9%) descent much lower. These people met a variety of unpleasant reactions but settled down to become worthy citizens. Their children, born in Britain, are now in the schools. All the parents have high aspirations for their children and great hope in education.

The careers and achievements of these pupils have attracted continual comment and been the subject of the Swann Report, *Education for All* (1985). To talk of them as a 'problem' is a gross mistake. What they have done is to highlight the problem of a white society unable to alter into a truly plural community. Those of Indian descent have, in general, succeeded in the system (though still less well than might be expected) but with great difficulties of social adjustment and language learning. Some of Pakistani and West Indian descent have highlighted the long-standing problem of education for children from manual backgrounds. For many years white working-class children have had a poor deal, but they slipped more or less quietly through the system, and out into manual jobs.

In the 1970s two things happened. The number of manual jobs decreased dramatically, and black pupils predominantly from that background were clearly identifiable. It was obvious that they were not achieving high academic success, though if the results are adjusted for class factors, the differences are not as great as at first apparent. They were in fact acting like the barium meal that shows what is wrong with the digestive system as a whole.

The Swann Report included racism — possibly 'unintentional' — as a major factor in their lack of success. There is no doubt that after school they faced discrimination — the Nottingham Report *Half a Chance* showed that white youths seeking work at 16+ were twice as likely to be taken on as equally qualified non-whites. But the Swann Report was looking at what actually happened in school. Part of the problem was inappropriate curriculum. While it might be dealt with in the chapter on curriculum, it is included here because it challenges not just curriculum but the whole of school management. The challenge is not met by adding a 'Black Studies' course, or modifying the history syllabus or including 'other religions' in RE as 'bolt-on' additions to a curriculum that is basically OK. Management is involved in three ways:

1. Knowing what is going on. You can't do anything about something you don't know is happening. If there is a careful check on who is suspended from school, who is put in lower sets, who is most frequently sent to Year Heads for discipline, it may appear that black pupils are over-represented. This should prompt investigation. There may be good reasons every time; there may not, in which case the bad reasons must be looked into. These could involve communications within the school and with parents; pupils' involvement; how buildings are used — trying to avoid cliques; how buildings are treated — trying to avoid racist graffiti; how pupils behave to each other.

2. Direction of resources. The easier part (though by no means easy) is ensuring that minorities get help they need — possibly language support for those whose home language is Urdu or Bengali. In some areas this will need massive resources. A 1987 report showed that ILEA deals with 170 languages, and in Tower Hamlets schools 40% of children have a home language other than English.

Another resource is books — reading books in primary schools, library books, text books. Many of these were written when the UK was all-white and other races were far away, at least beyond Dover. They may give images of other cultures which are narrow and limited, to the point of distortion and offence. Arranging a regular review of such material is a management responsibility.

The more difficult task concerns the largest resource — staff. Most teachers were not trained to deal with ethnic difference, and may feel threatened when they meet it. They are as liable as any white Briton to have stereotypes and expectations. These expectations can be self-fulfilling and result (as one research project showed) in high-achieving black children ending up in low examination groups. Management of staff, particularly highly-trained professional staff, demands great skill. Attitudes cannot be changed by proclamation on the staff notice-board. Confidence in the face of new relationships takes time and support. 'Racism awareness' courses have had some limited success, though they sometimes convince staff they are in a no-win situation. But management has to pursue a water-on-stone policy of monitoring, negotiating, suggestion, organizing mutual support, and trying to build up a sense of fairness. The task will not be easy. A study of two Midlands comprehensive schools in the *Times Educational Supplement* included the following:

'School A was originally a boys' grammar school which amalgamated with a boys' secondary modern in 1975 to form a mixed comprehensive. One quarter of the pupils are of Afro-Caribbean or Asian origin. There is still a strong grammar ethos among some senior staff, who are said to feel frustrated by what they see as the poor quality of the pupils, a frustration exacerbated by having to contend with what they consider "troublesome black pupils" . . . One black teacher told the researcher that some teachers just assumed that West Indian pupils would be intellectually inferior and were "amazed" when they were bright . . .

'School B, formerly a select girls' grammar school, was amalgamated with two single-sex secondary moderns in a rushed re-organization in 1972. Since then the proportion of pupils from ethnic minorities has risen steadily and it is now more than 60%. Some members of staff, still nostalgic for their old schools, have not adjusted happily to the change, so the report says. Many are said to share the views of one teacher who told the researcher, "This school is a low ability school because of its catchment area, which consists of a low social class and a high immigrant population. More fundamentally, it is the high proportion of immigrants in this school which is responsible for the lowering of standards" . . . The two deputy heads in the school acknowledged that there was a problem between teachers and certain groups of pupils but saw this as being inherent in the pupils. Other teachers, however, admitted that there were racist attitudes among staff.'

The *Times Educational Supplement* which carried this report (25.10.85) had a sad editorial headed 'Some teachers are racist'. It failed to make the point, which should be emphasized in the present context, that some of the blame must be put on management. Many schemes of reorganization were 'rushed' with little staff training or help. To neglect such training — even if it is expensive of time and money — when the ethnic composition of the schools was changing too, was irresponsible. County Halls were under pressure in the 1970s. They were being asked to reorganize the system in a way that amounted to the biggest in-service training exercise of all time. All too often schools were thrown together and told to get on with it as best they could. We shall be paying for the lack of resource and vision for a long time to come.

3. Feedback. There must be provision for pupils and parents to contribute their views and perceptions. This must be open and not seen as a secret threat by teachers doing their best. It must also be seen as genuine by pupils (who may feel they suffer discrimination), and produce an atmosphere where they can even consider that they may not be blameless themselves. At senior level, especially 16+, this is easier, and I have known outstanding participation by students of all ethnic groups with mutual esteem and goodwill.

The challenge is a difficult one, and there has been no shortage of instant answers. One call has been for 'positive discrimination', the idea that management should deliberately make extra resources available to those already disadvantaged. There is some justice in this. But the plea has been hardened into a demand that standards should be lowered for those who find it hard to achieve them. For example, that entry requirements for further or higher education should be lower for black pupils. This backfires by making them a special class who are patronizingly regarded as less suitable than others. Also (unless there are genuine reasons to expect they will develop very rapidly to the required base-line) it is no service to put people in a position of even greater hopelessness.

At primary level, the Thomas Report (ILEA primary schools 1985) had the wise advice:

> 'We hope that teachers will not be so afraid of being thought racist that they lower the standards they expect when dealing with black children. To do so would in fact be racist and an insidious way of achieving the opposite of what is intended — the maximum development of which every child is capable.'

Extra help where it is needed, by all means, but not a patronizing blurring of standards.

A lot comes back to the total ethos of the school. If we insist on our preoccupation with intelligence we shall confirm the growing belief among the black urban culture that their status depends upon certificates; that their forebears were servile and unworthy. In short we shall give them a view of society, status and value which will breed aspirations which are unattainable for many. But the alternative is not to pretend we can make everyone 'more clever', but to realize we have picked a wrong horse. Or, rather, we have made one good horse the only runner. We don't pretend everyone can be six feet tall or swim the Channel. The school exists to develop the gifts and potential which pupils already *have*. And management must see it happens.

All this is an example of the two faces of management — keeping the show on the road, and working out whether the show is a good one. The former takes up so much time and energy that the latter gets insufficient attention unless management deliberately builds into its programme regular review of the aims and objectives of the school.

LOCAL FINANCIAL MANAGEMENT.

A new facet of school management covers finance. The governors and headteacher have always been responsible for the 'General Allowance' or 'Capitation', an amount given by the LEA to each school to be spent as they like on textbooks and equipment. Allocating this to items for the good of the whole school and individual departments is an annual headache which leaves no one quite happy but most people with something to keep their department going. The total sum is in fact relatively small — from £1,000 for a small primary school to £40,000 for a large secondary school. All other expenses are now paid by the LEA.

The 1988 Act makes wide changes. The aims are:

● To ensure that parents and the community know how local resources are being distributed and how much is being spent on each school;

● To give the governors (of all secondary schools and primary schools of 200 or more pupils) freedom to take expenditure decisions which match their own priorities and the guarantee that their own school will benefit if they achieve efficiency savings. Special Schools are not automatically included, but the Secretary of State may make regulations for particular Special Schools to join the scheme.

The LEA are still responsible for:

● Capital expenditure and debt charges;
● Spending government grants given for specific purposes;
● School meals and midday supervision;
● Costs of dismissal or premature retirement of staff (unless LEA has 'good reasons' for making the school pay).

In addition the LEA must pay 'such other items as may be prescribed' — it is expected this will include the administrative costs of processing salaries; advisory and inspection services; welfare, psychology, library services and professional advice.

All these must be deducted from the total LEA educational budget and the balance divided up among the schools on the basis of pupils' numbers and age. The exact scheme must be submitted to the Secretary of State for approval. Pilot schemes have already been running for a year or two and shown various teething troubles.

An advantage is clearly that the costs of particular schools will be accurately identified. Governors, parents and staff will know what it all costs. This in itself may move them to look for greater efficiency, especially as any savings go to the school. But this is more complicated than it seems at first glance. There are a lot of variations in expense that even out over a large number of schools. So the LEA can budget for these expenses and spread it over all the schools. For example, teachers' salary scales provide for increments up to the maximum over ten years or so. This causes 'incremental drift' as the teachers as a whole move up the scale. The LEA allow for this in their staffing budget. But a particular school might have three staff retiring (at top of scale) and being replaced by three teachers straight from college. The wage bill would be cut by £15,000. Again the LEA budgets for redecorating — perhaps every five years. Will governors be faced with the whole cost in one year? Cover for long-term staff absence — long illness or maternity leave — will be borne by LEA under the 1988 Act provisions.

Governors will have more freedom to decide quite substantial matters — how many staff they can afford, and what sort — whether to have three top-scale teachers or four lower-scale teachers to reduce class size, for example. The LEA will fix the budget for the school, but not the details of how it is spent.

Governors do not incur any personal liability for anything done in good faith. These provisions raise problems also because governors have the power to appoint and dismiss staff, though LEAs are the employers and liable to any lawsuits that may arise. The Secretary of State has power (after consultation) to modify existing employment legislation accordingly.

Two cautions must be made — one practical and one of principle. In practice it is going to put a heavy burden on headteachers. Deciding how to spend £1,500,000 is very different from allocating a General Allowance of £40,000, even though most of it is fixed by staff arrangements. Headteachers are promised financial management training, but they must not turn from leading a professional teaching team to becoming amateur accountants. They need competent bursars who are experienced in dealing with such amounts. Obviously it can be done, but not necessarily as cheaply as at present.

The matter of principle concerns how decisions will be made. The governors make the decisions, though they delegate day-to-day running to the headteacher. Most of them will have no experience of such amounts of money, and it is doubtful if the 'training' they are promised will be more than understanding the mechanics. It is important that those who do understand finance are listened to; also that the headteacher is listened to. Simple majority votes could be dangerous. Governors with financial experience must remember that schools are a 'cost-accountant's nightmare' and analyses of performance are very difficult to carry out with any certainty. It is, of course, important too that the headteacher makes a carefully explained and reasoned case, and does not just talk about 'intangible benefits' or indulge a passion for trees down the school drive or a heated swimming pool. Headship will be an even greater responsibility, and should be rewarded accordingly.

MANAGEMENT AND VALUES

All the points I have made so far could be seen as routine matters — keeping the show on the road. It is impossible, however, to separate a management system from the values it contains or shows. It is part of the 'hidden curriculum' which teaches children, more eloquently than anything teachers say, what is really important. Tim Brighouse, Chief Education Officer for Oxfordshire, has said, 'Most of our schools . . . have unspoken assumptions in their organization, their timetables and their curriculum, which reinforce individualism and materialism and minimize the need for co-operation.'

Our society is no longer sure about the values it wants to conserve and pass on. Reports assume we know. The Swann Report, *Education for All*, pleaded for:

> 'a basis of pluralism which enables, expects and encourages members of all ethnic groups, both minority and majority, to participate fully in shaping the society as a whole within a framework of commonly accepted values, practices and procedures, whilst . . . maintaining their distinct ethnic identities within a common framework.'

And again:

> 'We would thus regard a democratic pluralist society as seeking to achieve a balance between, on the one hand, the maintenance and active support of the essential elements of the cultures and lifestyles of all the ethnic groups within it, and on the other, the acceptance by all groups of a set of shared values distinctive of the society as a whole.'

It doesn't tell us what the 'commonly accepted values' are. We are wizards at 'practices and procedures' but fumbling novices at values. The logical result of 'no fixed values' is that each group of people who have to live together must 'agree among themselves'. Heads and governors become experts in consensus, trying to hold a ring in which people can discuss differences and agree to get on somehow. Often it means a different value system in school from that at home, for both pupils and teachers.

This confusion of values is nowhere more clearly seen than in what we think about children. That's the next topic to look at.

CHAPTER 3

Children

and how to educate them

Everyone involved in the discussion says loudly that, 'Of course, it's all about children'. We assume that we all know and agree what children are, what they need to know and how they can be taught it. In fact, there is no consensus about any of these things. Because we rarely ask such basic questions, we may not even realize how ill-equipped we are for such analysis.

The 1988 Education Act aims to:

a) 'promote the spiritual, moral, cultural, mental and physical development of pupils at the school and of society'

b) prepare such pupils for the opportunities, responsibilities and experiences of adult life.

This has a fine traditional ring about it. The great educators of the past would warm to it. But over the last fifty years there has been an erosion of traditional religious and human understanding and a reduction to technical and 'scientific' frameworks of thinking. We are better at asking 'how' to do things than 'why' we should do them or what value they have. If things go wrong or children turn delinquent, we look for 'causes' in their circumstances. At its gloomiest, this reduces children merely to things, bits of humanity that develop (according to sociological principles) into units performing various functions in society. Education is one factor in this development. Let us look first at this gloomy picture and then at what it leaves out.

THE EVOLUTIONARY VIEW

At the end of the twentieth century, if we ask questions about the origin of the human species, we are given an evolutionary account. We are told that over millions of years, humankind has developed by biological and then psycho-social evolution, the development of the complex from the simple. This has been a process of 'chance and necessity', random mutations being worked on by fixed laws of biochemistry, the results being filtered by the 'survival of the fittest'. This is so much part of our mental furniture that it may seem odd to mention it. American fundamentalists who campaign for Creation Science alongside Evolutionary Science may worry about such things, but that's a long way away. Dinosaurs are popular with the children; many classrooms have colourful friezes to match the textbook story of development. You can even get plastic dinosaurs in the cornflakes. But it is worth a thought. It could be setting a mental mould. Evolution is a useful hypothesis for scientific description and discussion. Biologists would be lost without it. But when Evolution gets a capital 'E' and controls development of living things, it starts to take over. Humankind is nothing more than a product of impersonal, scientific forces. Where and how an individual starts to be responsible for himself and his surroundings is far from clear. C.S. Lewis tartly asked why we should trust our reason to tell us how we developed, if reason itself developed without reason, by random change. Also, the underlying message suggests that humankind is on the up-and-up. This optimism was held by the Victorians — that we are getting steadily better as we get cleverer and all will be all right in the end.

Survival is an essential part of this framework — humankind survives and succeeds by superior knowledge and using that knowledge to predict and control. Natural science (genetics, medicine and dietetics) and social sciences (psychology, sociology, economics and politics) will enable us to give our children a high chance of survival. This 'naturalist' framework influences educational thought in a number of ways and can be looked at under three headings:

- Controlling the 'child-machine';
- Developing the child's mind;
- The child's place in public institutions.

CONTROLLING THE 'CHILD-MACHINE'

The first aspect of this control we shall look at is the **physiological.** Many diseases can be eliminated; many handicaps can be identified before birth and aborted; many illnesses can be prevented by immunization; better health and growth can be achieved by appropriate diet. In a school context, a medical room must be provided, and provision made for medical and dental inspections. The Secretary of State has power to order a pupil to be medically examined — parents have a right to be present. This is a fascinating example of the interplay of social control and personal care. The medical room, often with a school nurse, is a haven for many sick children. It is also a symbol of society's determination to monitor and direct the health of the nation. Nearly everybody goes to school so nearly everyone can be checked up on. Statistics can be collected showing the incidence of disease, and how many children have hearing or sight impairment. Statistics can also show that children are getting taller and heavier than they were at comparable ages years ago. Remedies are to hand if the inspection shows they are needed. It's all rather like the MOT for the car, and just as valuable.

This 'naturalist' framework also has its particular understanding of the **psychological** make-up of the child. We know how the mind works — or rather, we know how learning takes place. The mind itself is a black box with inputs and outputs that can be measured.

At one extreme the American scientist, B.F. Skinner, believes positive reinforcement is the key to learning — you can get the right response every time if you find the right stimulus and 'reward' the right response. This is the basis of some teaching machines or computer programmes which are excellent for teaching specific skills or information (sometimes useful for pupils who miss a lesson through illness). A popular example is a pocket 'computer' for children learning number addition and multiplication, which gives a cheerful ring when they get the answer right.

For years some teachers have gone in for 'stick and carrot' methods, punishing pupils who failed to learn and rewarding those who did. Skinner majors on the carrots — rewards or self-esteem reinforce successful learning. Pupils chanting the two-times table show it 'works', though whether they understand multiplication is doubtful. In a world where you need to learn lots of irrelevant facts, this might be a happy state of affairs. I knew a Latin teacher who enthused first-formers, promising a sticky bun from the tuckshop at break for those who got full marks in vocabulary tests. But don't get this mixed up with 'deserts' — as primary children might deserve and get gold stars for good behaviour. Scientists don't deal in what you deserve, only in what works to produce the required change of behaviour.

Another area where psychologists' research needs careful application deals with what children *can* learn. Jean Piaget, a distinguished Swiss educational psychologist, published many books of his research into how children formed concepts — general ideas of space, number, time, and classes of objects. His 'results', when they filtered down to the humble teacher in training, were hailed as showing that young children just cannot form concepts. This meant that you must not try to teach them anything that involves abstract thinking until they are 7 or more. One teacher trainer disagreed:

> 'Children undoubtedly do develop concepts at an early age (some, of course, more rapidly than others) and the extent to which they develop such concepts may depend . . . upon the language used by adults when talking to them. Should nursery and infant teachers consider children to be unable to acquire concepts, then their own teaching behaviour could well help to justify their erroneous beliefs.'

And he deplored the uncritical 'half-baked Piaget' some students believed:

> 'Student teachers, even student teachers who are parents, have tended to ignore the evidence of their own experience in favour of the Piagetian view, such is the strength of the Piagetian legend.'

Now to look at the **social** aspect of this view: education is seen as a mechanism of social change. It is at school that children are initiated into socially acceptable lifestyles. This is an extension of the psychological approach mentioned above. Children learn to respond appropriately to situations — it's not about learning morals, it is only about observable behaviour. Manners makyth man, but molecules makyth manners. One teacher's guide says:

> 'all behaviour, good or bad, is learned . . . if all behaviour is learned, it follows that one can employ the principles of learning to bring about change in behaviour.'

The same guide gave therapeutic techniques to help children overcome 'bad self-perception' and go in for better self-fulfilment. As one reviewer put it: 'with love and lollipops there should be happy children and happy teachers.'

Another part of this process is allocating children to their place in society. Schools are the machinery by which society gets the operatives to keep it going. The child-machine takes its place in the society-machine.

This 'child-machine' view is true, but not the whole truth. The behavioural scientists are usually cautious, painstaking investigators, slowly building up an understanding of psychological and sociological patterns. The trouble comes when they or others try to apply their work. Skinner himself recognizes that this learning theory puts power into the hands of those who know it. 'What values,' he asks, 'are to guide the choice of goals towards which behaviours should be directed by the controllers?' and goes on to answer, 'Survival is the only value according to which a culture is eventually to be judged.' If it survives, it's good. But that comes from *his* value system, not his behavioural scientific research. Tyrannical governments have survived, but it didn't make them good.

DEVELOPING THE CHILD'S MIND
Mercifully, the modern 'machine' world-view is not entirely consistent. It might seem as if a child was just a 'black box' responding to various inputs in predictable ways. Paradoxically it is also believed to be a *thinking* black box. Unlike computers, we can think for ourselves. However we got it, *reason* is an important part of being human. It is the distinctive human characteristic. Two questions come up for consideration — what is this 'reason'? And, how should it affect the way we teach children?

First, reason. Is it the same as intelligence? And again, there is argument about intelligence — how far it is inherited and how far nurtured — but there is still extraordinary faith in IQ (intelligence quotient) measurement, which became a major way of categorizing children. In the days of selective schools, everyone did the 11+ test, from which their IQ was calculated. This was found by dividing 'mental age', as shown by the mark in the test, by the 'chronological age', as shown by the birth certificate. So 'average' children would have mental age the same as actual age and get an IQ of 100. Children with an IQ of about 115 or over would go to grammar school — the actual figure varied from place to place according to the accommodation available.

Whatever it is that IQ measures, it is only part of what we usually mean by 'reason'. Reason has to do with grasping concepts, arranging information, connecting ideas. The jokes about absent-minded professors, and clever people who have no 'common sense' show that there is more to 'reason' than IQ. The grammar school selection was supposed to take account of this. The Nottingham City report for 1957, for example, said:

'The headteachers' reports and recommendations were carefully considered by the Board and a number of children offered places in grammar school as a result of investigations into individual cases.' But overall, out of 4,700 children in the year, 1,550 were 'recommended' but only 749 got places — IQ reigns.

In most LEAs the 11+ no longer exists, but for some purposes 'intelligence' testing happens occasionally. There is less universal confidence in it now, and the debate continues as to how far it is inherited and how far the result of a child's upbringing. Ever since Plato's *Republic*, writers have dreamt of Utopias — beautiful societies where everyone (or at least everyone who rules) is clever, and where selective breeding ensures the steady development of super-brains. Behavioural scientists are more down-to-earth. They talk of 'regression to the mean' — which means that the distribution of intelligence (insofar as it is passed on from parents to children) will tend to show the same general pattern in the long run.

A very serious debate arose in recent years over the relation of IQ to race. The uproar arose when American educational psychologist Arthur Jensen contributed an article to a learned journal in 1969. He said his researches showed that:

'genetic factors are responsible for something like 80 per cent of all the variation which we find in IQs within a given population such as that living in England or the USA at the present time.'

Controversial, but not alarming, until, a few pages later, he gave the disastrous throw-away line, 'American negroes on the average score something like 15 points of IQ below whites.' In spite of the subsequent criticism of his research, this sadly confirmed the folk-wisdom of white Americans — black people are likely to be less intelligent.

The matter became urgent in Britain as many black people came to live here, and many black children came into the schools. The Swann Commission, set up to look into under-achievement of black children in school, commissioned a research paper. This paper, published as an appendix to the Swann Report *Education for All* (1985), examined all the research evidence and concluded that intelligence is not dependent upon racial group.

'Much of the difference has been due to the particularly poor performance of children who have only recently immigrated into this country . . . In the case of children of West Indian origin, this does not seem to be the whole story; while those born in this country have higher scores than recent immigrants, they still score, on average, about 5 to 12 points below the population mean . . . Much of this difference in IQ scores between West Indian and indigenous children appears to be related to differences between them in such factors as parental occupation, income, size of family, degree of overcrowding and neighbourhood. All of these factors are related to IQ among whites, and when they are taken into account, the difference between West Indian and indigenous children is sharply reduced, to somewhere between 1 and 7 points.'

However, it is all too easy for teachers to have lower expectations for some children because of their colour than for others. Certainly black children are over-represented in ESN (educationally sub-normal) classes and this could, in some cases, be because teachers expect them to 'have problems in learning'. In 1943, when IQ was highly trusted, the Norwood report made IQ testing the basis of deciding what was 'appropriate teaching' for various classes of intelligence. This report was the basis of the selective system that followed the 1944 Act, and was acclaimed as giving children the different sorts of education they needed. But it is dangerous to 'label' children — especially if the labelling method is doubtful. Perhaps, as Professor Eysenck said in reviewing Jensen's work:

'the question is whether it is more important to emphasize the differences between human beings, or their similarities.'

This introduces a related issue. How should the fact that children are — or will be — 'reasoning' creatures, affect the way we teach them? Education should develop the child's reasoning capacity, enabling the child to understand what is known of the world and to apply it to particular situations and problems. There is some dispute about what can be known, and whether knowledge comes by experience or intuition, but the child's mind is more than a mental filing cabinet — there is room for reflection, judgment, decision and action. So we have the great emphasis on understanding. Children must not only memorize things — at one time the rivers of England starting with the Tweed, or the Kings and Queens of England, were regarded as things every child should know — but they should be able to understand how things work, how particular things are connected in general patterns and rules. Concentration on rules alone is a limitation on the full possibilities of reason. Determination to reduce everything to rules has often affected how some subjects were taught — for example, the way endings of nouns and verbs change in various languages was taught as 'rules', and generations of pupils chanted '*amo, amas, amat*'. Caesar, of course, did not learn Latin that way. He just spoke what he heard and was corrected when he got things wrong. I remember being told that Hebrew was *the* rational language — a rule for everything. When I complained that half the verbs in the set texts were irregular, I was told that all their irregularities followed another lot of rules. I doubt if Moses understood that — he just spoke and wrote the language he learnt as a child.

The old public-school tradition thought that reason linked different areas of learning. Latin was a 'good training for the mind' and the skills developed transferred to other subjects such as mathematics. This could, of course, be simply a result of a clever child doing well in both. Research has not supported this, though common aptitudes can be used in different areas. Computer firms are happy to recruit good linguists as programmers.

THE CHILD AND THE SYSTEM

Survival is important, and is helped by a stable community. Children do not fend for themselves as isolated units, but must take their place in various institutional systems. The scientific explanation of these systems is that they are a deal — perhaps a sub-conscious deal — between individuals and rulers, known as a Social Contract. Individuals give up some freedom to the rulers. In return they get security in place of anarchy. Teachers are good at telling children, 'If people didn't obey the rules, we'd have chaos.'

It is therefore important that children are taught how these institutions work. For example, in 1985 the Secretary of State expressed concern that pupils were leaving school 'economically illiterate'. They didn't understand how supply and demand affected prices, or how labour costs affected competitiveness; they couldn't even write a cheque. Teachers reacted predictably with a fear that economic education might be politically slanted and be 'more from the viewpoint of the entrepreneurial provider than the consumer'. They agreed more could be done in Careers and Social Education to give pupils understanding of how the business world works. Some courses for older pupils (like TVEI and CPVE) pay a lot of attention to this.

So children need to be taught about the world of business,

politics, law and order. They must be trained to co-operate in these structures and to adopt appropriate roles. At worst this could be simply producing happy consumers; but at best, people who understand the social system in which they will be citizens.

LIVING TOGETHER

Traditionally children have to be taught what's right and wrong — 'they should learn 'em some morals.' In the reduced framework of natural and social science, this is problematic. Ethics and morality no longer carry authority but have become servants of social survival. This approach — known as 'relativism' — emphasizes how morality differs in different societies. Indeed, social survival depends upon consensus, and as society develops, various 'norms' are accepted and agreed. People know what is expected of them. When these accepted values are absorbed (internalized) by the child, 'conscience' develops and is a powerful guide to the child's behaviour.

The present dominant pattern in our own culture is utilitarian — pleasure is valued and pain avoided and all decisions must be made on the basis of maximizing pleasure and minimizing pain. This can be the individual's pleasure, but is extended ideally to the 'greatest pleasure of the greatest number'. Education therefore must train children to understand this principle and perform the necessary pleasure calculations. Because of the paradoxical mixture of 'machine' and 'reason' this has several results:

● **Some control will be necessary to deal with 'deviants'.** Children who do not follow the accepted values must be prevented from harming others and also 'treated' or reformed in some way to be more acceptable citizens. This 'medical model' thinks you can 'treat' youngsters for a bad bout of vandalism in the same way you can treat a dose of 'flu. It's just a matter of finding the right 'medicine'.

● **'Guilt' is seen as awareness of non-acceptance.** Not that you have 'erred and strayed from God's ways' but that society does not like what you have done. This can be used as a powerful pressure to conform. It thus becomes a social tool. Otherwise 'guilt' is to be avoided, and psychiatrists spend a lot of time persuading people that their 'guilt' is not necessary. The American psychologist, Herbert Mowrer, later in his life came to doubt this and caricatured the idea in the rhyme:

'At three I had a feeling of ambivalence t'wards my
brothers
And so it follows naturally, I murdered all my lovers
But now I'm happy; I have learnt the lesson this has
taught —
That everything I do that's wrong is someone else's fault.'

● **The majority can be educated to behave responsibly of their
own free will, even though a minority may need such 'control'.**
The ideal is autonomous behaviour based on reason. This will not
depend upon absolutes or rules by the State, church or parents,
but be the personally chosen behaviour within the accepted limits
of the society. Here the emphasis on 'reason' shines through.
Apparently the 'deviants' are less reasonable or refuse to use
it, so have to be controlled.

MOTIVATION
Exactly how children can be led to respond to the educative process within this framework is confused. Four different approaches
can be detected:

● **Mechanistic** — since the child is a kind of machine he can
be motivated by the right stimulus; praise, privilege, gold stars
can all act as 'positive reinforcement'; deviant behaviour can be
limited by less pleasant experiences.

● **Rationalist** — as a reasoning being, the child will enjoy finding
out and building up knowledge, so 'discovery' teaching methods
have been developed. Many ingenious examples will be seen in
primary schools, teaching number, measure and time.

● **Pragmatic** — a thing is 'right' if it works. So 'problem-solving'
is an important approach, by trial and error, devising and testing
out various ways of attacking a situation.

● **Existential** — linked to the others only in that 'nothing is
given', there is no absolute. So the child is encouraged to develop
by action and self-expression. The only restrictions are those
needed to stop her upsetting other children in the class.

All these have value and will be seen in teaching syllabus and
method in all schools. The trouble is that they lack unity or coherence and so any one is likely to take over. Parents often complain,

'They never learn anything, it's all self-expression nowadays.'

THE FUTURE

In the short term this framework is concerned to help the child grow into a full member of society, taking an appropriate role and fulfilling some function within that society. There is great optimism about this. Education carries a heavy cargo of hope. Today's children are the thinkers and scientists of tomorrow who will help the forward march of civilization. I vividly remember being at a training conference where a new teaching programme was being introduced, and bemoaning with another teacher the sad mess children inherit in our society. 'Never mind,' she said, 'we've got the next generation.' And there was real hope in her voice and eyes.

The longer-term goal of society is less certain and usually boils down to more and better of the same — a more powerful and affluent society in which the individual shares some of the goodies.

Still longer-term, death is the end for the individual. It is a topic to be avoided, but the individual's profit and loss account closes at death. In the seventeenth century Bishop Ken wrote:

> 'Teach me to live that I may dread the grave as little as my bed.
> Teach me to die that so I may rise glorious at the awful day.'

Fearless living may still be on the syllabus. The second line is definitely out.

MORE TO LIFE THAN MOLECULES

We can all probably recognize some features of the particular approach to life which I have described in this chapter in schools we know. Maybe administrators and planners are more likely to deal with abstractions. Teachers in the classroom may see children as more than learning machines. The danger is that under pressure people with this basically materialistic framework for thought will revert to materialistic solutions.

It may be the exasperated teacher, at the end of his tether, exclaiming, 'You behave like an animal; I'll treat you like an animal.' It may possibly be, in the smoother world of Parliament, that the 1988 Education Act has been seen by some as letting competition sort it all out. Survival of the fittest will weed out the bad schools, just as it weeded out the dinosaurs.

Many people fear that, in developing so rapidly in our science and technology, we have let slip values and viewpoints that are vital to real humanity.

One response in this vein comes from G.H. Bantock writing in *Dilemmas of the Curriculum,*

> ' . . . We have accepted too readily the surface agitation of scientific and technological change . . . forgetful of the human problems which underlie the superficial appearance of difference. We have become too concerned with "relevance" . . . to appreciate that for centuries men have thought and written on these problems, that the world was not born yesterday and that encapsulated in the past there may well be an illuminating wisdom.'

Bantock calls the scientific approach 'Newton's single vision' and regrets the loss of the wide-ranging human understanding seen in the Renaissance and great literature. Science tells us *some* things — valuable and useful things — but not everything about people.

Another response bemoans the loss of childhood. The 'machine' view of education sees children only as potential citizens, valuable for what they may one day become. At worst they are regarded as mini-adults already, judged by adult standards and expected to have adult seriousness to fit themselves for the future. Some parents sadly fall into the trap of worrying so much about their children's future and 'how they are getting on at school' that neither parent nor child has time to enjoy the experience of childhood.

A criticism is that this is all a planner's abstraction, which fails to take into account the individual child. Children are put in bundles and labelled like products in a factory: high-flyers, average, low achievers; indigenous, ethnic minority; handicapped or underprivileged (there are even six components of disadvantage solemnly listed by DES). This 'management' approach comes from trying to apply industrial techniques to education. It got its major push way back in the 60s in the USA when President Johnson, greatly impressed by the success of the previous administration in reducing Defence Department costs and increasing effectiveness by adopting business/engineering ways of thinking, mandated the use of management practices in federal agencies, including the Office of Education. So began a bonanza for 'testing' and alarm and despondency for teachers.

I met this view when I was one of the guinea pigs in a new management training course for headteachers. The tutors wanted to know what we were producing, how we measured it, what the raw material was — children presumably. 'No,' we said, 'the children are operatives, like us.' 'Then what are you producing?' 'The future,' we said — no doubt partly out of awkwardness. For administrative purposes such management techniques may be necessary, and it is better that at least some groups and their needs should be recognized. The danger is that divisions become fixed, and the treatment for each category is prescribed like medicine at the chemists. Accountability demands that the treatment is checked and shown to be effective. But how can we ensure that each child is known and nurtured as an individual, black, white, affluent, poor, nervous, brash, clever, slow, idle, sad or jolly? The tension is shown by a comment from a mathematics teacher:

> 'The managerial view of education leaves me, as a teacher of mathematics with two incompatible tasks. On the one hand my accountability to the tax-paying public is to be measured by my pupils' performance on an instant test that presents mathematics as a stagnant set of conceptual items and mathematical activity, and as the enunciation of grammatically acceptable and logically unexceptional statements incorporating these items. On the other hand, I am accountable to the great tradition of mathematics as a vibrant, living, growing metamorphosing activity, and to the memory of such men as Jacobi, who justified his involvement with mathematics as being "pour la gloire de l'esprit humaine". The better I do on the one count, the poorer will be my showing on the other.'

Even more radical would be a Christian critique which sees that the real problem with the mid-twentieth century framework is the artificial boundary drawn round the human story. By excluding — tacitly or directly — the idea of anything outside our scientific-humanist system, we sadly limit our understanding of humankind, and of children in particular. The difference can be stated in three ways: we are created, flawed, but capable of renewal and redemption.

● **People — adults and children — are not the products of chance and necessity.** It is an illogical jump to trust reason as our guide, if reason itself is the result of random changes in molecules. If a Creator is let into the picture we have a firm base for each child's individual value and dignity that does not depend upon their achievements or 'use' to society. We also have a firm framework within which reason (and other faculties) can show us how to use God's world responsibly together. Beyond that, we understand that some things remain 'hidden' — a continual quest of mystery and wonder, which seems to match human (and particularly children's) curiosity, delight, longing and sense of eternity.

● **All is not for the best in the best of all possible worlds.** Even children are not the pure hope for a better future. They are the latest subjects of the perennial tragedy of humankind. They grow up in a society that 'suppresses the truth' and tries to get along on its own. A touch of school RE will not counteract the steady message of most homes, media and other school teaching that for practical purposes God is irrelevant. Children also share the human bias to selfishness and evil, so they need positive instruction in what is good, not just what 'works' or is 'acceptable'. Even 'reason' is limited and cannot be the sole guide of life. At worst it can be used to unworthy ends.

● **The child is always an object of hope, not despair.** Background or behaviour to date does not extinguish this hope. And this hope extends beyond death in the 'life more abundant' that Jesus spoke about. To deny children knowledge of this is a betrayal of their humanity.

The Fourth R Report (1970) provides a sharp conclusion to this chapter:

> 'One of the basic educational questions is plainly what kind of being is this whom we seek to educate? Are human beings no more — though no less — than a combined topic of the natural and behavioural sciences? Do we differ as socially acceptable citizens at all significantly from house-trained dogs? Or are human beings anything more than extremely elaborate computers whose major distinction is that they are comparatively cheap to come by? If this is our view of the nature of man then the educational process need plainly be no more than a process of individual and social conditioning. For what is quite clear is that what we do in education depends quite basically on our understanding of what it is to be human.'

Perhaps these features are to some extent behind the 1988 Act's desire to 'promote the spiritual, moral, cultural, mental and physical development of pupils'. Not all of them are evident after clause one of the Act and it will take more than an Act of Parliament to effect such a sea change in society's view of life and children.

CHAPTER 4

Parents

and their choices

Parents are very much in the educational news. From every platform, in every programme, you can hear about the rights of parents. Politicians seem to take it for granted that here they have a real vote-winner. Parents have always had an interest in what goes on at school. A few of them have always been deeply involved. But they haven't always been very welcome.

I remember once calling on a headteacher at about 3.30 p.m. and commenting on the women gathering outside his primary school. 'That's the gate gang,' he said, 'We do our best to keep them out, but it's difficult.' And there are a few schools where you can still see decaying notices saying that parents should not come 'beyond this point' (that is, on school property) unless they have an appointment.

At most schools it's very different now. Why are parents so much more welcome? Why has the pressure for more parent power increased so greatly recently?

To begin with, does the pressure come from parents? By a process of elimination it seems to be so. It doesn't come from teachers, pupils or the world of education.

Traditionally, teachers are mildly suspicious of parents. It would be a surprise if they were actively campaigning to have parents telling them what to do.

Such pressure as there is from pupils — the National School Students Union may not be typical — is usually for greater *student* involvement, especially at secondary level. At this stage, children usually want to keep parents out of it, except so far as meals and pocket money are concerned.

County Hall officers are usually glad to be left to get on with their job. They treat parents courteously enough when they call, but it seems unlikely there is any urge from County Hall for more parent involvement.

Elected members of Education Committees are councillors with their own constituents who keep their ears to the ground. They may occasionally help an aggrieved parent sort out a problem.

So that seems to leave only the parents to account for the increasing pressure. But at the grass-roots level, headteachers complain about lack of interest, the difficulty of getting a strong Parent-Teacher Association going, or even recruiting parent-governors. On more than one occasion I have gone through the 'Election of Parent-Governors' procedure: sent out letters (via pupil post, so some may have got lost there) and put the box to receive nominations in the appointed place; only to find there are insufficient nominations even to fill the vacancies, let alone have an election.

A poll of 1,000 parents in 1987 produced the surprising result that only 19% said parents should have the greatest influence in school. 46% thought teachers should have most say.

So what is the truth about parent power? Who is pushing their case? Here are a couple of possibilities:

• Politicians and pressure groups who want to alter things see parents as 'folk with an interest' who might be recruited to support their cause;

• Parents do react to specific provocations, and when they do so, they are well enough organized to get media attention. The specific provocations may arise through the more radical innovations of some authorities. For example, parents get concerned about some sorts of sex-education, anti-heterosexism, and the like. This makes good headlines. White parents who objected to their children being allocated to an 85% Asian school got a lot of media coverage.

Putting these two factors together would explain quite a bit. Politicians and lobbyists may be seeing parent power as better than some other power — for example, the power of local authorities, particularly the so-called 'loony' ones. Even an official body like the Taylor Commission may have been influenced this way. (This Commission reported in 1978 and some of its recommendations were included in the 1986 Education Act.) They saw a need for a wider range of opinion, more democratic control of schools, and it seemed natural to increase the number of parents on the governing body. Parents, after all, represent the democratic ideal of ordinary citizens being involved in local affairs, people with no professional or political axe to grind, people who naturally care about children. It is significant that one of the questions the Secretary of State will be asking schools that wish to 'opt out' is about those who are willing to stand as governors.

PARENTS' POTENTIAL

What, then, do parents have to offer to the educational system? Several points can be made:

● Some offer very little — their influence on their own children is poor. An HMI investigation in 1979 reported that 20% of the schools visited said they had difficulty with parents who colluded in their children's truancy. All LEAs have procedures teachers must follow if they suspect 'non-accidental injury' to children. Sexual abuse is a hazard that too many children face at home. Divorce affects 200,000 children a year, sapping their trust in adults and in authority in general. Sixteen-year-old Dawn began arriving late every morning. Eventually the tutor found out that her mother had walked out on the family and Dawn was getting all the meals and getting two younger sisters off to school — but had been too embarrassed to explain. 100,000 children a year have their homes disturbed when Father is sent to prison. Some parents' idea of discipline is different from the school's; Peter Dawson (Secretary of the Professional Teachers' Association) refers to some parents' readiness to protect their own children's right to disrupt the school. He also comments on the lack of support Heads find from LEAs — 'the appeasement of parents is a first priority in the bureaucratic mind.'

● The majority of parents offer intimate knowledge of their own children and, by the same token, of many similar children. This knowledge is not just professional but marked by love and concern. Deeply held hopes and anxieties may colour the contribution they have to make, but it rests on detailed and firm daily acquaintance. Possibly greatest for younger children, such knowledge is still impressive in teenage years. Very many parents have open and confident relationships with teenage children and their experience is not to be easily set aside by some teacher who thinks he or she has more direct access to the pupil's feelings. In some cases, perhaps, but parents can tell teachers a lot.

● A few parents offer some expertise relevant to the school — legal, administrative, contact with employers, or driving the school minibus. The majority do not. In fact, one of the reasons why so many parents are reluctant to get involved as governors is that they 'don't know enough'. All governing bodies need to have a lot explained to them by the headteacher or local education clerk.

The average parent understands even less of current practice. This undermines the idea of school-parent partnership. A lack of knowledge and understanding of what the school is doing can sap parents' confidence in their own role as parents, let alone in relation to the school. It usually takes some particularly lurid happening to make them bold enough to make contact with the school. Sometimes the student has to act as interpreter if the parent is confident only in, say, Urdu. To maintain dignity as a parent in such a situation shows maturity, courage and concern.

● Although parents may not be experts in curriculum or structure, they do have normal human experience and insight. As Lord Justice Devlin said about the legal system, we pick twelve people at random to form a jury, not because they know all about the law, not because they are super-intelligent (there is no such test) but because 'God has set within them in equal measure the knowledge of right and wrong.' Perhaps the same is true about parents. They provide a valuable input into the system precisely because of their general common sense, and this common sense acts as a check on the narrowly-focused schemes of specialists or the broad-brush utopias of theorists. It would be nice to think so. But it is not the way the matter is usually presented.

● The usual emphasis is that parents have a right to close involvement because their child is at stake. This would be reasonable if the parents were involved only in matters affecting their own child. The Education Act of 1944 said children must be educated 'in accordance with the wishes of the parents' — though it hedged it about with the proviso that this must be subject to the efficiency of education and reasonable use of resources. The wording however is ambiguous and discussion seems to suggest that parents as a group should have more power — even controlling power. 'Put the control of the schools back where it belongs — with the parents' says one political pamphlet. There is some confusion here. Parents' usefulness as contributors to the *general* development of the school is mixed up with an idea of their right in *one* part of the school — their own children. This confusion is not helped by the apparent belief that the parent's interest finishes when their child leaves the school. Certainly parent-governors can't continue in office after that time. It would help discussion if these two possible interests and contributions of parents could be kept separate.

PARENTS' RIGHTS
The question of rights is a sticky one anyway. The philosophy of

human rights is a fairly recent industry. What rights are based *on* is difficult to determine, particularly since the situation changes as the children grow up. Fourteen-year-olds start complaining that parents have no right to tell them what hair-style to have, or what time they should come in. Civil Rights groups are ready to tell children what legal authority parents have over them at various ages, with the frequent suggestion that parents have no moral authority to do this or that.

This too is confusing. Legal rights and duties can be stated fairly clearly. But people don't always accept these — indeed civil rights' enthusiasts spend much time criticizing the legal position. They must have some basis for criticism — usually some form of self-evident natural right. The American constitution said citizens were 'endowed by the Creator' with basic rights. Modern apologists are less sure about any creator.

In practice, the situation broadly accepted in Britain regarding education seems to be something like this:

● The State has the right, certainly legally, probably morally, to require parents to educate their children.

● Parents choosing to do this themselves must demonstrate to the authority that they can educate efficiently.

● Otherwise, parents must send their child to the designated school, or to an approved independent school at their own expense.

● The local authority must ensure that its schools are staffed by competent teachers, maintained in a safe condition, and follow an approved curriculum.

● The headteacher (and other teachers delegated by the Head) act *in loco parentis*, that is, they must treat the children as a reasonable parent would treat them.

● Parents have a right to information and opportunity to consult with the school on matters affecting their child.

Each of these statements would get general agreement, though the basis for regarding any as a 'right' would tax the most ingenious philosopher. Their broad acceptance probably owes as much to long custom and practice as to any philosophical base.

An attempt could be made to establish parents' rights simply on the fact of parenthood. They are our children. But the 'our' is not as easy as that. The car we buy is 'our' car and we can sell it if we like. We can't sell our children, or do many other things with them. The State could say the children are 'our' future citizens but that doesn't give the State the right to condition them how it likes. The ambiguity is shown by the fact that 'our' children can be taken into care by the State if we are not treating them correctly.

It might be more helpful to drop the language of 'rights' and look for another approach. For example, the notion of responsibility. This would help in a number of ways. Parents and State could each have responsibilities, sometimes overlapping and sometimes complementary. Parents' responsibilities will alter as the children grow up and take progressively more responsibility for themselves.

PARENTS' DUTY

This could still be a powerful position for parents to take. It has been strongly developed, for example, by Christian parents who have set up their own schools. They would apply their reasoning to all parents, whether they take this drastic step or not. Parents, so the argument runs, are entrusted *by God* with the care of the children. The Jewish law laid the duty firmly on the parents to bring up the child in the community tradition, knowing how to live and worship. The later Proverbs reinforced the message: 'Train up a child in the way he should go.' The Christian tradition followed the Jewish law with the parents' obligation to 'bring up your children in the nurture and admonition of the Lord'. Some Christians feel it is impossible to do this without compromise in the present secular humanist climate of education. That is why they have chosen to set up their own schools. Some other minority groups have taken a similar view. There is pressure among Muslim parents for their own schools, as they feel they cannot fully discharge their responsibility to nurture their children in their tradition in a secular State school.

It could be argued that 'rights' are the obverse of 'responsibilities' but the case is shaky and parents would do better to base their case for involvement on their responsibility, a responsibility which they cannot hand over completely to the school or any other institution. It may seem like splitting hairs, but I would rather say to a parent, 'It is right that you are concerned for John,' than, 'You have a right to be concerned for John.'

PARENTS' DILEMMA

Is it 'concern for John' or 'concern for all the children'? And can the two concerns mix?

Take an example from the question of curriculum. An irate father writes to the Chief Education Officer outraged that John can't do O-level German in the sixth form. John wants to be an archaeologist and Dad has been told that German is a good subject to have for this. Asked for an explanation, the Head says that there were only four takers this year and the County regulation is that there must be at least eight. This is in the interests of efficient staff usage. Very small sets in one part have to be paid for by oversize sets or no sets in some other subjects. After discussion of John's archaeological aspirations, Dad accepts the situation with reasonable grace. To be honest, it must be said the Head did not try very hard to get Dad to put the common good against John's good, but spent the time showing that German was not all that vital really.

Take another example from classroom organization. Parents come to complain that Mary and her friend Charlene are being held back in Maths because the teacher spends so much time with the less bright children. Why can't the classes be set according to ability? Teacher explains that mixed-ability teaching is school policy in the first year. Children have come from all sorts of primary school background and this system helps even them out as far as possible. The techniques are well established and do allow for some individual attention. In any case the textbook has additional material for those who complete standard work quickly. They can pursue their own investigations.

The parents are followed almost immediately by Tom's mother who is worried that Tom finds it all very difficult and says Teacher spends all her time with the clever children. He lost a lot of time in his last year of primary school so has ground to make up. Both sets of parents say 'We realize you've got to take all the children into account, but . . .'

A third example shows a wider concern. It comes from a book by an Irish parent who is very critical of a health education programme which he feels is overriding moral reasoning by appealing only to pupils' feelings.

> 'Like most parents in Ireland I am a Christian. I am trying to teach my children that Christianity is true. The teacher acts *in loco parentis* . . . Part and parcel of being a Christian is holding that there are definite answers to the basic moral questions . . . Any teacher who tells my children that there are no right and wrong answers to those questions is betraying the trust I placed in him.'

In this case the parent is clearly concerned about his own child but would probably argue that the programme he criticizes is bad for all the children. In Britain the religious basis of the argument might hardly apply (except in a church school) but parents might object to some programme on a general principle which they feel is valid for everyone. They feel they speak on behalf of others as well as themselves.

The class teacher, the headteacher and ultimately the local authority have to try and fit together all the interests that are expressed, mostly on behalf of individual children and some by individual parents expressing what they see as good for everyone.

More serious are cases where, in pushing forward the interests of 'our' children, we may hinder others. This has been mentioned in a minor way in connection with curriculum. Sometimes the parent seems unaware of the advantage he is claiming. One of my first phone calls in a new job was from a parent requesting that his son be put in Mr X's Physics set. I said that no doubt sets would be arranged in the usual way. 'But it's important for him; he's going to be a doctor.' Presumably lesser students could manage with staff the father valued less highly.

Sometimes the search for advantage is acknowledged. Parents will move house to get into the catchment area of a 'better' school. Or in some cases parents will decide that it is better to face the hardship and pay the fees to get Simon into an independent school rather than stay with those awful children. This is not new — the *Edinburgh Review* of 1871 carried the following comment on the introduction of compulsory elementary education:

> 'A respectable artisan earning his two pounds a week will not willingly bring his child into contact with street Arabs . . . is there to be no conscience clause against the contagion of infectious disease, or the worse contagion of bad example, against the extreme dirt, roughness and degradation of the very lowest classes of the poor? . . . Many parents had rather make any sacrifice than plunge their children into such a low social atmosphere.'

Such incidents may be regarded as perfectly proper. After all, one's first duty is to one's own. Granted, but it undercuts the argument that more control should be given to parents because they care and know about all the children. They know about their own, and their attempts to exercise control will be from as many points of view as there are children, possibly conflicting, leaving the school and local authority to sort it out. Parents have a serious concern for their own children. They may also care about others. The dilemma can be sharp. Often you only realize how sharp it is when decisions have to be made. What are the choices?

PARENTS' CHOICE

One view of 'choice' seems to be the free market idea. Competition is a good thing in itself. Competition breeds efficiency. Parents differ in what they think their children need (and they should know), so let a thousand flowers blossom and let parents pick the ones they like. This 'market' view is double-edged. It combines concern for parental freedom with a passion for 'efficiency'. Rather than trust LEAs to ensure that schools are as good as possible, the competitive power of the market place is drawn in via parents. Some schools will fade and have to be closed. But they will be closed, not by some LEA judgment, but by popular demand or non-demand. But, again, will parents be acting for themselves or for the general good? Before looking at what is actually on offer, make a shopping list of what parents are hoping for.

The details of what parents may have in mind in choosing a school would need a chapter to themselves. In fact much of this book is relevant to the choice. It is a good exercise to make your own 'shopping list'. At Open Days headteachers set out their stall and let you walk round the (carefully prepared) school. From other parents, and children, there will be a lot of news and comment. Your list might include things like:

- Buildings and atmosphere that give a sense of security and care;
- A stable system of support, ideally based on religious or moral principles;
- Opportunity to meet a cross-section of society in a controlled setting;
- Accessibility of headteacher and staff;
- A balanced curriculum, giving skills, knowledge and understanding appropriate to the child's age;
- A variety of teaching methods, maintaining interest and allowing for the child's own creativity;
- As much individual understanding and attention as can be with normal class size;
- Contact with the wider community;
- (for older children) Adequate career advice and preparation in life skills needed on leaving school;
- Good communication between teachers and pupils, and between teachers and parents.

These are very broad statements and you may not agree

with them all (any difference would be worth thinking more about). They do give an outline of what parents are looking for from a school in the joint enterprise of educating their children.

Once the school has been chosen, there will be further choices along the way. Not a lot at primary stage, but certainly in secondary schools, parents will be consulted at the 13-14-year stage when children are allocated to 'options' for GCSE examinations. An Inspector's report says they were impressed with the general level of consultation, though listening to the parents' side of the story is less reassuring. Where it is well done, it is an enormous drain on the school's resources and it is not surprising (though regrettable) if interviews are sometimes perfunctory. You need to know the degree of consultation on offer at this stage, as well as the regular once-or-twice-a-year meeting of parents with teachers. Are parents taken seriously? They recognize they need advice from teachers, but sometimes feel teachers always 'know what is best'. Teachers, on their part, find that parents are strongly moved by examination goals, and may plead for courses that are over-demanding on pupils. Pupils are loaded with more subjects than they can usefully carry, especially with the advent of GCSE and its demand for hours of course-work. Parents may think the teachers have too low an expectation of the child and are out of touch with the competitive world outside. All this points up the need for the school to encourage a relationship of trust and openness with parents.

At each stage, parents want their child to be considered seriously as an individual and be shown care and advice. While recognizing that teachers have their job to do, parents want to be consulted and informed. To begin with, they want to know what options the system as a whole offers them.

CHOOSING A SCHOOL

Something has already been said in chapter 1 about the system as a whole. Now we can look at the parents' decision for their own child.

1. Independent schools. For perhaps one child in five, parents have a choice between sectors. They could, with varying degrees of hardship, send their child to a fee-charging independent school, or to a local maintained school — which could in some cases be a voluntary-aided church school. This could be seen as a personal decision on how to spend money. No one complains if a family chooses to save and go to Bali for a holiday, or spend all their money on bingo, so why not on the child's education? If this were agreed, the parents would then need to see what they got for their money. Money is not always the supreme consideration — there are scholarships and bursaries, usually with a special examination. There is also the Government Assisted Places Scheme designed to help the less-well-off family. These usually involve some sort of test, and all obviously involve interview of child and parents at the school. It *is* often a competitive business and before exposing a child to it, parents want to know what will be gained.

Advantages usually quoted include:

● Smaller classes — the pupil-teacher ratio is half that of the maintained sector.
● More individual attention.
● Likelihood of good exam results and possibly favoured consideration by university. (Certainly independent schools account for one-third of all A-levels and half of all Oxford and Cambridge entrants.)
● A network of friends, most of whom will grow up into professional or managerial positions of influence.

It is also widely believed that more of the staff have higher academic qualifications; pupils are generally of higher ability and taught by staff accustomed to this higher ability range. But this needs checking — the average and mediocre must not be allowed to ride on the reputation of the best.

Against this, possibly a narrower social experience — though that might be made up outside school, or we don't think the wider experience is very good anyway. So if the pupil can stand the pace — and we can find the fees — there seems to be an open door to 'success'.

A few years ago there was political uncertainty. It was Labour Party policy, if returned to power, to disband or take over the independent schools. This threat or promise was not included in the most recent manifesto, though there is little doubt that independent schools' privileges, resulting from their charitable status, would be restricted. The 'dilemma' factor remains, however, and parents will need to resolve it to their own satisfaction. The choice may seem fine for John or Mary. How does the choice affect children at large? Undoubtedly it buys privilege for John or Mary (if the school chosen lives up to reputation). It almost certainly means that the parents will take little interest in the local schools, so to that extent the local schools lose the influence of more powerful and articulate people. Also local schools will lose two clever children (assuming John and Mary pass the independent school entrance exam). This will add to the disparity of ability between the two sectors.

So far this has dealt only with day pupils, where parents can play the normal part in a child's growing up. The particular issues raised by boarding education (independent or State schools) will be dealt with a bit later.

2. Voluntary schools. For parents who have considered the private sector and decided against it, and for the other 80% of parents for whom such a choice is out of the question, there may still remain some element of choice among the schools maintained by the Local Education Authority.

There may be a voluntary-aided or voluntary-controlled church school, most likely in the case of primary schools. This will affect the options in the following ways:

● Such a school may well be the 'local' school for a neighbourhood. Some parents, convinced non-Christians, occasionally complain that their children cannot escape the 'indoctrination' of the church school which is the only one in the neighbourhood. They are entitled to choose a more distant non-church school.

● A voluntary school is also a possible choice for people living outside its immediate catchment area but who can make a claim to consideration. The admission policy is decided by the governors, and will normally favour applications from active church members. Cynics may say it is surprising how suddenly some parents get interested in the church when their children are coming up to school age.

● Choice for the distant church school (or against the local church school) will involve extra travelling, and separation from other children who all go to the local school. In many cases LEAs meet the cost of this travelling *to* the church school, but very rarely to avoid it — a discrimination the strongly non-Christian parent may resent.

● There may be a danger that aided schools give the impression of catering for nice children from nice backgrounds and so parents of no particular religious conviction may see them as 'better'. Most aided schools would indignantly reject this suggestion. It would amount to a form of selection on social or class lines.

● As with any choice, detailed knowledge is essential. Parents will want not only to visit the schools but also to hear from parents with children already there. Where it is well run with a specifically Christian programme and ethos, parents may well feel they should make this choice, even if it involves some travelling.

The case for these aided schools is rooted in history and was briefly looked at in chapter 1.

3. LEA-maintained schools. At secondary level the voluntary provision is much less widespread. In these cases, and where there is no voluntary primary school nearby, parents will still have some choice, among County schools. The 1980 Education Act extended parental choice, within the capabilities of the LEA's duty to ensure 'provision of efficient education' and 'the efficient use of resources'. In practice this meant that LEAs set overall admission limits, dictated by efficient use of all schools being run by the LEA. Admission was then dealt with in the following way:

● Parents would be notified of the 'designated' school — usually the one nearest their home;
● If they were happy with this, that's where the pupil would go.
● If they were not happy, parents could express a preference for another school. Local Education Officers considered the applications and in 90% or more cases parents were given their first choice.
● In the remaining cases an appeal procedure operated. Where appeals were turned down it was usually on the grounds that a school was 'full'.

The 1988 Act changes the meaning of 'full'. Previously, LEAs determined admission limits, and tried to keep viable numbers in all the schools which they thought should keep going. With rapidly falling pupil numbers LEAs had often to combine schools — for example, making one primary school out of the former infants and junior schools — or to close some schools. But as far as possible they tried to ensure that each school could provide an adequate curriculum. Hence the parents whose appeal was turned down were told that the efficiency of the service in general had to take priority over their preference.

The 1988 Act represents a change in this basic philosophy. It is no longer entirely up to the LEA to decide which schools should stay open. Parent power will now play a part. 'Full' will no longer mean 'up to LEA admission limit', but up to a 'standard number', that is, 'what the buildings will actually contain'. (That is the gist; the actual formula is more complicated, trying to take account of changes to the buildings or needs of new subjects since 1980.) This change stems from three considerations: the ideological commitment to parent choice; the conviction that competition will weed out the bad schools and improve the ones that are popular; and the fact that there are too many places available at present, which represents a waste of resources. LEAs have not been quick enough to eliminate these 'waste' spaces, and whenever they have tried, there has always been a parents' lobby using all the procedures available to 'save our school'.

LEAs fear this new meaning of 'full' will make some good schools impossible to keep going, as parents choose another school that is currently very popular. In any case it will make the LEA's duty of providing overall service more difficult.

Popular schools may suffer too, especially primary. As numbers dropped, many primary schools had surplus classrooms which were turned into libraries or music and drama rooms, or just convenient spare rooms where small groups could be withdrawn for special attention. This made a more relaxed and comfortable setting for the whole school. If these spaces now have to be reclaimed as classrooms for the surge of new children, the total educational package will be reduced. Governors or LEA can ask the Secretary of State to reduce the 'standard number', but the circumstances in which he can do this are very narrowly defined. Voluntary schools must be consulted by LEA to ensure that any increase in admission number does not alter the character of the school. For example, a Roman Catholic school may already cater for all the Roman Catholics in the neighbourhood, and any large increase in the intake would severely dilute the denominational character.

4. Special Schools. There are over 100,000 children in Special Schools. Not a lot out of more than seven million children, but of particular concern to their parents. Something has already been said in chapter 1 about these schools and also the 'Warnock philosophy', which aims to integrate as many of these children as possible in 'normal' schools. Considerable progress has already been made, particularly in primary schools, possibly because their structure gives children the security of long periods with one teacher. As they grow up we shall see how well the more fragmented structure of the secondary phase can cope.

Parents of children with more serious handicap will do well to visit a local Special School to see what is offered. For less serious disability — whether in mobility, sight, hearing or learning difficulty — the local normal primary schools will give details of the number of similar children they have and the resources to help them. If a 'statement of needs' is made, additional staffing is often available to the school. Sadly, some parents resist this, fearing that it 'labels' their child as in some way inferior, or limiting the parents' freedom to control what happens.

One effect of the 'Warnock' provisions has been that the dividing line between 'normal' and 'special needs' has become less visible. In the primary classroom it would be hard to pick out those who had been 'statemented'. Many 'normal' children have their problems too. One group of primary schools found that in their first and second years, 40% of pupils had some personal or background pressure that required special care. As mentioned in chapter 1, parents of 'normal' children need not fear that their children will suffer or be held back by 'special needs' children being in the same class or school. The living together and mutual understanding, where teachers have been able to get adequate training and experience, is a positive gain.

5. Grant Maintained Schools — 'opting out'
The Government provisions for Grant Maintained Schools — the first possibly to open in September 1989 — have been dubbed by the press 'opting out' of the State system. In fact such schools will still be funded by the State, but directly to the school rather than through the LEA. The administrative details of this scheme have been given in chapter 1, so here we can look at the implications for choice by parents.

Twenty per cent of parents can require the governors to ballot all parents. They can also obtain addresses of all parents, except those who expressly ask to be left off the list, so that they can put their case.

No one knows whether this proposal will catch on. The Secondary Heads Association (SHA) ran a seminar that attracted only about thirty Heads, but the Secretary said that there was 'substantial growth of interest' among his members. Clearly in some areas parents are going to be under pressure from one group or other — to opt out or to stay in. They will need to consult together and try to draw up a list of the factors involved to help them weigh the matter up.

It is easy to see the negative reasons for opting out — what might be called 'push' factors:

• Parents may have a jaundiced view of the present LEA policies. A move *away* from sex education or peace studies or some other media Aunt Sally may be a rallying cry.

• There may be a feeling that exam results could be better or discipline stronger.

• Parents may fear the LEA is about to propose a reorganization involving closing a school, or changing its status from grammar to comprehensive, or removing a sixth form. The 'opting out' procedure may be used to pre-empt this. (Once a school is designated for closure, 'opting out' is no longer possible.)

• Some headteachers will see benefit in leaving the burden of paperwork and having the LEA breathing down their necks — though they will realize there may well be different paperwork and different breath down their necks.

• Heads and governors may also feel frustrated by LEA staffing policies, such as a redeployment policy negotiated with unions that leaves governors little flexibility in staff appointment or dismissal. Actually, the local financial management provisions of the 1988 Act will go a long way to meeting this difficulty.

• Education has been a bastion of power in local government and so is tied up with non-educational political considerations. Grant Maintained status offers an escape from this political footballing.

• Parents may even think they will be able to get rid of a headteacher or senior member of staff they feel is not good enough.

On the positive side, what might be called 'pull' factors are harder to spell out. They are the sort of thing people 'have a feeling' about; hard-to-measure things like atmosphere, ethos, relationships, motivation to work. More specifically:

• The scheme could give opportunity for curriculum experiment or control, though still within the 'core curriculum' provisions laid down by government. This could, for example, include a more distinctively Christian or Muslim emphasis. It is unlikely the requirement to teach RE according to an LEA-agreed syllabus would allow a completely non-religious programme.

• Some parents may welcome the fact that the governors will have control of admissions and this could lead to a one-social-class, or one-ethnic-group school. The Secretary of State may, however, rule such things out in his criteria.

● There will be a little more freedom regarding staff appointments, but this will be offset to some extent by vastly increased responsibility for staff training and support. Also it involves balancing the needs of the school against the needs of teachers for security and confidence. (This will be discussed in chapter 10.)

It seems the staff have no say in this. If the school 'opts out' they go with it. If they don't like it, they are assumed to have resigned. One would hope, however, that anything they had to say would be listened to with respect, even though they have no 'vote'. To do otherwise would be counter-productive. Headteacher and staff are the driving force of the school and must be carried with the move for change. The official policy of the Teachers' Associations is strongly against these provisions, though it may be that in particular situations, in some LEAs, teachers may regard it as the only way to safeguard what they want for the school.

Parents involved in such situations should aim for positive rather than negative indicators. It is a mistake to think that '*anything* is better than the present system'. It is significant that the Centre for Policy Studies booklet advocating 'opting out' spends longer answering critics of the proposal than putting forward positive benefits. The key questions are: what does the Grant Maintained School positively offer that the present school does not? Could any of this be achieved at present by more energetic use of existing powers and resources (especially under the local financial management provisions)? Who will see that the vision is carried out? Can it be done with about the same resources and the same staff? Who will support and enthuse the Head and staff during the transition? Will the present enthusiasts be around for the next ten years, because it may be hard to change back before then?

Like a stone dropped in a pond, the decision to opt out will send ripples through the local system. When we've sorted out the answer for *our* children at *this* school, what does our decision mean for other schools?

The independent schools now attract parents who don't like what the LEA offer. In many cases parents are prepared to pay dearly for the escape. If Grant Maintained Schools did establish themselves with a reputation for high standards and good results, parents might well shift to this free provision from the fee-paying independent schools. The only card left to the independent schools would be the old school tie and the fact that they do not have to follow the National Curriculum. They might be reduced to what has been described as 'well-funded eccentricity'.

Voluntary schools have some freedom already, and some experience of managing their own show. They already get an 85% grant for external maintenance but the thought of 100% if they 'opted out' might be a carrot. Churches (Anglican and Roman Catholic) are very unhappy about this. Schools escaping from LEA control is one thing; to escape from diocesan control would be another. It might result in diocesan education plans being cut, training harder to mount and policy harder to enforce. The Secretary of State has given some reassurance on this. Voluntary Aided Schools will not be given grant-maintained status involving 'significant change' in religious character, without the agreement of the Trustees. In other matters they will be 'consulted', but it was made clear in debate that the Government does not intend to allow Trustees to veto the 'wishes of the parents'.

For LEAs the big question mark over all these 'competitive' devices is that they may help one lot at the expense of others. Overall planning may have disadvantages and present temptations to power-maniacs, but uncontrolled change of the system can be equally disastrous. For example, 'minority' subjects are a problem for all schools. Music classes are small; a second modern language is hard to staff. Some local authorities lay down minimum class sizes and all have to consider 'efficient use of resources'. If school A puts a lot of resources into Music and German it may attract more customers. Over a few years schools B and C may have to stop offering Music and German. This will mean they will also lose many pupils who want to do French or English GCSE or A-level along with the Music or German, so French sets may become non-viable. If school A decides to 'opt out' the LEA may have difficulty in providing Music, French or German in the maintained schools, because there simply aren't enough pupils with the aptitude and inclination left after school A has creamed the pool. It is true the Secretary of State is to take local effects into consideration in considering applications, but some of these effects will not be immediately apparent.

6. Boarding schools. For some parents the possibility of boarding school will be a serious consideration. Home circumstances differ widely, and 'home' may not be able to provide what the child needs in formative years. It may be, for example, that due to some disability, the child needs specialist medical or educational attention. There are both voluntary and some State boarding schools designed specifically to offer this support. Some parents want an education based on their religious convictions — for example, the Quakers. There are only a few Quaker schools to cover the whole country, so boarding becomes inevitable for many pupils.

In other cases the reason may be parental mobility — the need to work overseas where adequate education is not available. Members of the armed services, diplomats, civil engineers, media correspondents and missionaries in remote places are examples. For children from such homes, a boarding school gives a stable environment and alternative 'home'. In most cases they are funded by the employing agency and regarded as part of the total employment package. This often sounds like a second best to a 'normal' schooling — separation from parents being the price of a decent education in these circumstances — but there is a strong tradition that the boarding experience is good anyway, offering opportunities to build self-confidence, self-discipline and independence. They can certainly point to examples of self-confidence — young ladies of 16 who fly off to Jeddah to join the family for the holidays as easily as many young people their age catch a bus home.

The boarding tradition is seen as a good thing by those not forced by their career to choose boarding school, and who stump up the fees themselves. It is obviously a decision faced by very few parents — fees are about half the average UK total wage. And in some cases it is hardly a decision at all. It is simply assumed Alastair will go to XYZ as his father did and kind grandparents may have taken out the necessary insurance when he was born.

When reasons are weighed it is usually the 'hidden curriculum' that tips the balance. It is taken for granted that the academic education will be good (though this needs checking — mediocre schools must not be allowed to ride on the reputation of the best). The 'extra' is the emphasis on community, often in beautiful rural surroundings; the learning to live with other people (though in many schools this may be from a limited social range); the giving and receiving of support and progressively taking responsibility for others and the wide range of cultural, recreational and other group activities that can be provided in a residential setting. Such decisions must clearly be part of a total package which involves the parents' way of life, their view of family, and their aspirations for their children. It is doubtful whether children can return to 'normal' family life during holidays. They simply have a different growing-up experience.

Seventy per cent of boarding provision is in the independent sector (127,500 places). Places for 7,750 are maintained by LEAs. Community Homes account for another 20,000 and Special Schools (LEA and independent) for 27,600 of those with serious handicap. Those maintained by LEAs, of course, make no charge for teaching, only for the boarding element — and even this can be free under the 1988 Act if the LEA consider that 'special educational needs cannot otherwise be provided'. There is concern that the maintained boarding school places have dropped by a half in twenty years, though it could be argued that the need has increased. Boarding education is very expensive for an LEA and where it is well provided it is a mark of deliberate policy. In times of cuts and financial pressure the temptation is always to reduce the expensive minority provision. For some children, however, boarding is not a 'frill' or 'extra' but the only chance of a hopeful start to life.

EDUCATION VOUCHERS

A radical proposal to increase parental choice was the education voucher. Under this scheme parents would be given a voucher — say £1,100 for a secondary-age pupil and £800 for a primary-age pupil — and be able to 'spend' it at any school, LEA or independent, topping up fees for the independent if necessary out of their own income.

The scheme would be administered by the LEA which would run schools as at present but charge parents, using the vouchers. As matters stand at the moment it is illegal for LEAs to pay fees for private education without the approval of the Secretary of State, so the scheme would require fresh legislation. The advantages claimed include:

● Fairness — all parents would get the same amount of State help towards education. Those who chose independent schools would not, as now, pay twice — once in taxes and once in fees.

● Decision — parents would be likely to give more thought to where their children went if they had the idea they were 'spending' money. It would make people realize the cost of education.

● Competition — once again it is optimistically assumed that schools, competing for customers, would improve.

Against this could be put the uncertainty of the whole system. Fashions could swing between schools, giving alternately overcrowding and too few pupils to provide proper courses.

Staff would be insecure and might well seek more stable posts elsewhere rather than face being shuffled between schools as their sizes fluctuated. Independent schools might not be able to accommodate all the refugees from the LEA schools. Education is a long process. Institutions take time to establish and cannot fluctuate in response to demand like fun-fairs on Brighton pier changing with the seasons.

In 1978 the Kent Education Authority did an extended study of the system. They found 90% of parents in favour of more choice, but only 12% definitely ready to move their child from one school to another. More parents wanted to move to the independent schools than there were places available. The administration and transport costs were high, and the financial savings doubtful. A similar scheme tried in California had the ironic effect of giving less power to parents and more power to the school boards who allocated places.

A steady murmur of interest in voucher schemes surfaces from time to time, but it may be that the extended choice under the new Act (see above) will go a long way to meeting the parental feeling for 'choice' which the Kent study discovered.

WHICH PARENTS?

When the headline screams '70% of parents want selection' the small print says it is a sample of 354 parents. Probably all of them went to school in fully selective days and have little experience of the present system except what they hear from children. And the poll doesn't say what all the 70% of the 354 expect to gain from selection. It is likely to be many different and contradictory things.

Not all parents are equally active. One poll investigated the attitudes of parents according to occupation. It showed that half the social class AB parents (professional and managerial) belonged to Parent-Teacher Associations and only 15% of class DE (semi-skilled and unskilled manual workers). Social class AB parents already let their children travel further to the school of their choice. DE parents more often send their children to the local school. Incidentally party political allegiance varied too — 34% of Conservative voters were PTA members, 19% of Labour voters and 39% of Liberal/SDP voters.

There are other ways in which social class difference is reflected — in differences of opinion about what should be taught, how the school should be run, about homework, uniform, discipline. The call for parent power may mean in practice class AB parent power. It could be argued that this is fair enough if they are the ones who show interest. But then the argument has shifted from rights as parents (meaning all parents) to rights earned by participation or superior resources.

In some cases where parents seem to join across class difference, all is not clear. In 1987 the schools of Dewsbury hit the headlines. The (white) parents of twenty-three children were united in keeping their children away from the school they were offered by the LEA. They did so on the ground that 85% of the children in that school were Asian. Under the law as it then stood, the LEA's decision was supported by the Secretary of State. The parents stuck to their guns and for nearly a year the children were taught by a retired headmaster in a room over a pub. The Asian parents could well have said they welcomed the presence of white children to broaden their own children's experience, and perhaps as a symbol of commitment to a multi-cultural society. Some other parents branded the action as racist. One of the parents involved said, 'It's an issue of choice, not race. They said we had a choice of schools and when we made that choice they said our children couldn't go there.' Once again the LEA — and Secretary of State — were caught in the middle. Which parents should be listened to? Are parents (any of them) the crucial factor anyway? In the event, the Secretary of State considered the LEA acted rightly in providing education in a mixed community. That is, the social neighbourhood ideal takes priority over sectional parental interest.

Parents concerned about education — and anyone reading this is likely to be in that category — have to take seriously this dilemma of parents. The Hadow Report, as long ago as 1926, phrased it very well: *What a wise and good parent will desire for his own children, a nation must desire for all children.*

At a headteachers' conference, the chairman doubted if it could be done:

> 'Few schools have a homogeneous group of parents. And very few of those parents are objective or altruistic enough to look with complete impartiality at the needs of the school as a whole. They are interested primarily in the needs of their own child. Thus it is more important for schools to have adequate arrangements for dealing with parents as individuals, to welcome them into school and to keep in close touch with them about the needs of their own child, than it is to let a small number of articulate, middle-class parents with specific interests have undue influence on the aims and objectives, the curriculum, the

discipline and the use of resources which have to meet the needs of all and which are rightly the preserve of the Head and the staff. A proper professional judgment will always take into account the interest and wishes of all groups but will not allow itself to be unduly influenced by any one view.'

But even professional Heads and staff may need a few articulate people to check up on them in this imperfect world.

How can we keep our natural concern for our own children separate from our concern for children as a whole? First we must clearly recognize the need to do so. Then we might begin to realize how little we actually know about the hopes and fears of parents of different children, how rarely we ever meet them.

How can we earn the right to speak on behalf of *all* parents? Parents do bring to the debate a pile of knowledge about children and the world. They should be a valuable counter to theorists and cranks, to narrow enthusiasts and idle traditionalists. But they can only do this if they carry conviction as caring for all children.

Perhaps this all sounds hopelessly idealistic — just the sort of thing you'd expect from a teacher! But the alternative is to continue with rival pressure groups all mustering whatever power they can to further their own ends. What we desperately need is parents who will make the effort to recognize and wrestle with this dilemma, doing justice both to their own children and to 'children'.

It may be true to say that my children matter more *to me* and that I care for them more than I care for the children of a black unemployed father in inner Manchester (or Uganda). It is certainly wrong to say that my children are more important or valuable than his. If I am more articulate and confident than he is, my responsibility is increased. I *am* my brother's children's keeper.

CHAPTER 5

A National Curriculum

for all?

The 1988 Act has several pages about a National Curriculum. Politicians and commentators have spent much time defending or slanging it. Why the excitement? Hasn't there always been a national curriculum? Don't schools all teach the same? In fact, No. To get the picture, we need to delve into history a bit.

You probably value education highly and may well have good memories of your own time at school. For most present-day parents your memories will be of a grammar school or a secondary modern school in the 50s or 60s — relatively small schools of 500 or so. Memories will almost certainly be a mixture of people and subjects — Miss A trying to make us like poetry; I never was much good at Maths; Mr K was a dear, I'd never have passed Biology without him: remember how we used to do anything to get out of Games; and the sarcastic Miss B put me off History for life.

Now your own children come home from school with similar stories, but they seem to mean different things. The old familiar subjects don't seem to mean what they used to. So the cartoon shows boy presenting exercise book to father saying 'We only got six out of ten for *our* Maths homework, Dad.' If there ever was a time when all schools taught a fixed package, it isn't so any longer. It would help, perhaps, if schools took pains to explain to parents what has changed and what is the same as in their day. For the moment, let us look at how this change has come about, and in what seems so short a time. A flash-back in three stages will help.

1. YEARS OF EXPANSION (1944-64)

The 1944 Education Act was passed at a time of very high national unity and determination. The resulting system of grammar, technical and secondary modern schools offered 'secondary education for all', as part of the process of building a new society after the War. People responded with enthusiasm. The selective system developed rapidly, though technical schools did not take off in the way that had been hoped. In practice it amounted to education for the able with a view to further education, and vocational and social

97

training for the rest with a view to direct employment. Grammar schools developed along the same lines as the public schools. Modern schools sometimes, sadly, tried to be mini-grammar schools but some of them made great strides in working out programmes of study for those not academically gifted.

Meanwhile, in the independent sector there were some moves to change the content and style of teaching. SMP Mathematics (called 'modern maths' though most of it was around in the nineteenth century), and Nuffield Science pioneered more open and investigative ways of learning. Instead of just being told, pupils would find out more for themselves. It was hoped this would give greater understanding. These initiatives started in schools catering for the more able and spilled over slowly into maintained grammar schools.

The outstanding emphasis of these years is shown by the fate of two government reports:

- **The Robbins Report**, recommending a great expansion of university education, was accepted and fulfilled. More than twenty new universities sprang up, followed by as many polytechnics, to produce the highly educated top brass and managers we needed to keep our place in the world.

- **The Newsom Report** *Half our Future* recommended extra time and facilities, and a more imaginative programme for the half of the children who would leave school at 15 and have little or no further formal education. This report was the subject of much discussion, little action and less resources.

2. YEARS OF CHALLENGE (1964-74)

Slowly at first, then much more quickly (with government direction in 1965) the selective system was replaced by the comprehensive system. This was a response as much to parent pressure as to political dogma. Schools became larger and teachers began to meet the whole ability range instead of the part they knew all about. A Schools Council for Curriculum and Examinations was set up in 1964 with strong teacher involvement. Questions about what we teach and how we examine it were very fully, if not very fruitfully, aired.

One major result of comprehensive reorganization was the removal of the Eleven Plus. Many of today's parents will remember this hurdle, and either the rapture of receiving a bicycle for 'passing' or kind words from Mum which did little to appease the sense of 'failing'. But beyond the thousands of homes where this joy or sorrow reigned, in the primary schools of the country, teachers were suddenly wondering 'What do we do now? If we don't have to prepare children for the Eleven Plus what do we do? What are primary schools for if not to sift people out to the right school at 11?' So they began to think what children needed to know and do, and worked out a variety of programmes — often to the dismay of parents who saw only children playing in sandpits or milling about in chaotic activity.

Two other things which had a great effect on secondary schools happened during this time. First, there was a change in the nature of society. The old emphasis on heavy manual industry — coal, steel, shipbuilding, and so on — was giving way to a 'service' economy in which information technology was more in demand than metal-bashing, and typing and word-processing than assembly-line work. Secondly, in 1972 the leaving age was raised to 16 and schools were faced with the mammoth task of doing something with the many pupils who wanted to leave and get a job (possible in those days). Today's parents will remember, whether they were the good guys who stayed cheerfully and even went on into the sixth form, or the disgruntled conscripts who stayed for 'more of the same'. Teachers who lived through those days either learned fast, or moved to pastures new, or had breakdowns. They certainly were days of challenge and new programmes of work and study emerged with agony and hope.

3. YEARS OF CRISIS (1974-87)

The Prime Minister, Mr Callaghan, set the educational world by the ears with a speech at Ruskin College, Oxford, in 1976. His message was that we were not fitting young people for the real world. They couldn't cope with the new technology or the new requirements of the workplace. So there was intense discussion of 'relevance' and 'work-related' ways of learning. 'Life skills' began to appear on timetables, alongside the 'personal and social development' courses that were just getting established. The progression from school to technical college or apprenticeship scheme — and whether these were offering the right programme — were matters of urgent debate.

What happened in the toolmaking industry is a good example. (See diagram 11.) For years lads with average academic performance had joined apprenticeship schemes and become craftsmen toolmakers — among the elite of the factory workforce. Technological change altered all that, as the diagram shows. We

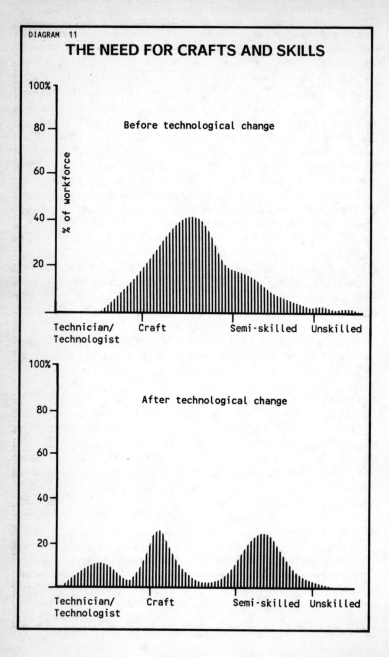

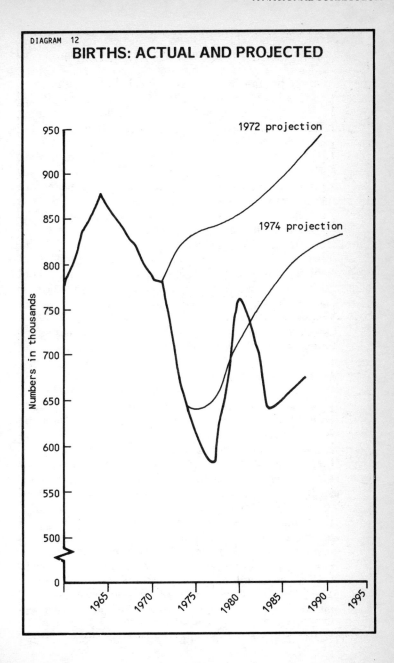

DIAGRAM 12

BIRTHS: ACTUAL AND PROJECTED

1972 projection

1974 projection

Numbers in thousands

950
900
850
800
750
700
650
600
550
500
0

1965 1970 1975 1980 1985 1990 1995

now need a small number of *more* highly qualified technicians to oversee the machines, many fewer craftsmen and still some semi-skilled and unskilled people to take things from A to B.

The situation became even more critical as the number of pupils entering school began to fall. The statisticians had egg on their face in a big way. They had planned for a continuing rise in the birth rate from 1972 onward. Instead there was a big drop (see diagram 12).

So, instead of needing more teachers, it seemed we needed less. But the whole system was geared to expansion, and, like a tanker trying to do a U-turn, it was some time before anything happened. Schools hadn't enough pupils to make the usual size groups in minority subjects like German and Music. Every part of the school programme was under scrutiny to see where staff saving could be achieved. Primary schools were hit first, of course, with sad results for proud, homely little infant schools dwindling and being amalgamated with the junior school next door to make one, still small, primary school. Many teachers were retired early and very few new ones could be taken on.

As if this wasn't enough to worry about, the changing pattern of employment hit the 16-year-old leavers. World recession and the results of automation meant that unemployment grew rapidly, particularly among the less academically able. Whereas in 1937 70% of jobs were manual and 30% white-collar 'thinking'; by the year 2000 the proportions will be reversed. It is greatly to the credit of the schools that during these very pressing years, a lot of good thinking still went on about what we should teach and how we should teach it.

The independent schools were not so seriously affected by these changes. They deal mainly with able pupils and their goal is usually higher education. The main problem was one for parents — finding fees in times of recession. There was, however, a twinge or two of self-examination, especially at the younger end. Preparatory schools had traditionally prepared pupils for the senior independent schools. The hurdle was the 13+ 'Common Entrance' examination, and schools became very good indeed at coaching pupils for this. A few preparatory school teachers were uneasy — as can be seen from a *Times Educational Supplement* feature in 1984, 'Flogging down the Common Entrance Trail', which put the dilemma of a prep. school Head who wants to provide a broad and balanced and modern education for his pupils. 'We can't risk harming the children's chances of getting to their next school,' he said sadly, 'by doing what is good for the children.'

A NATIONAL CURRICULUM

After all these years of trauma, made even more traumatic by several years of dispute between teachers' unions and government over pay and conditions of service, we are presented with Mr Baker's answer to Mr Callaghan's prayer. The 1988 Education Act instructs the Secretary of State, the LEAs, governors and headteachers to provide a basic curriculum, designed to give pupils a broad and balanced education. This comprises the National Curriculum:

'the core and other foundation subjects and specifies in relation to each of them

a) the knowledge, skills and understanding which pupils of different abilities and maturities are expected to have by the end of each key stage (that is, at age 7, 11, 14 and 16);

b) the matters, skills and processes which are required to be taught;

c) the arrangements for assessing pupils at or near the end of each key stage.'

The core subjects are Mathematics, English and Science. The foundation subjects are History, Geography, Technology, Music, Art and Physical Education. For third and fourth stages (secondary schools) a modern foreign language is 'foundation'. Welsh is 'core' in Welsh-speaking Wales and 'foundation' elsewhere in Wales (they think of everything). A National Curriculum Council (NCC) is being set up to oversee the development of this curriculum. In addition, RE is included in the basic curriculum, but not under the national curriculum 'core' or 'foundation', because its content is not determined by the NCC but by an Agreed Syllabus Conference as described in the next chapter. LEAs are also charged with the duty of setting up 'arrangements for the consideration and disposal of any complaint' made by anyone who thinks the new curriculum is not being properly provided.

In the discussion leading up to the Act a figure of 85% was quoted as the proportion of school time taken up by this national curriculum. Minority subject teachers, particularly of Latin and Home Economics, fought a strong campaign and, when the Bill was published, a figure of 70% was given. So more time is left for subjects not mentioned — Classics, Personal and Social Education (PSE), Careers, a second modern language, RE and Drama. The Act specifically says that no fixed proportion of time shall be stated for any subject. Just for comparison, long ago in the days of 'payments by results', the 'three Rs' alone took 90% of teaching time.

Although nearly all parties to the discussion claim to want a national curriculum, they loudly say they don't like the one they've been ordered. This is partly because the Act puts more power into the hands of the Secretary of State than ever before, and people don't like 'centralization', and because Teachers' Associations claim the scheme is inadequately funded. The existing teacher shortage in some subjects — especially science and languages — will be made much worse. The Secretary of State recognizes this and the introduction of the curriculum may be 'staggered' over a number of years as more teachers are trained. Also, and probably most seriously, many teachers fear it will hinder the development of new courses and new methods of teaching and assessment on which many schools pride themselves.

To give an example, a small secondary school in Wensleydale (450 pupils) runs an integrated first-year (11-year-olds) course which takes up 40% of the week. It is not divided up into traditional 'subjects', but all focused round the local neighbourhood and farming industry. The course includes work in English, Maths, History, Geography, Music, RE and Rural Studies, but these are not divided out into separate slots. Instead all the skills, concepts and knowledge are brought in as they are needed for the topic in hand. Early in the course a week at a residential outdoor pursuits centre gives an unusual experience for many children, as they do a survey of the coastal area, land use, town, abbey, and other outdoor work. On return to school this is analyzed and written up. All the 'subject' components are used. The great spin-off benefit has emerged as greatly increased pupil confidence, and quicker settling in at a new (larger) school. The seventy-three pupils are in effect one 'friendship group' and are very well known by the four staff who spend 40% of their time with them.

There is a considerable amount of assessment, but not a series of 'subject' tests. Testing is 'diagnostic', to show what each child *needs*. Every pupil is well known and the very fluid teaching arrangements make individual or group help easy. Sometimes all are together for a 'lead lesson' followed by development work in larger groups. Sometimes pupils work in threes or fours and teachers move among them helping as necessary. When I visited them, they were preparing a magazine to tell next year's entrants what a good idea it was. They themselves will move on to a similar second-year course, this time focused on information technology and science. They are already well skilled on the word-processors that are now regarded as a normal part of the furniture. Another spin-off is the close co-operation of staff involved. They learn from each other and the pupils, and do not see each other as belonging to separate departments with rival territorial claims.

Will the new Act allow this type of thing? Can the Act's assessment provisions be fitted into this 'integrated' programme? The discussion papers before the Act suggest the answer to both questions could be 'Yes' — 'there must be space to accommodate the enterprise of teachers, offering the staff flexibility in the choice of content to adapt what they teach to the needs of the pupil.' The Act is hopeful, too, saying that 'for the purpose of enabling development work or experiments to be carried out' the Secretary of State may remove or modify the need for a particular school to follow the National Curriculum, for all or some pupils. He may also make regulations enabling headteachers to make exceptions for individual pupils. LEA and parents must be notified.

But will parents be seduced to the school in the next town that offers 'proper subjects'? Parents who have visited the school and seen it all happening are enthusiastic. Perhaps they will spread the good news.

How can those who haven't been closely involved in all this development catch up with the discussion? Television programmes, very informative at times, show a lot of examples of what is going on and provoke earnest or spirited, certainly conflicting, views on it. They help, but they also need some guide by which to judge *them*. Three very large questions have to be faced about curriculum:

● Curriculum for all?

● Curriculum for life?

● The 'hidden' curriculum.

Large questions indeed, and only an outline can be given here. This will be mainly about secondary schools. More will be said about primary schools later.

CURRICULUM FOR ALL?

In the grammar-school days everybody did more or less the same things. A daily dose of English, French and Maths; two lessons a week for History, Geography, three sciences, Art, Music, RE, PE. At age 14 'options' were decided and pupils pressed on to O-level and many to A-level and higher education. This was fine for 20-25% of the pupils. The rest followed a similar programme but watered down. Then the CSE examination was devised for 60% of the ability range, though in fact it was taken by 80% or more in some subjects. It was still single-subject; still focused on examinations.

In comprehensive schools some system of streaming or banding was often used, according to the pupils' abilities. But still programmes for all bands were similar, at least to begin with. One kind of curriculum for all, but not a suitable curriculum for each child. Many parents have agonized: 'Sue gets on with it fine. But Steve just doesn't cope that way. I wish he could do more of the things he's good at.'

This one-menu diet is largely the result of university influence. Universities want students who can cope with their degree courses, and they also want easy ways of finding these folk. A-level examinations are used as a filter (not a very accurate one, according to the research) and also to ensure that students have covered the work they will need for their degree studies. In turn, O-level was used as a preparation for A-level. Everybody thought it was a good thing — it wasn't too bad for those going on to higher education — and so modelled the programme for other pupils on it. The single-subject, exam-directed system required and developed mental abilities (known as verbal reasoning) which IQ was thought to measure. So the same thing must be good for those of lesser IQ, they said, provided you water subjects down a bit for them.

It is extraordinary that though universities have no interest whatever in 80% of the children, they have exerted this influence on the curriculum. Maybe it is partly because they have influential support through the independent sector which, of course, is almost totally university-focused. Some recent projects have tried to break free from this and work out what the 80% need, as we shall see later.

CURRICULUM FOR LIFE?

Unease about examination pressure increased as the nature of society changed. 'Leisure' is likely to increase and people will need to find resources of personal fulfilment and recreation. HMI (1977) raised questions about

> 'a curriculum which is, for the majority of pupils . . . in the last two years of compulsory education, almost entirely geared to examination objectives. How can a school ensure that preparation for examinations does not stunt the development of qualities of curiosity, inventiveness and imagination?'

When teachers thought about the possibility of life after school, they realized that what was happening in school did not match what would happen for more than half their customers when they left school. Diagram 13 shows the almost total mismatch. So they set themselves to start at the other end. Instead of working from what you need in order to go into higher education and then trying to simplify it for the rest (the so-called 'top-down' approach), they looked at the 'rest' and asked what they needed to become responsible members of a plural, democratic society (the 'bottom-up' approach).

For a start, they realized that man does not live by verbal reasoning alone. The adult world needs many skills of co-operation, perseverance, communication, self-esteem, self-discipline, handling equipment and problem solving, which neither need nor come from high academic ability. Employers say these skills are vital to modern industry and commerce and that traditional syllabuses were not giving them. Looking at it this way, the limitations of specialist 'subjects' became clear. The world outside does not deal in 'subjects' but wants whole people who can solve problems by drawing on skills learned across the board. 'Subjects' dominate the curriculum because they are easy to examine. But examinations themselves can be counter-productive. If you train all horses as if they were racehorses, you may destroy some children's much-loved and useful ponies. So along with the search for new programmes of learning and preparation for the world of work, there has also been a quest for better methods of assessment.

Teachers are traditionally suspicious of the 'world of work' and of employers looking for 'hands', but they are increasingly looking for ways of matching what goes on in school to what is needed outside. How they are trying will be considered later.

DIAGRAM 13

SCHOOL AND LIFE AFTER

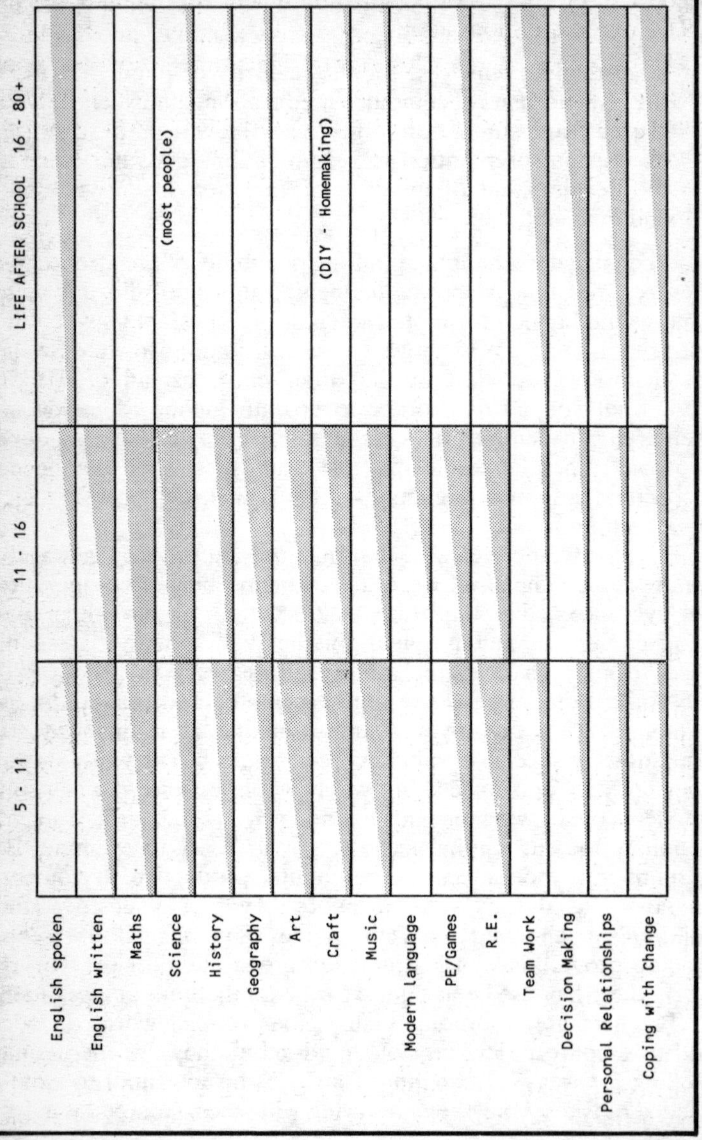
5 - 11
11 - 16
LIFE AFTER SCHOOL 16 - 80+
(most people)
(DIY - Homemaking)
English spoken
English written
Maths
Science
History
Geography
Art
Craft
Music
Modern language
PE/Games
R.E.
Team Work
Decision Making
Personal Relationships
Coping with Change

THE HIDDEN CURRICULUM

It isn't only what happens in 'lessons' that children learn from. The so-called 'hidden curriculum' includes all the other things that happen to Donovan in the course of a week at school: the whole atmosphere of Donovan's school; the way pupils and staff talk to each other; tutor group, assembly, lunch-time activities, sports and such hard-to-describe things as a place to be Donovan; a chance to be somebody; to be worth attention. This can come across in the way you are taught — do you have responsibility for your own learning sometimes or do you sit tight and copy from the board? The structure of the school — do the 'clevers' seem to get most of the resources? Do disruptive children get most of the teacher's attention? Is the atmosphere one of competition or co-operation? How does the school deal with difference — of ability, colour, home background?

Many years ago in a grammar school I tried to enthuse the gentlemen of fifth-form Maths Set 5. They heard me patiently, then told me, 'You're talking like the headmaster. But we can't do Maths. We know we're thick. Everyone tells us we're thick.' Grammar school boys, they were in the top 20% of national ability, but the 'hidden curriculum' had told them differently.

Outside the school there is another curriculum — what the French call 'the parallel school' — all the influences that affect pupils — parental attitudes; television, advertising, newspapers, magazines and comics; the hoardings they pass on the way to school; the peer group pressures. The HMI again: 'Schools are not the only providers of education. They complement other influences or may compete or even conflict with them.' So schools have put increasing resources into 'pastoral' organization, and courses designed to help young people make their own and group decisions, to deal with difficulty, to use resources, to learn how to learn, how to make a reasoned reaction to all the messages they get.

THE AIMS OF A NATIONAL CURRICULUM

What has come out of all the discussion reviewed in the last sections? What will a national curriculum mean in practice? What will it do for the children?

In 1980 the DES published a 'Framework for the School Curriculum', summarizing the work of the previous few years and forming the basis for most present-day statements of aims. It gave six broad aims:

● To help pupils to develop lively enquiring minds, with ability to question, argue rationally and apply themselves to tasks, and physical skills.

● To help pupils acquire knowledge and skill relevant to adult life and employment in a fast-changing world.

● To help pupils to use language and numbers effectively.

● To instil respect for religious and moral values, and tolerance of other races, religions and ways of life.

● To help pupils understand the world in which they live, and the inter-dependence of individuals, groups and nations.

● To help pupils appreciate human achievements and aspirations.

This is much the same as saying what we want children to be (see chapter 3). Other publications have extended the list considerably. It shows what a big and complex job it is to grow up in Britain at the end of the twentieth century. Most parents would be happy with the list given. Allowing for the fact that children differ widely in ability and temperament, it is nevertheless a good general picture. The next question is, 'How shall we get this highly desirable state of affairs?' To achieve these aims, what do you teach and how do you teach it?

WHAT TO LEARN?
As explained already, there is a move away from 'subjects'. What children need to learn is not like neatly arranged boxes on the shelves of an educational supermarket — 500g of history, 1kg English, and so on. In this respect the 1988 Act's persistent reference to 'subjects' is a bit backward, though perhaps it will be interpreted more hopefully.

The HMI defined nine 'areas of learning and experience'. This, they felt, was more helpful than narrower 'subject' division. History and Geography, for example, would come under the 'Human and Social' area but so would come Biology, RE and Health Education. The nine areas are listed below with very brief comment:

1. Aesthetic and creative. Primary schools are good at this. Many a granny has a kitchen wall full of the artistic efforts of her grandchildren. My grandson has a life-size picture of himself on his bedroom door. Apparently all the children lay down on large sheets of paper; teacher drew round them; then they cut out and coloured it all in. Nothing as exciting as that ever happened to me when I was five. Music, drama, dance, writing all liven the day. Later on, children learn to appreciate and criticize the work of others, to recognize and value beauty around them. Creative writing and other expressions of imagination get squeezed out too early in the serious business of examination preparation. But what you think up for yourself always has a fascination greater than what you are told, and in this expression you learn a lot about yourself as well.

2. Human and social. Children love to find out about people; where they live, how they live; what they were like long ago. They need to learn, too, to appreciate the world in which they grow up, to learn about themselves, and their own culture. In a rapidly changing world they especially need a sense of time, place and history, and to develop this into an understanding of political and economic factors that influence our common humanity. Some of this has been controversial (and overlaps with the 'moral'). For example, the 1986 Act lays down that sex education must be in the context of 'moral considerations and the value of family life' and political education must be 'balanced'.

3. Linguistic and literary. Reading, writing, speaking and listening are essential in our society, though the first two tend to oust the others as children move up the school system. Grammar and spelling are sore points between some parents and some teachers — particularly over marking. The Thomas Report (1985) offers the explanations: 'It is not desirable to give children the lasting impression that things are right when they are not. But nor should children be discouraged from using words or making efforts that have a touch of adventurousness for fear their faults will attract a prolific red pen.' It does add the wise comment: 'Schools should explain their marking policies to pupils and parents.' Certainly fluency and confidence in speaking and writing, ease and clear comprehension in reading and listening are vital ingredients of the educated person. There is also a world of literature to enter and schools (and perhaps home) battle against the instant impact of television for children's interest. The 1988 Act makes a second language a 'foundation' subject too in secondary schools — a worthy aim for the traditionally isolated Englishman, though the level at which children will cope will vary. Many of our new neighbours are already fluent in Urdu or Punjabi. It is to be hoped these will count (as Welsh does!).

4. Mathematics. This is much more than the mechanical ability to do sums and recite tables. They may still be useful sometimes, though calculators have revolutionized life. Very few people ever need to multiply 574 x 974 in their heads or on paper. The Set 5 mathematicians I taught eventually got really good at working out cube roots by logarithms. I doubt if they've ever needed to do it since, and anyway calculators have put logarithms on the shelf. Still, they enjoyed it and that is an important aim of mathematics as well as developing a useful tool for dealing with many problems. Concepts of number, shape, size, comparison, arranging data, all turn out to be much more difficult to teach with understanding than was supposed. Applications to money, time, measure, estimating and problem solving follow from real understanding. Recent emphasis has been on the use of mathematical concepts and techniques to formulate and solve problems in many areas — as well as to investigate ideas for their own sake, for fun.

5. Moral. Understanding the values by which people and societies live. It is a controversial area because adult society is floundering. The old landmarks are being moved. The boundary between 'acceptable' and 'unacceptable' is increasingly hazy. Sex education (mentioned above) has been much discussed. In many ways standards at home may differ (higher or lower) than standards at school so teachers are in a sensitive position. But to disregard the area is to sell pupils short, and give the impression it does not matter. Pupils need guidance into moral reasoning and decision. They are tomorrow's citizens and need knowledge and skills to criticize as well as understand the different value-systems they will meet. Even if it is not formally taught as a timetabled subject, it will enter into many areas (such as values in English literature, History and Geography) and be more subtly 'taught' by the school structure and ethos.

6. Physical. Some pupils love sport; some do everything they can to dodge PE and games. Balanced personal development includes physical awareness, the understanding and use of the body. Health education, diet and fitness will be part of this, also the ability to control emotion, to work co-operatively, to lead and be led.

7. Spiritual. This is the world of inner feelings and beliefs; reflection on experience; asking 'ultimate questions' about the purpose and significance of human life and the world around us. This is not only RE (which will get more space to itself in the next chapter), but will be met in literature, music, art, drama and even (ideally) in the sense of wonder in science and the feeling of responsibility in humanities. Sadly it is often restricted to RE, if anywhere, and pupil growth is stunted. In a plural society, respect for a variety of religions is important and the nature of religious language needs to be understood.

8. Scientific. This starts with curiosity and enquiry. It is a pity that the 'wonder' element gets lost as 'explanations' multiply. A six-year-old fascinated by water pouring over her hand, or listening to the sound of a rabbit crunching its lettuce is expressing a fundamental human response to the world around. Concepts develop understanding, prediction and control. Pupils learn accurate observation, recording, logical inference, how to design and perform experiments — though at school level most of these are simply contrived illustrations of what the book says. If Rajeev in the fifth form finds an unexpected value for g (acceleration due to gravity), he will be told he's careless in his experiment. If Professor XYZ found any such thing it would be news.

9. Technological. A new name for many old things and some new ones. It is about applying knowledge to design and making things, but not only the skills of drawing, woodwork and metalwork (and now electronics). It draws on these and other skills and knowledge to clarify and define problems, evaluate possible solutions, and select the best on grounds that include economics, scientific knowledge, and moral considerations. Then you have to communicate the solution clearly. It gives an insight into the way industry and commerce and public services operate to give society what it needs.

The 1988 Act starts off at Section One with acceptance of this pattern of 'areas of learning and experience' demanding

'a broad and balanced curriculum which

a) promotes the spiritual, moral, cultural, mental and physical development of pupils at the school and of society; and

b) prepares such pupils for the opportunities, responsibilities and experiences of adult life.'

Unfortunately Sections Two and Three relapse into talk of core 'subjects' and foundation 'subjects'. Working parties are being set up for each subject to lay down attainment targets at various ages. We must hope that they do their work in the spirit of Section One.

This is to be for all pupils in maintained schools. The application to independent schools is hazy; maybe they are trusted to do the right thing without legal direction. Pupils with special needs — physical or emotional handicap, slow-learners and the very gifted — are still entitled to this curriculum as far as their circumstances allow. The special attention they need due to their limitations (or giftedness) must not crowd out a balanced 'normal' course. Great efforts are being made to include as many as possible in 'normal' schools. Much remains to be done.

LEARNING TO LEARN

The nine 'areas' are mainly *what* ought to be learnt. You could look at education another way and ask *how* children learn. The old rhyme gives one method:

> Ram it in, jam it in, children's heads are hollow.
> Cram it in, slam it in, still there's more to follow.

That was probably never quite true (except in Dicken's *Hard Times*) but certainly the present emphasis is very different. Child-centred or child-related teaching is the model, using 'discovery' methods. This could be pushed too far, and provides good stories and jokes:

> Teacher: Why aren't you doing anything, Johnny?
> Johnny: I'm discovering what it's like doing nothing.

However, it does emphasize the learner rather than the teacher as central, the process of learning rather than the content.

Employers keep saying they want employees who can think for themselves, find out information, work as a team, solve problems, show initiative, be flexible. It is, incidentally, ironical that, having said all this, they used to put so much weight on O-level results, which say much more about the information people have remembered than about other qualities. Particularly ironic was employers' reaction to the CSE examination which was designed to include more course-work and self-directed study. Anyway, they say they want these qualities. How are they going to get them? A DES paper posed the questions:

> 'How do we help children to understand sexual relationships and their implications? Do we prepare children well enough for more leisure and less work as unemployment becomes more structural and less cyclical? How do we prepare them to understand the social and political impact of unemployment? . . . Do we

give pupils an understanding that they are living through a third industrial revolution which may lead to social and personal disturbance . . . ? When pupils can legally marry at 16, and vote at 18, what should the curriculum do to help pupils with these matters of fundamental importance to adult life? It is in this context that the conviction has grown up that all pupils are entitled to a broad compulsory common curriculum to the age of 16 which introduces them to a range of experiences, makes them aware of the kind of society in which they are going to live and gives them the skills necessary to live in it.'

This 'Entitlement Curriculum' has been described under four headings: Skills, Attitudes, Concepts and Knowledge. This does not rule out the content-based view of the 'areas of knowledge and experience'. It is complementary to it and does state an important principle. What is the use of a teenager being good at Chemistry and being able to describe the molecular structure of alcohol if he has a serious drinking problem? How will a clever person get on in marriage or employment if her attitude is arrogant or unreliable? Less clever people may be more at home in society if they have developed attitudes of perseverance, self-confidence and adaptability. It may be said these attitudes are learnt at home, or picked up somewhere along the way and it is not part of the school's job to 'teach' them. Yet it is good to draw specific attention to them. This is a large part of what children need. We look at the four parts of the programme in more detail.

1. Skills. A skill is a capacity or competence: the ability to perform a task successfully, whether intellectual or manual. Skills include:

● Communication skills, broadly defined to include not only reading and writing but speaking, listening, drawing diagrams, demonstration and acting a role.

● Numerical skills.

● Skills of observation and recording and interpreting what is observed.

● Imaginative skills.

● Skills of organization, to get, arrange, classify material; make the best use of time.

● Physical and practical skills — manual dexterity; knowing which tools to use and how to use them.

115

● Social skills — ability to co-operate, negotiate, express your own ideas in various contexts, consider and judge other points of view.

● Problem-solving skills — deciding what is important, devising hypotheses and testing them, evaluating results, persevering with alternatives.

These skills come up all over the place in the school day, of course. Sometimes they are specifically 'taught' at some point in a particular 'subject', but it is haphazard and chancy. Attempts have been made to find out where they actually arise, and then ensure that specific guidance is given in mastering the skills themselves and applying them to a variety of situations.

A lot of 'note-making' occurs. But unless pupils are taught how to do this efficiently, a lot of time is wasted and learning is hindered. If each teacher has to explain for her own class, pupils don't see it as a general skill that can be applied everywhere, especially if Miss X likes notes done this way, Mr Y doesn't seem to bother and Dr K gives you a printed handout anyway. So 'life skills' are now on the timetable, teaching study skills, library use and how to get information, group-work skills, personal confidence building, and so on.

2. Attitudes. An attitude is a disposition to think or act in a particular way, a tendency to face a situation with a particular expectation. Some people have developed an attitude of 'I can't do it' when faced with anything new; some people expect to be told; some people can't stand being told.

All this will have something to do with basic temperament, but also something to do with what and how you learn. If you are always at the middle or bottom of the class, in a competitive situation, you don't expect to get everything right. Worse still, your teacher builds up a similar expectation. Nor is all sweetness and light in the world outside. One girl who went off on a work-experience placement enthusiastic and eager to learn, returned disillusioned and furious at the apathy and slovenliness of the office she had been in. Even so, it is worthwhile finding out what attitudes are needed, how people acquire them and what can be done in school to help.

Life skills and careers lessons talk about group attitudes of co-operation, reliability, self-confidence, self-discipline, tolerance, perseverance, consideration of others. Individual attitudes of curiosity, openness to new ideas, commitment to a purpose, honesty and integrity are in short supply in society at large and it is unfair to expect teachers to be markedly better than other citizens. Nevertheless, they do have a responsibility as models, and the school ethos and structure can strengthen rather than weaken these attitudes.

3. Concepts. A concept enables you to organize and understand knowledge and experience, usually as a generalization or abstraction from many isolated things. This key feature of the ability to learn was given insufficient attention in the past. Masses of facts can be memorized but unless they are organized into patterns and understood you only have a lot of walking filing-cabinets or tape-recorders. At one stage, following the heyday of Piaget's child psychology, educationalists were pessimistic about young children grasping concepts at all. Particularly in RE it was said children could not cope with the concept of God. The pessimism has receded, though it is widely acknowledged that teachers must give careful attention to the formation of concepts.

Parents who have been mystified by primary school 'number' ('Why don't they just teach them to count and say their tables?') will find on discussing with the teacher that the aim is to form a strong number-concept, so that whatever it is that three dogs, three cats and three houses have in common is understood. Not like the mythical fishmonger who is alleged to have exploded, 'Blow me down, I've been working it out in herrings and they're mackerel.' In secondary school the quest for understanding continues and some concepts are very sophisticated — wave, molecule, perspective, diminished seventh. Most of the interesting parts of living are connected with understanding and the relation between concepts. Pupils should at least recognize one when they meet it, and know how to look for the unifying concepts in any new field of experience.

4. Knowledge. Some knowledge will arise from natural curiosity and the daily business of living. At some ages children amass information like squirrels collecting nuts. They astound parents by knowing that Mercury has no moons, Zachariah was the father of John the Baptist and the new boy at school comes from a school with outside toilets. Often the least successful pupils surprise their teacher with detailed knowledge of a hobby or interest. In terms of curriculum planning, in the 'subject' pattern the teacher is a specialist in an area of knowledge and will select the 'knowledge' which needs to be covered to give a pupil an adequate acquaintance with the area. This can be

117

exciting and many people have a life-long interest in novels, or Geography, because of such an introduction at school.

Overall, a selection of knowledge is needed to build up the skills, attitudes and concepts necessary to cope with the areas of knowledge mentioned and the needs of life in the world. So, for example, there has been a move to give 'economic awareness' — knowledge about how the world of business works, concepts like exchange, inflation, price-mechanism, and skills like writing a cheque or filling out a claim for unemployment benefit. There is a case here for letting children know about the great and the good (provided they really are good), tales of courage, perseverance and achievement by people of all races.

'WHAT TO' WITH 'HOW TO'

In primary schools the division of what is taught in subject areas is less marked and both these ways of looking at educa-tion — areas of knowledge and general factors — are worked in together by the class teacher for her class. In some subject areas there may be a person with responsibility for seeing that that subject is understood by all class teachers and the material properly prepared. Occasionally this specialist takes lessons with all classes — in music or a foreign language, for example.

Secondary schools until very recently have been dominated by the subject divisions and the immense complexity of timetabling has solidified this still further. Children who have been accustomed to the broadly 'one-teacher' world of primary school have to get accustomed to being taught by seven or eight different people all selling their own specialism in their own classroom. Some schools try to reduce this by having English, History, Geography and RE taught as 'Humanities' in one block by one teacher per class. Later in the secondary school, especially for the less able pupils, courses involving larger blocks of time with one teacher are arranged. Some courses are specifically designed, as we shall see, at 14-18 years to present an integrated development of the pupil as a whole person. The problem is by no means resolved and is most acute for the 14-year-old who may have done nine or ten subjects but has to choose six or seven for the two-year GCSE course, starting 'a vague two-year journey towards nebulous and distant goals' (as one report puts it). This means he has to stop doing a number of things he may have enjoyed — Art and Music and RE are usually sad casualties. Motivation is a problem, too, as the report continues: 'The very structure of two-year courses disadvantages many working-class pupils. We need to find ways of motivating pupils that do not rely on appeals to goals two years ahead.'

There is some pressure for the introduction of a 'modular' course, enabling a pupil to do a number of 'modules' (free-standing units of learning) of less than the full two years. For example, she could do a standard two-year course in English, Maths, Physics and Chemistry, one year in Home Economics, Electronics and Biology and one year in Art, History and Economics, as well as a weekly dose of RE and Recreation. Even one-term modules could be possible, grouped together to count for a GCSE certificate as long as they have 'coherence'. Examination groups set up by the government are looking at this. One group invites schools to submit schemes. An encouraging sign is the report of a working party set up by the Standing Conference of Regional Examination Boards to find 'another approach to the curriculum which would be complementary to the new GCSE'. Their conclusion states:

> 'The alternative approach to the curriculum outlined in the previous pages has attempted to get away from the standard, single-subject, academically orientated curriculum. It has emphasized process rather than content, the development of skills which are transferable from one curriculum area to another and the association of learning procedures with the future needs of pupils in terms of living and working within the community. The fact that the skills listed under separate headings often appear to be the same or very similar serves to emphasize the inter-relatedness of these areas and underlines one of the key aims inherent in this framework. It is recognized that many schools will not wish to alter their existing organization in order to accommodate what is outlined here; this is why a pattern of modules is suggested which would still enable a school to develop a cross-curricular approach.'

The examiner is still king, so perhaps we shall see movement in this direction soon. It would certainly give a broader and more flexible curriculum.

CURRICULUM FOR THE OLDER STUDENT

Since the new thinking in secondary schools has been sparked off by the school-to-work change, it is natural that many of the new ideas have been at the older end. Some of this will be dealt with in chapter 9 on Careers. Here we look at how the curriculum as a whole has been slanted towards the needs of students soon to be in the world. Several principles compete for attention:

- Nothing must be done to hinder the 15-20% who will go on to polytechnics or universities — all schemes allow A-level or equivalent courses to continue;

- The needs of the workplace must not crowd out broad general education;

- An industrial trading nation must have an adequately trained workforce;

- Students need to make their own decisions about careers, but need information and guidance;

- Equal opportunities must be available for both boys and girls. The Sex Discrimination Act 1975 says so, but it has been general practice anyway in many schools.

TVEI AND CPVE EXPLAINED

For some time many schools have arranged 'work experience' — a week or two for students, usually in the fifth year. This can be a sampling of a particular job, and then some go on into that kind of job, often taken on by the firm where they did the work experience. It can be more broadly an experience of the disciplines and relationships of a workplace, and students who are going on to higher education, as well as others, have found this experience personally valuable. A few schools have this work experience integrated into a careers programme with preparation and feedback from the placement. In general it is a fairly small intrusion into the traditional school pattern — a demanding intrusion for teachers as there will be some disruption of normal classes and students will have to be visited at the place of work.

A similar arrangement is often made between a school and a nearby college of further education so that students can attend technical and vocational courses run at the college — so-called 'link-courses' — to broaden their curriculum. This does not have quite the same effect of learning what a real workplace is like, but does give a chance to learn skills not available at the school.

Technical and Vocational Educational Initiative, known as TVEI, is a more sustained attempt to bring school and industrial learning together. The Initiative was announced by the Government in 1983, through the Manpower Services Commission (MSC), now called the Training Commission. Eventually about 80% of LEAs took part in pilot schemes, heavily funded by MSC, to develop industry-related courses of study for students aged 14-18 years. Government hoped the pilot schemes would be so successful that LEAs would want to extend the system more generally — though how they would be funded was less clear.

Among the stated aims of these courses are:

● Preparation for adult life in a society liable to rapid change;

● To encourage initiative, problem-solving and other aspects of personal development;

● To give technical and vocational elements which are broadly related to potential job opportunities;

● Planned work experience throughout the programme;

● Regular educational assessment and careers counselling.

Great emphasis is placed on information technology and computing, and first-hand experience of industrial situations. There is a wide range of short courses (modules) offering experience of work — anything from animal husbandry to robotics.

Assessment goes on throughout the programme, building up a 'profile'. The student is involved in this by self-evaluation and discussion of the details of the course. Students can take traditional GCSE and A-level examinations, but also other more vocational examinations usually taken at colleges of further education. About 40% of time is spent in the TVEI programme and the other 60% on core curriculum (English, Maths and some GCSE options), so TVEI students are not cut off from the rest of their peers, but spend over half their time in 'normal' classes.

The programme involves a great deal of staff training as teachers need to become confident in the new 'integrated' approach. Careful co-ordination is needed as a student progresses over the four years, using school, college and industrial workplace. This scheme has proved attractive to students of all abilities, boys and girls alike, and is to continue beyond the pilot stage. LEAs are preparing to develop the whole 14-18 curriculum along TVEI lines, though without the present generous MSC funding. To some extent the success of the scheme will be clearer when the first contingent of 4,000 students finish in the summer of 1988.

Certificate of Pre-Vocational Education, known as *CPVE*, started in 1985 following much discussion of the needs of young people just leaving school at 16. It aims to provide a one-year bridge between school and employment or further study. Before CPVE, many students had insufficient examination qualifications to fit them for some employment or for diploma courses at further education colleges. They either stayed on at school and repeated O-levels (not a very inspiring task) or went to take further education college courses introducing them to a vocational area (about which they were not certain).

CPVE aims to be 'pre-vocational', giving added basic education and also a chance to look at several vocational possibilities. For teachers it is, like TVEI, very different from normal 'subjects' as all work is focused on 'occupational families'. Each student has an individual programme which is negotiated with the tutor.

The aims of CPVE are stated:

● To assist the transition from school to adulthood by further equipping young people with basic skills, experiences, attitudes, knowledge and personal and social competences required for success in adult life including work;

●To provide individually relevant educational experience which encourages learning and achievement;

● To provide young people with recognition of their attainments through a qualification which embodies national standards;

● To provide opportunities for progression to continuing education, training and/or work.

This is achieved by core studies grouped in ten areas: personal and career development; industrial, social and environmental studies, communication; social skills; numeracy; science and technology; information technology; creative development; practical skills; and problem-solving. Motivation is achieved by focusing these core studies on vocational studies, arranged in five categories: business and administrative; technical services; production; distribution; and services to people. Students do three or four of these at introductory, exploratory or preparatory level. They may also do 'additional studies' for 20% of the timetable and this is usually a GCSE subject in which they have shown ability — once or twice an A-level has been taken as additional study.

An elaborate record is kept in which every topic is analyzed into the core skills it contained. Tutor and student hold regular discussion as the course record is filled in, giving a steady personal relationship of support and guidance. For example, the core area 'Personal and Career Development' has the main aim:

'To bring about an informed perspective as to the role and status of a young person in an adult, multi-cultural society, including the world of work. To enable the young person to maximize his/her potential.'

122

and sub-aims:

• 'To develop a young person's critical awareness of his/her abilities, needs and interests and how to make best use of these;

• To develop the skills, knowledge and experience necessary for young people to understand the variety of roles played during adult life and to be enabled to play an appropriate part;

• To provide a basis on which the young person can consider a range of social/moral/ethical issues in contemporary society and formulate his/her own values.'

Each sub-aim is broken down into smaller items that can be identified in the student's work and recorded. The role of the tutor is therefore very different from usual teaching. The documentation is formidable and the jargon daunting, but the scheme has proved good at motivating students who have had a poor school experience. Further education colleges are prepared to accept CPVE as entry to diploma courses and altogether more than 80% of CPVE students go either into employment or such FE courses.

A FOUR-YEAR PACKAGE

CPVE was designed specially for the average or below-average student who had often found the 'normal' two-year 'examination course' at school dull and uninspiring, and possibly shown this by an unco-operative attitude. TVEI aimed at all abilities and strengthened motivation by relating study to the world of industry. The question naturally arose 'Why should anyone have to cope with a 14-16 course that was uninspiring and irrelevant?' GCSE courses in various subjects might be all right for some — especially the 20% going on to A-level and higher education, though even for them a less piecemeal style of teaching might be an advantage. Can there not be more flexibility?

In 1987 the National Association of Headteachers (NAHT) produced *A policy 14-18*. This urged an integrated scheme for all young people. It would have four elements — academic, practical, technical and vocational. The present system makes age 16 a watershed (with GCSE for most pupils) when some leave and pursue training in the Youth Training Scheme (YTS) and some stay in school or colleges of further education and start new (possibly unrelated) studies. In practice, most young people are in some form of training till age 17 and very many till 18. Why cannot the whole process be planned as a single four-year programme appropriate to each young person? This would have advantages of great flexibility, so that late-developers (or any students who changed career ideas) could modify courses. Also, it might avoid the sense of 'sheep and goats' division at 16 when those who stay in 'education' seem to be successful and those who leave for 'training' are second-class citizens.

NAHT spell out the components:

● **Curriculum** — a full curriculum based on a large common core with extensive use of modules and ease of movement between them. This curriculum would bring together appropriate elements of traditional academic subjects, cross-curricular developments, personal and social education, vocational and/or pre-vocational education, information and other technologies and work experience.

● **Assessment** — assessment of modules linked to a system of records of achievement which sums up the progress and achievement of young people throughout the preparation phase (14-18) and including such things as initiative, motivation and commitment. At least to begin with, existing public examinations could be incorporated into this.

● **Counselling** — to support and advise young people and their parents when negotiating each individual's programme.

● **Teachers** — a broader contribution from specialist teachers; more flexible contracts for teachers so that 'twilight', 'evening', and 'holiday' teaching can be accommodated.

● **Structure** — greater responsibility given to pupils above the age of 14 for their own safety and welfare; alterations in attendance regulations so that pupils could be based either in a school, college or workplace as most appropriate to the programme.

● **Financial support** — Child Benefit as at present to be paid to age 16 and then a new common personal allowance of an appropriate level paid directly to the young person regardless of the institution or workplace or type of preparation being undertaken.

This is a bold vision which goes some way to making Britain's training of its young people as comprehensive as many of its competitor nations. Yet the emphasis on individual programme and the strong base of general education means that the industrial tail does not wag the preparation-for-life dog. The scheme received favourable comment. The Secondary Heads Association

(SHA) produced a similar scheme shortly afterwards. It may be some way in the future yet, however. John Swallow, who chaired the committee, quoted Machiavelli, 'The innovator has for enemies all those who have done well under the old system.'

THE VALUE OF WORK

These initiatives aim at the youngster on his way from childhood to adulthood. They all aim to establish purpose, value and dignity — a dignity that does not depend upon academic excellence, but on each person as an individual in a community, contributing a variety of skills and interests. What is very different from traditional schooling is the close relation with the world of work. Traditionally, teachers have been a bit suspicious of employers and 'work' which they have often pictured as nasty, boring, repetitive, noisy and probably dangerous. It seemed almost as though pupils leaving the cultured world of school were going to submit to nameless barbarisms at work. This has been a common view among many 'educated' people. Work has seemed a necessary evil, part of the human condition — probably Adam and Eve's fault for getting thrown out of the garden of Eden where everything just grew for them. Ironically such people often put up with 'work' to get money which they spend on garden or do-it-yourself about the house, which they don't call 'work'.

The new emphasis is not only about 'getting a good job' but on the value of work, whether paid or unpaid, good both for the person working and the person being served. Voluntary 'work' and house 'work' (what Americans call 'homemaking') might get a welcome boost in status. Work, paid or unpaid, is a true part of the human calling, co-operation with others (and God) dealing responsibly with God's world. As the ancient Wisdom of Ben Sirach commented — after mentioning those 'whose conversation is only of cattle' and many other craftsmen — 'yet by these is the fabric of society maintained, and their work is their prayer.'

CHAPTER 6

Religious and Moral Education
the debate

One part of the curriculum touched on only incidentally in the last chapter deserves fuller treatment. Religious Education — called 'instruction' in the previous Acts — is fixed in the curriculum in name if not always in practice and has been a source of long and often heated debate. The 1944 Act greatly strengthened the position of RE. The Agreed Syllabus was compulsory. Butler was very anxious to get his reform 'secondary education for all' through Parliament, so was prepared to negotiate with the churches. The churches were hard pressed to afford the great extension and improvement of property that the 1944 Act required, and many schools passed to LEA control for lack of church funds. The churches were anxious to ensure protection for Religious Instruction. The Act provided that 'religious instruction shall be given in every county school and in every voluntary school'. The Act gave details of how an 'Agreed Syllabus' was to be made by a conference of interests arranged by the LEA — representatives from the Church of England, other denominations, teacher associations and the Authority. This did not satisfy everyone, of course. The Archbishop of Liverpool described it as 'the religion of nobody, taught by anybody and paid for by everybody'. Winston Churchill called it the 'County Council Creed'. But it was an attempt to stop extremism and give a fair basis of knowledge.

In those days, 'other denominations' meant 'Christian denominations' — Roman Catholics, Baptists, Methodists and so on. In recent times, especially in some inner-London authorities, this group has been 'other religions', reflecting the ethnic nature of the neighbourhood. The 1988 Act says 'such Christian and other denominations as, in the opinion of the authority, ought, having regard to the circumstances of the area, to be represented'.

Similar stories can be told of other European countries — the Durham Report (1970) found that RE was compulsory in Northern Ireland, Scotland, Spain, West Germany, Sweden ('informative and neutral'), Denmark, Norway and parts of Switzerland.

The first clause of the 1988 Act might give the impression

that here we have a major educational purpose — 'to promote the spiritual, moral, cultural, mental and physical development of pupils at the school and of society'. In fact, the Bill as originally published simply left governors and headteachers to see that the 1944 requirements were continued. These provisions were not working very well, however. Many schools gave little attention to it, law or no law. It needed at least the boost of being put into the Basic Curriculum, or it would get lost in competition for the small amount of time left for 'other subjects'. So its advocates claimed, and the Act as passed now provides as follows:

● Religious education is part of the Basic Curriculum, which the Secretary of State, LEAs, governors and headteacher are all charged to provide. It is not a foundation or core subject, because it will not have attainment targets set by a working party like the other subjects. The syllabus will continue to be worked out by the Agreed Syllabus conference.

● The 1944 provisions for the 'daily act of worship' are widely amended. This need no longer be at the beginning of the day, nor of the whole school: 'all pupils . . . shall on each school day take part in an act of collective worship.' And the arrangements 'shall be made by the headteacher after consultation with the governors' either for 'a single act of worship for all pupils or for separate acts of worship for pupils in different age groups or in different school groups.' The character of the 'collective worship' is much more closely specified, as explained later.

Parents' rights granted in the 1944 Act are unchanged:

'If the parent of any pupil in attendance at any county school or any voluntary school requests that he be wholly or partly excused from attendance at religious worship in the school or from attendance at religious instruction in the school . . . then until the request is withdrawn, the pupil shall be excused such attendance accordingly.'

All this applies to Grant Maintained Schools too.

THE DEBATE ABOUT RE
This is one of the longest-running features of the education story. In 1870 'undenominational religious instruction' was a compromise. Radicals wanted completely secular schools, leaving religious education to the churches, out of school time. Some high churchmen didn't like State schools at all — education

should all be the churches' job. Following the Act, the London School Board settled for 'the teaching of the Bible . . . with such explanations and instruction therefrom in the principles of morality and religion as is suited to the capacities of children', and at the time that satisfied most people.

Report after report mentioned RE as an important part of the child's experience:

● *The Spens Report of 1938:*
'No boy or girl can be counted as properly educated unless he or she has been made aware of the fact of the existence of a religious interpretation of life.'

● *The Crowther Report of 1959:*
'The teenagers with whom we are concerned need, perhaps before all else, to find a faith to live by. They will not all find precisely the same faith and some will not find any. Education can and should play some part in their search. It can assure them that there is something to search for and it can show them where to look and what other men have found.'

● *The Newsom Report of 1963:*
'The best schools give their pupils something which they do not get elsewhere, something they know they need when they receive it, though they had not realized the lack before . . . given in a way which does justice to the mixed society in which we live, recognizing the range and degrees of religious belief and practice to be found in it, and respecting the right of the individual conscience to be provided with the material on which freely to decide its path.'

● *The Plowden Report of 1967* assumed continuance of RE in primary schools though a minority report opposed it for young children mainly on the grounds that the material was unsuitable for young children.

Many of the colleges for training teachers had Christian foundations and it was taken for granted that RE was an important part of the school programme. In the schools (especially grammar schools) in the 50s and 60s there was a strong growth of voluntary Christian groups and sixth-form conferences organized by the Christian Education Movement (CEM) and Inter-School Christian Fellowship (ISCF). These conferences often linked State schools with the independent sector, which had long-standing religious traditions. The conferences have become less frequent, but voluntary groups linked with the ISCF (now called Scripture

Union in Schools) flourish still in very many schools of all types.

So while the world outside the school system became progressively secularized, the schools (especially grammar schools and independent schools) maintained a fairly high commitment to religion, at least in name. In the 1960s a strong campaign was mounted by the National Secular Society and the British Humanist Association to have religion removed from the curriculum and replaced by 'Moral Education'. The 'battle of the surveys' raged as parents told pollsters they wanted RE (90% in one survey), and the opposition said the parents really meant morality, not religion. Parliament debated the subject quite often — a debate in 1976 under the Labour Government; a Select Committee in 1981 (Conservatives). The Lords returned learnedly to the subject from time to time. Always there were a few speeches saying RE should be dropped. Always there were some strongly supportive, so it stayed put.

The discussion surrounding the new Act brought the lobbyists out again. For example, pleading for RE to be put in the foundation subjects and to ensure a substantial place for Christianity. Others argued that being 'compulsory' by law hadn't done much for RE in the past. Good RE happens when its educational value is developed by good teachers, not when reluctant teachers comply with the law. Others again argued that compulsory RE was likely to be seen as the school doing its legal religious duty, when actually matters of faith and value should pervade the whole curriculum.

THE ARGUMENTS FOR RE

Why does RE stay on the boil like this? And what should be done about it? There are two shaky, though popular, arguments and one educational argument:

1. National religion? In its extreme form this argument talks about a 'Christian country' and a 'Christian tradition' into which children must be initiated. The Queen is 'Defender of the Faith'; Parliament starts with prayers (for the few who attend); royal occasions take place in St Paul's; people swear in court on the Bible; most people have a religious funeral and very many are still married in church. Sixty per cent or more tell the pollsters they are connected with some denomination or other. Therefore, children should learn all about it — not for a particular denomination, or to make them 'join', but to get the general background to the culture.

This is a poor argument for three reasons:

- The 'folk religion' of present-day Britain has little in common with the serious structure of belief and practice a school study would deal with. It may be a nostalgic and even useful link with an earlier age of more direct belief. It is not traditional or New Testament Christianity.

● The idea that Christianity is a 'national religion' and in some sense a social cement, keeping Britain British, is unfair to the facts and unfair to loyal British minorities of other religions. Muslims outnumber Methodists and you may meet as many Hindus as Anglicans in Leicester. They value their Britishness and to pretend this depends upon religion is wrong and may even lead to racist intolerance. It may well be that much of our national culture got into the system from Christian roots. Our laws were strongly influenced by Christian as well as Roman models. But these features of our law and culture do not now stay there for those reasons, but by their wide acceptance by people of all faiths and none who see them as self-evidently for the common good.

● Some convinced Christian minorities do not accept the idea either. They are happy to live and serve in a folk culture as long as they can urge individuals to become truly committed. In some cases they have set up 'Christian schools' where their children can be protected from the soggy unprincipled mess.

2. Religion = morals? The other very common view is that we need religion (and children must be taught it), because we need morals. In the debate on the 1944 Act, one MP proposed that Religious Instruction should be limited to the 'accepted Christian principles of truth, honesty, kindness, clean living and self-respect.' Such a reduced version was not accepted then and is not adequate now. It is true that religions of all sorts do have moral outcomes, and make moral demands upon their adherents. But their adherents usually sell them as *true*, not merely morally useful. The Christian commands are 'Love the Lord your God' and 'Love your neighbour as yourself'. Most people regard the second as the real essence, with the first as a useful support. But in fact the first is 'First'. There are several difficulties in this 'Religion = Morals' view:

● If morality does depend only on religious commitment, a plural society could not function. Religious commitments differ and many citizens have none.

● Secularists are constantly saying that morality can be worked out by common sense and goodwill, and pupils should be encouraged to do this for themselves. Even allowing for some over-optimism in the argument, government does depend upon everyone, of any faith or none, being able to see the reasonableness of required behaviour. Secularists have, in fact, argued it is *dangerous* to link morality with religion since, when religion is given up in the early teens (inevitable in their view), morality will be left rootless.

• There is some strength in this particular argument as far as education is concerned, though not as far as individuals' behaviour is concerned. It was forcefully put by Lord Justice Devlin:

'A man who concedes that morality is necessary to society must support the use of those instruments without which morality cannot be maintained. The two instruments are those of teaching, which is doctrine, and enforcement which is the law. If morals could be taught simply on the basis that they are necessary to society, there would be no social need for religion; it could be left as a purely personal affair. But morality cannot be taught in that way. Loyalty is not taught in that way either. No society has yet solved the problem of how to teach morality without religion.'

That was written in 1969. Certainly all religious groups train their children in behaviour along with religious instruction. In Britain, moral education was for centuries given in the context of common religious belief. But now, in schools, religious commitment cannot be assumed, and a lot of effort has been put into giving all children moral training, irrespective of religious belief. Devlin might still be unimpressed.

3. The educational argument. So what argument remains for RE in the curriculum? The major reports focus on its educational value.

• RE deals with matters at the root of identity and value. There is an area of mystery, wonder and perplexity which gives both richness and depth to experience. This has already been mentioned in chapter 3. Where social science might reduce children and their behaviour to machines, RE introduces a 'new interpretation' which adds much greater meaning. Children are not only social units but creatures of God and potentially *his* children; the world is his creation and we are responsible to maintain it and use it to serve each other. This interpretation has its own language — spread among many religions — and its own method of understanding. It is 'worthwhile' knowledge which children should be made aware of. What they do with the awareness is up to them.

• Incidentally, RE offers training in a variety of skills, many shared with other subjects, but some related to the wider world-view given by a religious dimension. The Avon County Resources Centre suggested the following:

— ability to handle and interpret different kinds of evidence (historical, sociological and textual);

— ability to use different methods of enquiry (reading, observation and reflection);

— ability to grasp the meaning of unfamiliar and often quite difficult ideas and concepts;

— ability to deal with a large body of information and to select what is important and relevant;

— imagination and sensitivity in seeking to understand the beliefs and attitudes of others;

— awareness of the factors influencing one's own attitudes and judgments.

● Religious ideas and allusions abound in literature. Religion played a great part in history. Some understanding is necessary to enable pupils to deal with the study of their heritage.

● RE gives information and understanding. In educational terms it is 'teaching about' not 'induction into'. Voluntary schools may possibly regard nurture in the particular denomination as a goal, but in county schools the aim is understanding, personal reflection and judgment. Such an approach can lead to mutual respect, along with difference of judgment in classes where pupils of many religions meet. It could help tomorrow's citizens live in peace.

● RE can give a framework of thought which includes and goes beyond non-religious systems. Diagram 14 may explain. It is drawn in a Christian context, and other faiths might modify it a little. To be a person is to be involved in many relationships. Viewed from the inside, these are things that happen to me, parts of my experience to which I respond. Viewed from the outside, from a religious point of view, these are ways in which God expresses his care for me and provides the raw material out of which I make myself. We could say there are four 'channels' through which God's care is shown: *society* — a structure in which to develop; *family*, with its duty of love and care; the *personal experiences* of wonder and the 'knowledge of good and evil'. These three are all

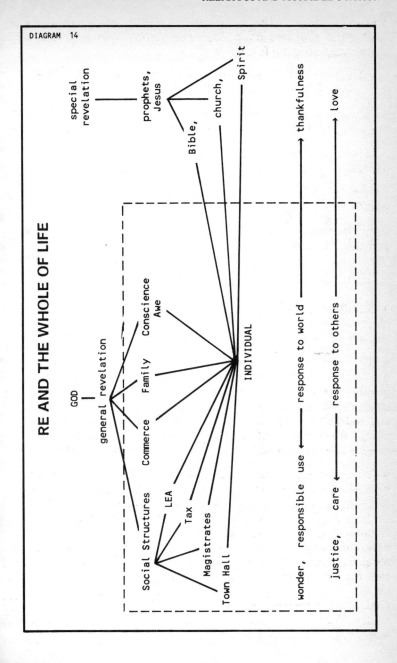

DIAGRAM 14

RE AND THE WHOLE OF LIFE

widely accepted as the place in which youngsters grow up, even if not seen as God's giving. The 'fourth channel' is that of *special revelation* which religions claim to deal in. It gives knowledge and assurance that cannot be obtained from the other three.

A humanist or non-religious morality would be contained inside the dotted line. RE lets pupils know that most cultures (and especially Christian ones) have seen all this as part of God's ordering of the world, and that there is a fourth channel on which he broadcasts and which requires a response.

If children were kept in the dark that the Town Hall had certain reponsibilities towards them and their families, there would be an outcry. On what ground then, can the child be denied the possibility of finding the fourth channel, with its particular responses and its clarification of all that comes through the other channels?

This 'whole-curriculum' view of RE — and of the demands it makes of teachers in a secular society — is expressed in one of the many representations made to the Secretary of State (from Christian Action Research and Education):

> 'We are disturbed at the extent to which it appears that increasingly in the school curriculum, where Christianity is dealt with, it is treated superficially, ignorantly and dismissively, to the distress and disappointment of Christian pupils and parents. Here we are mainly concerned not with religious education as such, but with those many occasions when religion is touched upon in a multitude of other subject areas (Literature, History, Social and Environmental studies, Science, etc.) We are not here concerned to criticize teachers; our perception is that the problem most usually arises because teachers themselves, from their own background and training, lack knowledge and understanding of the importance of religious belief in general, and have not been alerted to the need for sensitivity in dealing with religion in the classroom. We ask, therefore, for attention to be drawn to the need for sensitive and sympathetic treatment in schools of Christianity, and indeed of the deeply held beliefs and convictions of other, minority, religious communities, wherever in the curriculum reference may be made to religion.'

THE ARGUMENTS AGAINST RE

Objections come from all sides. Clearly, committed atheists like the National Secular Society quite logically want RE dropped.

So do some convinced believers who doubt if it can be taught properly in a compulsory setting. Some educationalists doubt if RE can be taught in an open way as they think other subjects are. The main problems have been: fear of indoctrination; the place of other religions; and a history of difficulty and neglect.

1. Indoctrination. The National Secular Society reported with glee in the 70s that it had succeeded in 'fixing the label "indoctrination" to Religious Education', and certainly the word is bandied about on all sides. Are innocent children being bullied into beliefs they don't understand? Can a teacher hide her own convictions, especially if she must really hope the children will believe as she does? Or how can an agnostic teacher teach what he does not personally believe?

Professor Basil Mitchell in the Durham Report *The Fourth R* of 1970 gave what is still probably the best analysis of indoctrination. Very briefly, he analyzed three aspects of indoctrination:

● **Method**. You indoctrinate a child if you cause him to believe something without understanding adequate reasons for it. Teachers and parents do this all the time — children are taught to obey parents and school staff, to be kind to some animals, and a whole welter of factual material they have no chance of checking up on.

● **Content**. You indoctrinate a child if what you cause them to believe is 'a debatable or controversial statement'. Mitchell shows that this still leaves a lot of information and values (which all parties would want to teach) as 'indoctrination'.

● **Aim**. You indoctrinate if you aim to prevent the child doubting what you teach, even in the face of stronger evidence. This amounts to giving a pupil a closed mind and would be rejected by all teachers.

Mitchell goes on to argue that the first two aspects of indoctrination are inevitable. The idea that children can work everything out for themselves is an illusion. They must have a framework at least to start with. No one starts from scratch.

> 'It is not only false but dangerous for the individual to think he is capable of doing this. Society depends for its proper functioning upon a multiplicity of shared beliefs, values and attitudes, and will suffer . . . if the individual feels that these have no claim upon him except in so far as he can independently validate them.

> 'Educators who scrupulously refrain from introducing any bias into the educational process will not thereby ensure that their pupils escape bias, only that the bias is imparted by other agencies.'

So some 'indoctrination' is inevitable, and it would be better to use the word generally and qualify it as 'good' or 'bad'. Then the last type, the aim to close the mind, would be 'bad' indoctrination.

Along with this discussion has gone a concern for the teacher. What is she to do about her own (maybe strongly held) convictions? After a flirtation with 'neutrality' in the 60s it is now widely agreed that teachers have convictions and biases that they simply cannot bury. What matters is how they deal with them. Any attempt to be completely 'neutral' involves personal contortions, and may in the end result in giving the children an 'initiation into agnosticism'. Edward Hulmes (then of the Farmington Institute for Christian Studies) was one of the critics of this pseudo-neutrality. He came to the conclusion:

> 'It is reassuring to know that openness does not exclude commitment, if this is taken to mean the finding of truth by the individual. To the extent that the teacher has himself been involved in this process of seeking and finding he will be entitled, and indeed obliged, to use his commitment explicitly as a primary teaching resource. For the moment it can be said that the declaration of personal commitment, not as a constantly repeated routine, but with sufficient emphasis to make it clear (and not only after children have asked for it) is one of the surest ways by which any teacher can avoid indoctrinating those whom he teaches.'

The teacher should:

> 'present the evidence in favour of religious commitment in as challenging a way as possible. It is the responsibility of a music teacher to present music as powerfully as possible so that children can judge of its value for themselves. The controversial nature of religion does not make it an exception, provided that free and critical engagement is guaranteed to the child in considering the evidence. This is the only safeguard against indoctrination in any subject.'

2. Other religions. Part of the argument against RE has been connected with non-Christian religions. In the 60s the debate was mostly about 'non-religious stances' such as humanism and communism and some Agreed Syllabuses tried to take account of these. Now there is greater pressure to consider the living world faiths that are practised by sizeable minorities of our fellow citizens. Some parents, following the 'Christian country' idea would limit RE to Christianity. In some LEAs this is policy in primary schools, on grounds that it would be confusing to introduce something so far from children's experience. In many LEAs the classrooms are already ethnically mixed, and it would be confusing if the teaching seems to suggest Christianity is the only religion. Attempts to find some 'Lowest Common Multiple' religious mix — 'they're all the same really' — is an affront to believers and misleading to the rest. It is better to present information about a number of faiths as practised by their adherents. This should make plain the truth-claims of each and the reality of personal commitment. Christianity may feature more largely if necessary to understand the culture, but to ignore the beliefs and culture of significant minorities is an unwarranted discrimination.

This area was very fully covered in the House of Lords debate. There was strong pressure to make the act of worship 'Christian' and to avoid the 'multi-faith confusion' some noble members feared. The Act now provides that any new agreed syllabus for RE 'shall reflect the fact that the religious traditions in Great Britain are in the main Christian whilst taking account of the teaching and practice of the other principal religions represented in Great Britain'.

This will make RE teaching even more demanding, but it is not a reason for dropping the subject.

3. Doubt and neglect. The present situation of RE is not good. This is due to a number of factors:

● RE has been a shortage subject for some time. This may reflect its 'Cinderella' status in many schools. Heads of department will usually be on lower scales than for comparable subjects. RE has a reputation for being a very demanding subject to teach, so relatively few opt for it in initial training. In a chicken-and-egg situation, many headteachers don't take RE very seriously because they see no hope of recruiting a really good teacher.

● Throughout the 60s RE pundits ran an agonizing soul-searching examination of what was happening in RE. Were we indoctrinating? Were we giving children enough opportunity to reflect and decide for themselves? *We teach them wrong* was one of the more hopeful books to appear. There was also doubt (as mentioned in chapter 3) about whether children could form the concepts necessary for RE. There was flirtation with 'neutrality' mentioned above.

● The situation has changed since the 1944 Act. Not only has society as a whole become less certain about its beliefs or values — it never was very sure — but the leaving age has been raised twice, and most secondary schools are now comprehensive. The 1944 Act was passed when children could leave on their 14th birthday. RE till then did not seem a problem. But 15- and 16-year-olds are developing their own attitudes and values in a bewildering world and RE needs a different approach and content. This was masked to some extent because grammar school teachers had been teaching older pupils for years — but of course they were the more academic who could cope with detailed examination of texts. Lessons prepared for them went down like a lead balloon with the others. It is arguable that much O-level RE teaching was not *religious* at all but biblical history.

● The 1988 Act does not help by simply repeating the 1944 requirements. The Secretary of State, saying 'It's protected by law' either does not know what is happening in his schools, or does not know what to do about it. Even making it a basic subject in the curriculum, though welcome, does not solve problems of past neglect and shortage of competent teachers.

Various surveys show that in the majority of secondary schools, RE stops at the third form, except for small sets working for examination. Advisors and Inspectors are aware of the situation, but also recognize the Heads' dilemma. The HMI Report in 1985, on sixty-two schools, found that eighteen had no RE in fourth or fifth years apart from examination options, and that in two-thirds of the remainder 'ethical and social problems . . . were considered to the exclusion of other aspects of religion.' The 1987 religious education statistics bulletin showed that 62% of fourth-year (15-year-old) children and 58% of fifth-year children were not given any religious education.

In many of these situations it is no good for parents to press the headteacher or governors for instant compliance with the law. If pressed, a headteacher will put RE on the timetable somewhere and coax a few unqualified but willing teachers to 'do something with them'. What is needed is a serious initiative to train more teachers and gradually improve individual schools. Many schools cover the subject well. Much training is good and takes account of the changed circumstances. Much more needs to be done. As one MP said in the debate: 'Whatever fine words we may place on the statute book, good religious education, which will bring tremendous benefit to pupils, depends upon detailed follow-up matters such as teacher training, recruitment and school priorities.'

In fairness to the Secretary of State he has made RE a national priority for in-service training, though the need for suitably trained RE teachers is likely to exceed supply for some time to come.

None of these problems is justification for dropping RE from the curriculum. In some schools Mathematics or History may be badly taught — no one suggests they should be dropped; only that they should be properly staffed and maintained.

PERSONAL AND MORAL EDUCATION

The debate about RE simmered merrily in the 60s and 70s but of late seems to have gone on the back burner. Some schools do it well; a lot ignore it beyond 13. But the needs of 14- and 15-year-olds for education in relationships and moral judgment has not gone away. It was a mistake to lumber the hard-pressed RE teacher with this — as if she were the custodian of pupil morality, and this area of education now receives attention in its own right. Usually it has no explicit religious base, so Lord Justice Devlin may say it is doomed from the start. However, Christian teachers could say it is based on religious values of personal responsibility and dignity which are shared as basic human concerns by most teachers and parents, whether or not they root them in personal religious commitment.

Personal and Social Education (PSE) courses deal with a range of topics such as health education (including alcohol and drug abuse; sexually transmitted diseases); relationships with authority; making and taking decisions; personal relationships and sexual behaviour; preparation for career; and choosing a lifestyle. The 1986 Act puts any sex education at the discretion of the governors and says it must be 'with regard to the values of family'. The 1988 Local Government Act forbids LEAs to 'promote homosexuality'. Clearly a lot will depend upon the skill and commitment of teachers and parents may still be apprehensive.

The Irish author quoted in an earlier chapter was very critical of one Health Education Programme, which he regarded as giving no moral guidance and effectively telling children that there are no rules, ridiculing those they might have been given. Many other programmes and classes try to help pupils towards clear thinking and responsible decision. It requires great skill to guide discussion so that pupils learn to question without destroying themselves or others; particularly when school may be the only place where open discussion of values and aims takes place, and when the media bombard them with every imaginable lifestyle model. The Durham Report commented:

'An education in any of these fields would be a failure if it produced people who were subservient and uncritical; it would also be a failure if it produced people who supposed that they could themselves rewrite the entire subject from scratch.'

There is, in fact, as the Report stated, a danger of bad indoctrination in moral education if teachers or writers try to short-circuit discussion and sell their own moral or political hobby-horses.

The 1988 Act says nothing about all this — except the general statement in Clause One. Any PSE lessons will have to come out of the time not allocated to core and foundation studies. Specialists in the field, naturally, feel PSE is a vital ingredient of education and fear it may get squeezed out in competition with other 'minority time' subjects. There is also the danger that, as in the past, PSE, like Careers and Tutorial time, is seen as less important than 'proper subjects' that lead to exams. Yet for many pupils, skills of living as a human being in the twentieth century are hard to come by and what they most need. Some of the recent syllabuses, like TVEI and CPVE specifically include this type of education in their programmes.

ASSEMBLY

The 1944 Act provided that 'The school day in every County school and every Voluntary school shall begin with collective worship on the part of all pupils in attendance at the school.' Although it didn't say so specifically, it assumed the 'worship' would be Christian. This was nothing new. Schools already started with 'prayers'. And so it continued for twenty years or so. But during the 1960s 'Morning Assembly' came under fire. Criticism came from various quarters:

● Fewer teachers, parents and pupils had a personal religious faith or practice.

● Those who did, doubted if 'worship' is possible in a mixed community. The Act spoke about 'collective' rather than 'corporate' worship, so perhaps hinted that not everyone would be actively and sympathetically involved. Some people said it was good for children to 'watch' what they did not 'share'. On the other hand, it was increasingly difficult to provide a genuine 'act of worship' which was not shared by the majority of pupils.

● As mentioned earlier, various anti-Christian organizations mounted a vigorous attack on the provisions.

● The increasing number of pupils from other religious backgrounds made a 'Christian' assembly difficult.

● The traditional five- or ten-minute 'assembly', often mixed up with notices, was seen as undignified and a very poor introduction to 'worship'. Some schools began having one, longer, assembly per week, when a topic could be dealt with more fully. A Government Education spokesman gave this at least tacit blessing saying 'the letter was broken so that the spirit of the Act could be followed more fully' and a few headteachers slept a little more easily.

● The 'right of withdrawal' had been put in the 1944 Act as a safeguard for parents who objected to a particular, or any, type of religious service. This was progressively less and less used. Parents realized that children 'excused assembly' hung around like spare parts with nothing useful to do, and felt very isolated. Cynics said some assemblies had become so bland that they weren't worth withdrawing a child from.

By the 1980s few secondary schools would be having a religious assembly for all pupils. Some larger schools broke up into house or year groups (the 1944 Act allowed this if there was not space for the whole school). Most regarded assembly as good for community spirit and school ethos, but not every day. Many interpreted 'worship' to mean 'celebration of worth', not necessarily religious worth, but the values and achievements of the school and society.

Primary schools have kept up assembly much better, though the content has tended to become less specifically Christian. Hymns are still sung but usually of a more general than confessional kind. Also, where there are pupils from other religious traditions, schools have tried to find some 'general' religious or community theme. This is rarely completely successful, and can be offensive to parents who see it is a woolly attempt to make all religions seem the same.

In both primary and secondary schools speakers from outside

the school have been welcome.

The 1988 Act suggests some change is necessary in 'School Worship' arrangements, but in its original form was far from grasping the nettle. In fact, it showed no recognition of the extent to which the 1944 Act is being flouted, especially in secondary schools. It puts upon governors and headteachers a task which in many places is impossible.

Any government is under pressure here. Most MPs went to independent schools (where chapel was compulsory, and 'didn't do us any harm') or to grammar schools twenty years ago before the present breakdown occurred. Many parents hold school assembly as part of their 'folk religion' and while not practising Christians themselves, somehow feel it would be a bad thing if it were stopped. Teachers are keenly aware of the difficulties of making a meaningful assembly. Even those with strong religious convictions would wish to see more flexibility. Some would say that, if the compulsion were withdrawn, assembly would still go on in many schools and be good. Almost all teachers would wish to retain some community functions — whole-school if space allowed, or by years or houses — because of their social value. On occasion, for example at major festivals, these could be religious.

Before looking at possible ways forward, it may be useful to summarize the hints given above as to the root of the problem. 'Collective worship' is a mixture of two worthy aims: 'worship' is the response to the highest we know, usually described in God-language though not, for example, for humanists or some Buddhists; a 'collective' occasion is one which unites the school. In 1944 it was assumed that the great majority responded in a similar way to a similar 'highest' and in this were united. This is a splendid idea — that there is something or someone before whom pupils, staff, governors and even LEA officials stand on level ground — but it is no longer a common belief. Attempts to talk as if it were have become an embarrassment to teachers trying to conduct an 'act of worship'. In many schools the presence of different religious groups highlights the difficulty. 'Worship' would be divisive rather than uniting. Unity and group-identity are important, so most schools came up with 'community values' and things — like good causes — in which all the school could share. 'Worship' took the more secular of the dictionary meanings: 'recognition given to worthiness or merit'.

Possible ways forward include:

- **Forget it**. Admit things are different from 1944. Leave it to headteachers to have a meeting of the whole school or parts of it whenever they have something to say. This would appear to be 'giving in' to the failure and faithlessness of the past, and saying the worship was not an important enough part of life to let children know about. It would also be politically controversial, as mentioned above. The least religiously active parents, citizens and MPs leap into action when they think anyone is mucking about with their heritage.

- **Less frequent**. Keep 'collective worship' as a national ideal, but make it once a week. A more worthwhile occasion can then be arranged, which may well raise the status of the function. This option was pressed by a wide group — churches, RE organizations and Christian groups — who submitted views to the Secretary of State on the discussion papers.

- **Choice**. Some schools already provide a choice of assembly — Muslim, Christian or secular — and children can opt between these. This need not be divisive, since children can be quite honestly 'just looking'. It also has the advantage that the actual functions can be more explicitly religious or secular. The 1988 Act allows this to happen in one of two ways. One way is for parents to use their 'withdrawal' rights, in which case the headteacher and governors can make such other provision for those withdrawn as they think good. The other is for the headteacher (after consulting the governors) to ask the Standing Advisory Council for RE (SACRE), to rule that, in the special circumstances of the school, Christian assemblies for all pupils are 'not appropriate'.

- **Voluntary attendance**. Where parents request, a religious assembly (non-denominational for Christianity) must be provided on, say, one day a week. Where no member of staff is competent or willing to conduct this, parents might be invited to do so. The disadvantage of this solution is that unless it took place outside school hours, the children not attending would have to have other work, or be supervised. This might lead to a feeling of division in the school.

- **Regular assemblies of parts of the school** should be held, at which matters of belief and value are dealt with. These would usually aim to provoke thought rather than assume religious response. The frequency, and also perhaps some proportion of 'religious' assemblies, could be laid down.

THE STATUS OF RE

It has to be said that the 1988 Act, following much debate and amendment in the House of Lords, has made a serious attempt to raise the status of RE, and define its position in a plural society. The Bishop of London expressed the concern to uphold five main principles:

1. The importance of maintaining the tradition of worship as part of the process of education, giving proper place to Christianity;

2. The contribution of collective worship to establishing values within the school community;

3. The undesirability of imposing inappropriate forms of worship on certain groups of pupils;

4. Yet also the importance of not breaking the school up into distinct communities, making some feel they are not really part of the school;

5. The whole approach must be realizable and practicable in terms of school organization.

All this is to be achieved partly through Standing Advisory Councils for RE (SACRE). Previously LEAs could, if they wished, have a Standing Advisory Council. Now this is compulsory and LEAs must appoint members to represent LEA, teachers, Church of England and other religious denominations. This SACRE will be a kind of watchdog for RE and collective worship. It will 'advise the authority' on such matters as methods of teaching, choice of books and teacher training. It can initiate the review of the LEA agreed syllabus. It must advise the LEA on the daily act of worship, which must 'reflect the broad position of Christian belief without being distinctive of any particular denomination' and be appropriate to 'the age, aptitude and family background of the pupils'. Not every assembly must be 'Christian' but 'most' must be, taking the term as a whole. It must publish an annual report of the advice it has given to the LEA and the reasons for this advice. The DES is to issue a circular explaining all this, and especially that RE must 'engender mutual tolerance and understanding between faiths and denominations'.

All this is still at the level of statute, and the previous statute was disregarded wholesale. Speaker after speaker said it all depended on getting enough willing and well-qualified teachers. 'Without having effective training facilities and properly trained teachers of RE, we can pass as many laws as we like, but they will not happen.' But the debate, and possibly the complaints procedure available to parents who feel the law is not being observed, will have concentrated a few minds. As the *Times Educational Supplement* commented: 'Heads and governors will now need clear policies where before they could reject the whole issue.' It is a basis to be worked on. It will take time, good will, understanding and resources for training.

A CAUTIONARY TALE

The last word has not been said on the matter. Governors may well weigh up their new responsibilities with distaste. One hopes that some of them will come up with arrangements that can be carried out with integrity for the good of the whole school community. Parents may rub their hands at the slight boost to RE being in the Basic Curriculum and the new complaints procedure. They need guidance and understanding, as is illustrated by the following apocryphal happenings one spring afternoon at the Alderman Green Comprehensive School in Little Hassle.

The headteacher notes with some apprehension his diary entry for 4.00 p.m. 'Mr Jake and parents re. RE'. Helen Jake is a pleasant pupil in the fifth year. The Head doesn't remember ever seeing her father before. The next entry is more hopeful: 'Mr Hussein' — an LEA governor who is a great help to the school, particularly as representing the Muslim community from which about seventy pupils come.

Mr Jake and cohort arrive — one or two parents the head-teacher recognizes. They are not happy that RE has been dropped this year from the third years, and there's no general RE in fourth and fifth years — 'only this Personal and Social stuff'. The Head explains it's all due to Father James' departure to work abroad last summer. The RE component in first and second year humanities continues as he had set it up. This is not a winner with the parents: 'all they do is the church in a mediaeval village and go to the parish church drawing stained glass windows.' Examination classes continue with a bit of part-time supply teaching. Father James could not be replaced as pupil numbers had dropped and the school was one overstaffed, so the LEA had frozen the post. Parents are not impressed. The LEA is acting unreasonably. The governors ought to be pressing the case harder. The law is being broken. They are all set to call a meeting and make a formal complaint.

Incidentally, while they are at it, they are not very pleased with assembly either. Reference to the Muslim festival of Id the other day was a bad thing. From the sound of it they had Abraham and Ishmael and Isaac mixed up anyway. They don't get a really straightforward message except when the local pastor or a parent comes in and does it. They're not being racist of course. They don't mind these other pupils being here, but they just don't want these foreign religions pushed down our children's throats, like Father James used to do in his fourth-form 'Introduction to Islam' lessons.

The Head says he will report their visit to the governors. They sweep out.

Mr Hussein is shown in. He greets the Head with his usual courtesy. He is delighted to serve on the governors and he and members of his community are full of praise for the Head and his staff. So it is all the more difficult to complain. He nervously produces a typed note 'In accordance with Section 25 of the 1944 Education Act I wish to withdraw my son Arshad Hussein from religious assembly.' The Head acknowledges that it is of course the parent's right, but asks if he might know what has set this off. He has always tried to remember the wide range of pupils present at assembly and to respect them all. There were readings sometimes from the Holy Qur'an as well as other religious texts. Speakers from outside are told of the composition of the school. Mr Hussein agrees. Everyone respects the way the headteacher conducts assembly — his explanation of the festival of Id was very much appreciated. But . . . clearly embarrassed, he produces a further seventy-three forms all duly filled and signed by Muslim parents. 'The Community is very deeply offended,' he goes on. 'At the assembly last week the parent conducting it said all religion except Christianity was of the devil and that the prophet Muhammad (peace be upon him) was a fraud.' The Head winced, remembering the unfortunate incident and his not very successful effort afterwards to counsel more moderation by the speaker. But Mr Hussein has tried hard to be constructive. He has arranged with the Imam at the local mosque to come into school, if the Head agrees, and conduct Muslim prayers if a room can be found. He would be happy for both boys and girls to attend. Incidentally, the parents would wish him to say how sorry they were that Father James left. His third-form explanations of Christian belief and custom were much appreciated — very necessary for the young people to understand the culture they are growing up in. He hopes the LEA will soon relent and a worthy successor can be appointed.

The Head thanks his visitor for his great courtesy; apologizes for the affront. Would the parents perhaps reconsider their requests if the Head could guarantee there would be no repetition? He would be very sorry if the present community atmosphere of assembly was broken by one group hiving off. He is grateful for the Imam's offer, but doubts if it will do. Worship has to be 'undenominational' and the Imam's presentation might not be acceptable to Muslims of other sects. Certainly he will see it is on the governors' agenda next month and he hopes Mr Hussein will speak about it then. They part on friendly terms and the Head makes his way home. His car radio brings the familiar voice of the Secretary of State — 'no one need have any fears about the position of RE; it is in the National Curriculum and is still fully supported by law; parents have the right of withdrawal if they wish; a complaints procedure is available if all this does not work properly.' Can things get worse? he asks himself. Yes, they can.

Next morning (Tuesday) Mrs Mbasi calls in to see the Head and submit her resignation as she has obtained another job at the Poly. Pity. Mrs Mbasi was doing a good job in establishing the Maths GCSE. It will be hard to replace her, especially with another black teacher who will be such a good role model to black pupils.

Wednesday morning Mr Jake is on the phone: 'I hear that Indian Maths teacher is going (actually she's not Indian but Nigerian, says the Head, determined to score any tiny point he can) . . . Anyway, now you'll have a space on the staff so you can advertise for a replacement for Father James.' 'It would be nice if we could,' agrees the Head, 'but Mrs Mbasi leaves a big gap in the Maths GCSE team. We shall have to ensure proper cover there for all the pupils on that course.' Mr Jake can't agree. 'It's RE I'm concerned about, and that's protected by law, and I want to see the law observed. And, if you take my advice, don't be too eager to take another Roman Catholic in place of Father James. It would be fairer to have a change. He did his best I'm sure, but his prejudices were bound to show through and he was often cross if pupils made fun of the Pope.'

The moral of this tale is that the law does not solve everything. There may be some cases where headteachers need to have a few sleeping dogs roused. But most situations are complicated; misunderstandings are easier to raise than to calm. Parents, governors and headteachers have to work hard to establish confidence and mutual respect so that when differences and difficulties arise, there is an atmosphere in which they can be hopefully discussed.

You can make up your own version of the next governors' meeting.

CHAPTER 7

Assessment

tests and grades

Assessment is a large, important and complicated subject. It will be considered in four parts: the examination system before GCSE; changes brought about by GCSE and the 1988 Act; recent thinking about assessment; and proposals for the future.

Discussion of 'standards' and whether they are rising or falling — and how you might know — is left to the next chapter.

EXAMINATIONS BEFORE GCSE

Written examinations have been a feature of the British education system for a long time. In 1917 the Secondary School Examinations Council was set up. The following year came the School Certificate and the Higher School Certificate, which will be remembered by the grandparents of some of today's children. Between 1% and 2% of a year group passed the Higher Schools Examination (18+) in the 1930s.

This all changed in 1951 when, following the Norwood Report of 1943, the General Certificate of Education (GCE) was launched. This was hailed by the *Daily Herald* as 'the exam everyone can pass', but was in fact designed for the top 25% of the mental ability range. It was taken normally at 16 (Ordinary Level) and 18 (Advanced Level), mostly in the grammar schools and independent schools, though some secondary modern schools had a 'GCE set' for those who wanted to stay on and take the O-level.

Everyone could *not* pass it, so yet another committee swung into action, producing the Beloe Report in 1960. From this came the Certificate of Secondary Education (CSE), which aimed to provide for the next 40% of the ability range. Grade 4 CSE was intended to be the performance of the average child at age 16 — a fact that needs to be often repeated since most people, and employers in particular, seem to have taken in the *Daily Herald*'s story. In practice many more pupils took the CSE, in some schools 80-90%, so that in 1985 only 11.7% of leavers had no graded examination result in any subject.

During the 1970s a number of things happened which affected examinations still further:

● Comprehensive reorganization, in most areas, stopped the division between grammar schools (where all pupils expected to do O-level) and modern schools (where few would).

● The school-leaving age was raised to 16 so more pupils had to stay till O-level time. This had the unfortunate effect of making an exam at 16 virtually inevitable, whereas previously everyone had been a volunteer. Pupils who didn't pass the examination now were failures; previously they had simply left school early.

● Parents became more examination-conscious and anxious for their children to take the prestigious O-level — even if 'double-entered' with CSE. Examination fees from hopeful parents poured into the Examination Boards' coffers along with the millions from LEAs who paid for one entry per pupil per subject only.

● Perhaps, too, teachers had got gradually better at getting the wider ability range to O-level standard. At any rate, by 1980 52% of the age group had at least one 'higher grade' (A, B or C) at O-level and in 1985 it was 52.9%.

GCE A-level continued. More pupils stayed on at school. By 1985 17% of the age group obtained at least one A-level pass.

After much discussion, in 1976 the Schools Council finally recommended a new examination to replace GCE and CSE. In 1978 the Labour Secretary of State approved the idea and plans were set in motion. In 1979 the incoming Conservative Secretary of State disapproved of the idea and cancelled the plans. In 1984 the Conservative Secretary of State finally approved the idea and plans went ahead — far too fast, the teachers' unions said — so that courses could start in September 1986 and the first GCSE examinations be taken in summer 1988.

Throughout these changes the original 'credit' standard of the old School Certificate has been maintained as diagram 15 shows. From 1945, alongside this examining at 16+, there was the 11+ 'intelligence test'. This is almost phased out now. 10% or so of children take such tests in the few remaining 'selective' authorities, so no detailed account is given here. Incidental references to the 11+ tests occur in other chapters. For the moment diagram 16 shows how GCE and CSE were related to verbal-reasoning ability ('IQ'). This is still followed in the main by GCSE, though GCSE does give some opportunity to test other abilities.

149

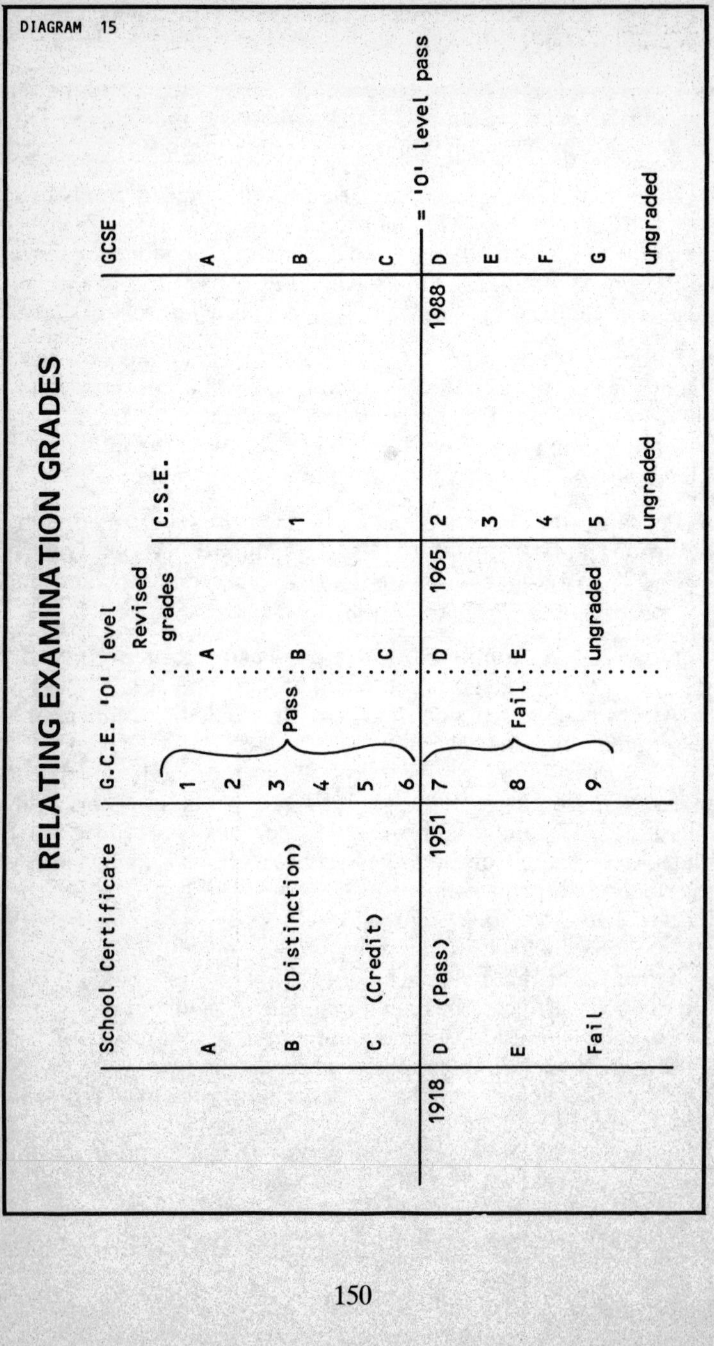
DIAGRAM 15
RELATING EXAMINATION GRADES
School Certificate
A
B (Distinction)
C (Credit)
D (Pass)
E
Fail
1918
G.C.E. 'O' level
1
2
3
4
5
6
Pass
7
8
9
Fail
1951
Revised grades
A
B
C
D
E
ungraded
1965
C.S.E.
1
2
3
4
5
ungraded
GCSE
A
B
C
D
E
F
G
ungraded
1988
= 'O' level pass

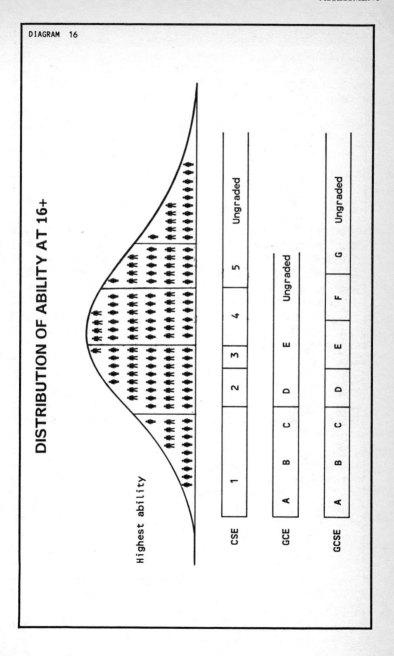

DIAGRAM 16

DISTRIBUTION OF ABILITY AT 16+

RECENT CHANGES

Despite the changes brought about by the introduction of GCSE, **A-level** keeps going, at least for the time being. After nearly twenty years of discussion, yet another committee, the Higginson Committee, has recommended ways of broadening the 16-18 curriculum. They recommend five A-levels, 'leaner and tougher', emphasizing skills and use of material rather than memorizing a lot of detail. The Secretary of State immediately rejected this outright, which was a tragedy since the proposals represent a wide consensus and would do a lot to break out of the present narrow A-level overcrowded syllabuses. Perhaps when he has got the GCSE going smoothly and his 1988 Act in place, he will have sense and time to re-examine these proposals.

At sixth-form level (16+) a new exam, the **Advanced Supplementary Level (AS)** was introduced in 1987 for first examination in 1989. This is intended to broaden sixth-form courses. A student used to be limited to three (or exceptionally four) A-level subjects, and these were often closely connected — for example, Physics, Maths, Further Maths. The AS-level is given half the time of an A-level course — usually two and a half hours a week for two years — so a student could now do A-level Maths and Physics plus AS-level Geography and French. The AS-level is supposed to be 'A-level depth', but only half the content.

This new examination did not get off to a good start for various reasons: teachers were knee-deep in trying to get the new GCSE going and they were also in dispute with the Government for most of the preparatory time. They tended to suspect the scheme of being a cost-cutting exercise, and not properly resourced. There was talk that A- and AS-levels would have to be taught together — just possible in some subjects but quite impossible in others. There was doubt whether the universities would accept AS-level for entry purposes. Whatever Vice-Chancellors *say*, it all depends what admissions officers do, and teachers were doubtful. The content of the new courses was important. Would they cram in a lot of content, or try to stimulate interest? Would students think them worthwhile?

In spite of this shaky start, the AS-level did begin in 1987 and the Secretary of State pronounced himself 'pleased' with the modest take-up. Universities are slowly declaring their hand. We shall know in 1989 just what value they put on AS-level. Schools are adapting AS-level to their own timetables and resources with their usual ingenuity. So AS-level could be a small step towards a wider range of study for 16-18-year-old students.

The **GCSE** (General Certificate of Secondary Education) is the 'single system' to replace the previous GCE and CSE. The many examination boards have been reduced to five 'Groups'. A Secondary Examinations Council (SEC) will monitor the syllabuses. It is hoped this will make it easier to get a uniform standard among them, and to avoid unnecessary multiplication of syllabuses. The system is governed by 'national criteria' — requirements that any syllabus must satisfy if it is to be accepted by the SEC as a proper GCSE. These national criteria are of two sorts — general (what every subject must follow) and subject criteria (what every syllabus in a particular syllabus must follow).

General criteria apply to all examinations and lay down the 'Modes' of examining, how many marks for written papers and how many for course-work; methods of marking and 'moderation' (ensuring that all markers have common standards); avoidance of political, gender or ethnic bias; recognition of cultural diversity of candidates; and other things that apply to every syllabus that is submitted. These general criteria include a vigorous defence of course-work assessed by teachers. O-level had a very small amount of teacher-assessed work in some subjects. CSE had quite a lot. GCSE allows anything from 20% to 100% to be internally assessed by teachers and 'moderated' — either by inspection (an external examiner looks at specimens of work) or statistically (comparison with other work by the same students). The general criteria state:

> 'Assessment by the candidate's teacher is fundamental to the use of course work in examinations. The candidate's teacher is the only person who can take into full account the candidate's personal contribution to the work which is being assessed and the extent of any assistance from the teacher or other outside sources. Consequently, the teacher is likely to be in the best position to judge the merits of his or her own candidates in relation to each other.'

Then there are national criteria for each subject. These specify the aims of the examination in that subject; how the aims will be turned into 'assessment objectives'; what actual content will be covered; how questions will 'differentiate' between pupils of differing ability; and how the assessment will be carried out.

For example, the *Mathematics* national criteria give the introduction:

> 'Pupils must not be required to prepare for examinations which are not suited to their attainment nor must

these examinations be of a kind which will undermine the confidence of pupils. [There must be] differentiated papers so that by choosing an appropriate level, pupils are enabled to demonstrate what they know and can do rather than what they do not know and cannot do.'

It goes on to give fifteen aims, including:

● To develop their mathematical knowledge and oral, written and practical skills in a manner which encourages confidence;

● To develop a feel for number, carry out calculations and understand the significance of the results obtained;

● To solve problems, present the solutions clearly, check and interpret results.

This is followed by seventeen assessment objectives, listing skills and abilities which the examination should test, such as 'perform calculations by suitable methods, use an electronic calculator, analyze a problem, select a suitable strategy and apply an appropriate technique to obtain a solution.'

Then come two pages of 'content' — most of the familiar subject matter, algebra, arithmetic, geometry, trigonometry, probability, statistics, upon which these skills and abilities are to be demonstrated. Finally details of assessment and 'grade definitions' are given. In this case there will be overlapping papers, for pupils of differing abilities rather than one paper which all pupils take.

This all amounts to a very detailed outline to which any syllabus must conform, and shows how difficult it is to provide the detail even for one subject.

Other subjects may need very different criteria, as for example, *Religious Studies*. Here the aims include things like 'to promote an enquiring, critical and sympathetic approach to the study of religion, especially in its individual and corporate expression in the contemporary world.' Assessment objectives include 'language, terms and concepts used in religion; principal beliefs of the religion or religions being studied, the meanings given to those beliefs by adherents and the ways in which beliefs are related to personal and corporate practice.'

The content provides that syllabuses will be 'based on the study of one, two or three of the major world religions. Each Examining Group will ensure that at least one syllabus concerned wholly with the study of Christianity is available.'

All pupils will take the same paper, and there must be questions of differing difficulty to differentiate between them.

Marks must be given according to three areas: Knowledge 35%-45%: Understanding 35%-45%; Evaluation 15%-25%.

These two examples will give an idea of the thoroughness with which GCSE has been worked out. A further refinement, not yet completed, is that of 'grade-related criteria'. This will attempt to relate the final grade to specific items of achievement. For example, Physics is divided into three 'domains' — knowledge with understanding; handling information and solving problems; experimental skills and investigations. Each of these is given four levels and marked 1, 2, 3 or 4, so a pupil could get a maximum score of twelve points and that would be a grade A. Eleven points would be an A as well and Grade B would be ten. To get these scores pupils would have to do well in all three areas. To get grade C (8/9 points) scores of 4, 4, 0 will not do because they do not show overall ability. Similarly at the lower level F (3/4 points) the pupils must score in at least two areas.

The grade-related criteria are still being worked out and will come into force over the next few years. It is a difficult task and no one has ever attempted before to give such precise information. In O-level examinations your marks for each question were simply added together to give a total. So you could get a grade C without touching half the syllabus. As one wag put it: 'An O-level pass is like a marriage certificate — it allows one to function in a certain way without guaranteeing the efficiency of the operation.'

Teachers fear the tests may cramp their style of teaching and have an even more rigid grip on what is taught. If the system works, it will be a big improvement in the information that can be obtained from certificates. In the meantime the GCE Board members on each Examining Group are to ensure that grades A, B and C for the new exam are for the same quality of work that gained these grades in the old O-level.

TWO KINDS OF EXAMINATION

Before going on to the 'new' tests a word of explanation of technical terms may be useful.

GCSE is dramatically different from the exams it replaced because it is 'criterion-referenced' whereas GCE was 'norm-referenced'. What does this jargon mean?

If you want to know how someone gets on in a test, you can ask one of two questions:

• What can she do?
• Where does she come in the pile?

The old O-level was (and A-level still is) asking the second question. Papers are marked by assistant examiners, checked, and arranged in rank order. The chief examiner then 'makes an award' — that is, he says where the dividing line between various grades will be. What this does can be illustrated by two sets of results from Joint Matriculation Board A-level in 1982 (diagram 17).

In the English examination very few candidates got high marks and very few made a complete mess so the marks are bunched together. In Mathematics, the marks are much more spread out — perhaps it is possible to get everything exactly right in Maths more easily than in English. Certainly it is possible to get it all wrong. So when candidates are lined up, we get a different pattern.

But why draw the grade lines as they are? Because the examination regulations lay down that on average (over all exams and all subjects) 70% must get grades A-E. So 40% gave you a grade E pass in English and a D in Maths. 30% was a pass in Maths and an 'O' (near miss, now called 'N') in English. On the other hand, to get grade A in English you needed 60%, but in Maths over 70%. This is known as 'norm-referencing'. The 'norm' is 70%, the proportion that 'normally' pass. (Since 1987 there has been a slight alteration. The A/B boundary and E/N boundary are fixed for 'a quality of work that has normally resulted in those grades' and the marks between them divided into four equal parts, B, C, D, and E. This still leaves the norm-referencing of the past in control.)

Not surprisingly there has been criticism of an exam that, by regulation, makes three candidates out of ten fail. The percentage works out over a whole range of exams, so there is a lot of variation here and there. For example, 57% got grades A, B or C for O-level English in 1982, 78% in Latin and 69% in Art. Some Boards, catering for special groups, passed 75% in English and 81% in Latin. So 'norm-referencing' answers the question 'Where do you come in the pile?' and only the top 70% of the pile can win. The standard stays roughly the same because the spread of ability in the population stays about the same and teachers perform about the same from year to year.

Criterion-referencing on the other hand has no built-in failure rate. It may vary widely from year to year. It is geared to what a given candidate can do, irrespective of whoever else may be being examined at the same time. The attainment targets are there and if he reaches them, he gets the grade.

156

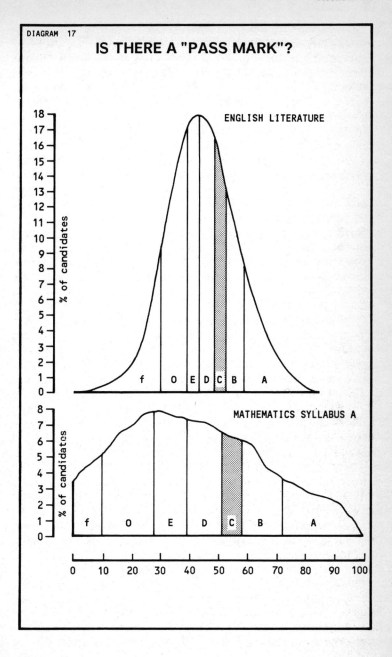

The GCSE has added greatly to teachers' work. The volume of course-work has increased — it needs very careful planning to ensure pupils are not overloaded, too. At one school it was found that for English, History and Geography assignments alone one candidate had written 26,000 words (about one-third of this book). HMI had previously said many pupils were writing too much. Parents need to know this and not press for children to take seven, eight or nine subjects. Schools need to know it and plan reasonable workloads. It all has to be marked and the marks moderated to make sure everyone is keeping the same standard.

The emphasis on practical work in some subjects, and problem-solving and application of knowledge in others, makes teaching more demanding, and again involves more assessment. The assessment of oral English or French takes a lot of time. Clearly it is better to have an examination that takes account of pupils' ability to speak the language. O-level English had no compulsory oral test. In-service training has been available to teachers and they learn fast, but confidence will take some time to develop. If more time had been allowed GCSE would have got off to a better start. As it is, it will be good in the end, we hope.

A less welcome suggestion put forward by the Secretary of State (then Sir Keith Joseph) during the GCSE discussions was for Distinction and Merit certificates. These would require 'higher grades' (at least 2 A's and only one C) in seven subjects chosen from a specified list. Merit needed six subjects at higher grades. The intention was to make pupils take a wider coverage of subjects. It was fiercely resisted by teachers of minority subjects since it would stop most pupils taking, for example, both a second language and Religious Studies or some other sensible choices. The idea seems to be in limbo at present. It would be better still if it were given a decent official burial.

1988 ACT — NATIONAL CURRICULUM TESTING

The 1988 Act provides for 'assessing pupils at or near the end of each key stage (age 7, 11, 14) . . . what they have achieved in relation to the attainment targets for that stage.' The attainment targets are 'the knowledge, skills and understanding which pupils of differing abilities and maturities are expected to have by the end of each key stage.'

Some authorities already have regular testing — for reading in primary schools, for example. Most schools have some sort of regular testing. What is new is the *national* targets in every subject at three specified points, and nationally-controlled tests.

These tests are to be criterion-referenced — that is, not competitive. Each pupil will be compared, not with other pupils, but the attainment target laid down. No individual pupil's test scores will be published. They will be notified only to that pupil's parents and to governors and LEA if necessary 'for the purposes of the performance of any of their functions'.

The Government intend to start testing in 1991. Children who were 5 in the autumn of 1989 will take this first test. It will be a 'trial run' with no reporting of results. The 1992 test results will be reported to parents, but not published.

Such testing had been under discussion for a long time — in fact a *Times Educational Supplement* poll in 1977 showed a majority of teachers in favour of testing at 8, 11 and 14. However, the version that has now appeared aroused many fears about these tests:

• Pupils differ so much in where they start from (and even how long they will have been in school by the time of the first test);

• The tests might damage pupils instead of helping, if they make emotional pressure;

• Parents might misunderstand the tests, reading more into them than possible;

• Teachers would be under pressure to teach narrowly for the limited targets — and testing would take up a lot of time;

• If results are published, league tables might give an unfair picture of some schools;

• Age-related tests are bad; children mature at different rates. It is widely accepted that there can be as much as seven years' difference in achievement in mathematics in some cases;

• The single-subject framework goes against the trend of unified learning;

• Tests are only one aspect of assessment and must not get out of proportion.

Obviously the crucial thing is what the tests are like, how they are administered, and what use is made of them. A Task Group was set up, with Professor Black as Chairman, to give general guidance about all this. It produced its report which had some reassuring things to say:

'the assessment process . . . should be the servant, not the master of the curriculum;'

'results should provide a basis for decision about the pupil's further learning needs;'

'publishing results poses many difficulties and is definitely not recommended for the 7-year-olds' test.'

The Task Group proposes a ten-level scheme, each level having a 'profile' — a statement of the knowledge, skills and abilities at each level. The levels form a continuous staircase, each step building on the previous one, which children can go up at their own pace. This is the answer to the fear that an age-related test would mark children off as 'failures'. What is proposed would be more like the Associated Board music examinations in which you can get grades 1 to 8 at any age. Level 4 would be the average for a child aged 11 and level 6/7 would be equivalent to GCSE grade F at age 16; level 10 would be GCSE grade A.

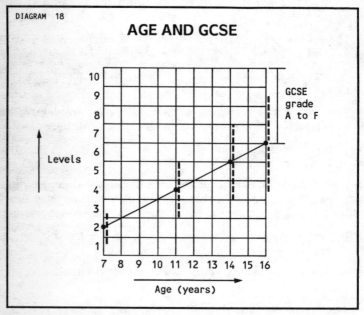

DIAGRAM 18

AGE AND GCSE

GCSE grade A to F

Levels

Age (years)

Diagram 18 was given to show how it would work out. An important recommendation concerns the manner of testing. Those whose image of 'testing' is everyone sitting at desks with the same printed questions will be disappointed. It would be quite inappropriate to younger children, says the Task Group. They recommend that:

'tests should be devised that, from the children's point

160

of view, are similar in form to their normal school work, should be based on familiar material, and should allow children to exhibit different levels of knowledge, understanding and skills in their responses . . . to take account of the varying maturity of pupils and the burden of testing on the class teachers, considerable restraint in the number of assessment tasks will . . . have to be exercised at the 7- and ll-year-old stage.'

The report looks at 'common and overlapping aspects of pupils' work' so that not every subject needs to be tested exhaustively. The report shows a general pattern that overcomes most of the fears, but is, of course, general.

Meanwhile, working parties are beavering away in each subject area to say what the attainment targets should be. That will be more difficult.

Another question that lingers in the minds of headteachers, especially in primary schools, is 'What effect will this testing have on "special" education?' As mentioned in chapter 1, children with physical or emotional learning difficulty are being integrated in 'normal' schools wherever possible. If schools are forced by competition to struggle for higher average test results, will they be so ready to accept disadvantaged children? Will Grant Maintained Schools be reluctant to take their share? It is suggested that 7-year-old pupils with a 'statement of needs' would not be tested, and the Act gives some latitude to headteachers in general to decide if the National Curriculum, and resultant testing, is appropriate to all pupils. This highlights the confusion over the purposes of testing. The lower achievers, as much as anyone, need testing diagnostically. It is only when their — lower — scores are included in a published average in a league table that misunderstanding may arise. It will be a tragedy indeed if the good work being done in integration is slowed down because of the idolatry of 'success' in one area that happens to be easily testable.

ASSESSING THE ASSESSORS

Testing is justified on many grounds. Diagram 19 shows what various people get out of it. This diagram was, as you may have guessed, designed by someone in the examining industry. It looks as if we couldn't live without them. In fairness, as things are now, they do do some of the things listed very usefully.

For the present purpose five uses of tests are most important:

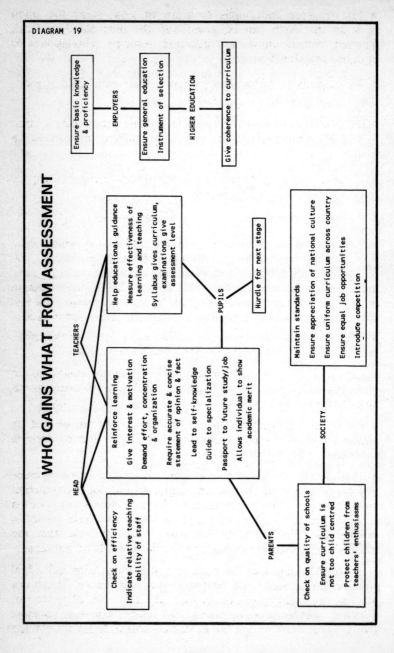

DIAGRAM 19

WHO GAINS WHAT FROM ASSESSMENT

EMPLOYERS
- Ensure basic knowledge & proficiency
- Ensure general education
- Instrument of selection

HIGHER EDUCATION
- Give coherence to curriculum

TEACHERS
- Help educational guidance
- Measure effectiveness of learning and teaching
- Syllabus gives curriculum, examinations give assessment level

PUPILS
- Hurdle for next stage

HEAD
- Check on efficiency
- Indicate relative teaching ability of staff
- Reinforce learning
- Give interest & motivation
- Demand effort, concentration & organization
- Require accurate & concise statement of opinion & fact
- Lead to self-knowledge
- Guide to specialization
- Passport to future study/job
- Allows individual to show academic merit

SOCIETY
- Maintain standards
- Ensure appreciation of national culture
- Ensure uniform curriculum across country
- Ensure equal job opportunities
- Introduce competition

PARENTS
- Check on quality of schools
- Ensure curriculum is not too child centred
- Protect children from teachers' enthusiasms

● For teachers and pupils to know at what stage the pupil is at so that help can be given and the next stage of work planned (usually known as 'diagnostic testing'). This applies to both fast and slow learners.

● For parents to know what progress their own child is making.

● For teachers to know how pupils overall are progressing — that is, to have some guide to the success of teaching methods being used.

● For the public to know that standards are being kept up or improved.

● For parents to decide which school to send children to.

Testing for the first reason goes on all the time, and is vital to make sure each child gets the teaching and help needed. The second reason is the reporting to parents which is usual at parents' evenings and in reports. The third applies all the time, though marked tests are by no means the only things teachers use. The last two reasons are where argument is hottest. Issues raised include:

● Individual children's results should be confidential to the child, the parent and the school. The Act does provide for this.

● Published total figures for a school are almost bound to be misleading. They need interpretation. All sorts of background factors affect them.

● Public, or DES, interest in national standards can be met by taking a sample of schools anonymously. This is already done in some cases quite successfully.

● There is a great danger that attention is focused on *one* feature of schools, which gets a trust and importance it does not warrant and cannot bear. Other factors are neglected. If towns were graded according to the number of people in them who have passed a driving test, that would be interesting. But to make that the main factor in deciding whether to live there would be nonsense.

It could be said that the better a test is for helping individual children the worse it will be for 'selling' the school. If schools must compete for business, let them do it by overall picture of the care, performance, openness, and relationship with parents. Don't force them to get paper results which could distort the teaching. Remember the prep. school head who lamented that he 'couldn't do what was good for the children' because he had to get them all through the 13+ examination.

The fear that examinations will become the only thing people care about is one of the main causes of unease about assessment. Other fears are: what does it do to teachers and curriculum? What does it do to pupils? Must 'judgment' always be 'damnation'? Before looking at proposed 'better ways' we spell out some of these fears.

GETTING THE WRONG MESSAGE FROM THE RESULTS

If parents, employers and politicians take the results of written examinations as gospel they can make two errors. It is *not* the only way of measuring a child, nor even the most important. And the raw grades do not all mean the same thing.

Assuming for the moment that everyone realizes written examinations leave a lot unmeasured, why can't they just accept that a grade C is grade C? First, as explained above, one grade C Mathematics could be 50% obtained over the whole paper and the other could be 50% without the least understanding of algebra. Second, selecting young people by 'five O-levels for clerical assistant', for example, was arbitrary, assuming that any content would do. English, French, Maths, Art and Home Economics was as good as English, Physics, Chemistry, Music and RE. What have any of these except English got to do with clerical work?

Third, and more important, Grade C from an inner-city school may represent twice the achievement of Grade C from a school in the leafy suburbs. School environment, neighbourhood resources, catchment area, parental support, all affect results. It is not just the pupil's ability. In 1983 the DES undertook a major analysis of background factors in relation to examination results and they have continued to produce similar figures since then. They use six 'additional educational needs' variables which show difficulties children may have:

● Children born outside UK or belonging to non-white ethnic groups;

● Children whose head of household is a semi-skilled or unskilled manual worker;

● Children living in households lacking one or more of standard amenities or having density of occupation more than 1.5 persons per room;

164

RELATING EXAM RESULTS TO SOCIAL FACTORS

DIAGRAM 20

Percentage of maintained school leavers achieving

Local Education Authority	No graded results		2 or less graded results		6 or more graded results		1 or more higher graded passes at 0 level/CSE		5 or more higher graded passes at 0 level/CSE		1 or more passes at A level	
	Actual	Fitted	Actual	Fitted	Actual	Fitted	Actual	Fitted	Actual	Fitted	Actual	Fitted
Barking	18.6	15.5	29.6	23.5	41.8	57.5	37.7	41.9	13.4	14.6	9.6	9.1
Barnet	8.8	6.0	15.4	10.3	65.5	68.3	64.4	64.0	35.8	33.3	27.9	22.7
Bexley	7.6	8.0	11.1	15.7	70.4	65.3	53.1	54.6	25.3	25.2	15.3	15.7
Brent	15.0	17.3	23.5	24.0	54.3	51.4	49.5	48.5	17.8	17.4	13.4	15.0
Bromley	9.0	7.3	15.0	12.9	64.3	70.4	55.7	60.9	28.8	32.8	19.3	23.2
Croydon	10.3	10.9	15.8	17.2	62.9	61.0	53.5	53.2	25.3	24.3	16.1	17.7
Ealing	13.9	14.7	22.1	20.9	56.1	56.4	49.1	49.8	19.3	19.8	13.1	14.9
Enfield	11.1	8.9	18.0	15.8	62.3	63.8	55.9	56.4	22.9	24.3	16.3	15.9
Haringey	20.0	17.2	26.6	25.2	51.3	47.5	44.9	48.0	14.8	17.2	11.4	14.1
Harrow	6.3	7.3	9.8	11.3	67.2	69.9	67.4	63.0	37.2	31.0	25.9	23.2
Havering	7.0	10.3	14.7	16.0	62.1	66.4	57.3	53.7	25.2	24.0	17.0	16.7
Hillingdon	10.9	10.9	14.9	16.1	64.6	64.5	53.9	52.7	21.4	23.8	15.2	16.7
Hounslow	12.9	12.9	19.4	20.8	60.4	59.1	56.0	51.9	22.2	19.7	17.1	14.2
Kingston-upon-Thames	9.4	6.4	15.3	13.0	63.6	69.1	60.7	63.0	31.3	32.3	21.6	21.3
Merton	12.7	10.5	16.3	16.6	65.1	63.4	52.8	52.4	24.5	24.0	15.8	15.9
Newham	25.1	22.0	33.3	32.0	45.3	45.7	36.9	36.5	11.3	11.4	7.4	8.3
Redbridge	9.3	9.1	19.3	14.4	55.7	66.9	57.6	57.6	25.7	27.3	18.1	18.1
Wiltshire	7.5	8.7	13.2	14.1	68.4	66.7	54.9	52.6	24.1	22.1	13.0	14.2
England (excluding Isles of Scilly)	11.1	11.1	17.7	17.7	64.1	64.1	51.2	51.2	22.7	22.7	14.6	14.6

165

- Children in one-parent families;

- Children in families of more than four children;

- Children receiving free school meals in maintained schools.

A formula is then used to show how national average performance would be altered by these factors. The results are shown in diagram 20. So although the national average in 1983 for 'no graded result' was 11.1%, in Barking you would expect 15.5% and in Barnet 6%. Similarly, nationally, 22.7% got five or more O-level passes, but in Barking 14.6% would be OK and in Barnet 33.3%. It is against these 'fitted' figures that results must be judged. To compare a Barking school with a Barnet school on examination grades alone is illogical. LEAs are to be charged with the duty of giving socio-economic statements for each school so that the results can be put in context.

Of course, you could say that background features are themselves results of low intelligence. Cattell (an American researcher) says so quite brutally:

> 'the analysis shows . . . that educational achievement in schools depends on many things besides intelligence, e.g. personality qualities and home attitudes to learning, among others. But unless it can be proved that these are for *independent* reasons (i.e. not as a by-product of low intelligence), poorer in the lower achievement communities, the statistician must accept as the *most probable* conclusion that lower achievement in communities is partly due to lower intelligence.'

This was written in the USA and fiercely contested. It is just as 'probable' that social and political pressures keep inner-city children where they are. Plenty of very intelligent people crumble under unemployment or other stress and end up on skid row or under the arches on the Embankment.

If children are underprivileged, we want to know how they cope with that. Are they resourceful, resilient, courageous? You don't get that information from Mathematics O-level grades.

HOW EXAMINATIONS AFFECT TEACHERS
'Do we have to?' 'Yes, it's on the syllabus.'

So runs a frequent classroom exchange. The examination syllabus justifies what is taught. What is examined is important. What isn't is not. Worse than that, what is important is what gets written down on the candidate's paper. If she understands it, so much the better, but make sure she knows the drill. So generations of children have passed O-level Mathematics using a few tricks of the trade. If they then go on to try A-level, it becomes clear that they did not understand the tricks.

The advantages claimed for the National Curriculum and the tests that go with it are:

1. Children will be 'protected from teacher enthusiasms' — which means bees-in-bonnets about content or method. A few teachers may think every child should know local history rather than the economic goings-on in the nineteenth century; or rock music rather than the school song book. 'Creative writing', discovery and discussion may go over the top and limit the input of hard information.

2. Curriculum will be cleared of 'clutter' — Sir Keith's word for things he did not like, such as peace studies, race studies, green studies, etc. There will be no danger that these extras will drive out the necessary 'core' and 'foundation' subjects.

3. Teachers will have limited and attainable goals and not feel overwhelmed by all the lobbies wanting to get their interest taught in school.

4. Broadly similar material will be taught all over the country for a given age-group. Teachers will not be faced with newcomers to a class having done something totally different.

Teachers doubt if more than a tiny minority go in for odd 'enthusiasms' or 'clutter' and fear that the more rigid framework will go to the other extreme. Teachers will 'shrink to the middle' of the syllabus instead of doing the interesting extras at the edges. Since the National Curriculum is 'tested', things it does not mention will be starved of time.

Already examinations severely affect lessons. One report shows that traditionally practical subjects like Home Economics and Craft now use more time in 'written evaluation of practical conclusions' than in practical skills. It is easier to mark written work.

In A-level modern languages one Board offered: Paper 1, prose/essay (31%); translation/reading comprehension (25%); oral (19%); literature (25%). But in practice it was shown that, whatever the syllabus *said*, in French, Paper 1 counted nearly twice as much as any of the others. In Italian it was three times as important. What are teachers to do? Marks on Paper

1 are what we need, so time actually *speaking* the language or enjoying the literature gets cut.

News of the new tests will soon be out. Teachers will analyze them closely to see 'what counts'. Parents will push teachers to 'do the best for the children', meaning get as many test marks as possible. Most teachers would be happy with 'bench marks' saying what a child ought to know and do at 11 and 14 (less sure about age 7) and would achieve these incidentally to good and interesting teaching if left to themselves. Perhaps by some miracle the Working Groups will do just that in their recommendations for test procedures for individual subjects.

HOW EXAMS AFFECT PUPILS

The big problem with examinations for pupils is that examinations can't do everything. They can test you and show what you need help with. Pupils welcome this. I have often had work volunteered — 'Could you please look at this and tell me what's right and wrong with it?' A very pleasant co-operative interaction. Half-yearly internal school examinations are intended by teachers to do the same things. 'Going over the paper' is a time-honoured way of explaining things, clearing up misunderstandings, and most teachers put individual notes on pupils' answers and discuss them individually. Pupils usually welcome this too, with reservations. They look first for the total mark and wonder, 'Where did I come?' and then, 'What will Mum say?' If Mum has common sense to 'go over the paper' and make constructive comment, things are not too bad. In both these situations the assessment and the assessor are linked in a personal relationship with the pupil. It is a personal, encouraging, business.

But O-level or GCSE or A-level are another kettle of fish. They are quite impersonal. In fact, this 'objectivity' is held to be their great virtue. The purpose is not to help the pupil, but to evaluate five years' secondary school experience at a stroke (GCSE does allow course-work to count which helps a little). It is a now-or-never, instant death situation. Pupils are nervous; so, to be honest, are teachers. For five years they have struggled to help pupils understand; now pupils and teacher are united simply to 'get through'. Agonizing last-minute sessions to plug gaps mix with attempts to 'spot questions'. Behind these are two fears — (a) I might not get the grades I need for the next stage and (b) I might be a 'failure'.

'JUDGMENT' — OR 'DAMNATION'?

Our society is shaky on judging. Things that used to be clearly right or wrong are now 'up to the individual'. So criticism of testing must not get sucked into this mistakenly 'tolerant' view. Some things are right and some are wrong, and pupils and teachers need to know it. It is quite right for a teacher to pass judgment on a piece of work. Quite right for an examination marking scheme to require correct reference to literature, or the right dates in a History essay, or the right equations in Chemistry. But we easily confuse two kinds of judgment — the pronouncement of fact and the apportionment of blame. The judge on a racetrack tells me that my 100m dash took twenty seconds, and I am nowhere near the world record of 9.2 seconds. But he does not say I am a bad or disreputable person. All too often examination results do both. They show a pupil clearly that he is not up to a 'pass' standard, and also make him feel it is his fault and he is a 'failure'. In some cases it can be partly his fault, through idleness or obstinacy; but by no means always. We must keep 'failure' as a moral word, something involving behaviour and character, not skill and knowledge. Ruth Etchells, Principal of a Durham College, wrote of the need to 're-instate the concept of judgment':

> 'We must be prepared to work out what we understand in terms of judgment as the first rate in each particular case, not only for the high-flyer, but at every level of teaching. When I was in Canada teaching a high-powered group of teachers and clergy, they found it very difficult indeed to accept judgment when they got their papers back . . . quite the most difficult students I have ever met . . . But any evaluation we make has to discriminate but yet be loving and open. It must reflect the Christian integration of mercy and justice. We are called upon to judge, as teachers, as thinkers, as counsellors, as people, and yet to do it in such a way as not to destroy. And we are called upon to accept judgment and yet not be destroyed.'

This is the guiding principle behind much recent thinking about assessment. It is combined with a concern to break the fascination of numbers. Politicians have backgrounds in industry and commerce where you can measure output. 'Objective' they call it. They want figures to measure things by, not waffly words. Many parents are in these fields too, and soak up the same attitude. But 'not all that counts can be counted, and not all that can be counted, counts.' Several recent schemes try to act on this principle.

PROPOSALS FOR THE FUTURE

The old 'school leaving certificate' carried weight with local employers because they knew the school and the headteacher who signed it. For most pupils it had no examination grades because pupils leaving at 14 or 15 had not taken examinations. But the certificates did say a lot about skill and character, attitude and reliability. This wider reporting has been revived. The Hargreaves Report (1984) identified four 'achievement aspects' which are so important that they are quoted at length:

> **Achievement aspect 1.** This aspect is strongly represented in the current 16+ public examinations. It involves most of all the capacity to express oneself in a written form . . . to retain propositional knowledge; to select from such knowledge appropriately in response to a specified request and to do so quickly without reference to possible sources of information. The capacity to memorize and organize material is particularly important.

> **Achievement aspect 2.** . . . to apply knowledge rather than knowledge itself, with the practical rather than the theoretical, with the oral rather than the written. Problem-solving and investigational skills are more important than the retention of knowledge. This aspect is to some degree measured in public examinations.

> **Achievement aspect 3.** . . . concerned with personal and social skills; the capacity to communicate with others in face-to-face relationships; the ability to co-operate with others in the interests of the group as well as of the individual; initiative, self-reliance and the ability to work alone without close supervision; and the skills of leadership. This aspect of achievement remains virtually untapped by the 16+ examinations.

> **Achievement aspect 4.** . . . involves motivation and commitment; the willingness to accept failure without destructive consequences; the readiness to persevere; the self-confidence to learn in spite of the difficulty of the task . . . working-class pupils are particularly vulnerable

here, since some of them, because of disadvantaged circumstances, come to school with already low levels of aspect 4 achievement; they rely upon teachers in a way that most middle-class pupils do not.'

Two initiatives are worth comment in this connection:

1. Records of achievement. This is a term the DES have adopted to include a report on all sorts of educational progress. It would include 'credit for what pupils have achieved and experienced, not just in terms of results in public examinations but in other ways as well . . . Young people leaving school or college should take with them a short, summary document of record which is recognized and valued by employers and institutions of further education. This should provide a more rounded picture of candidates for jobs or courses than can be provided by a list of examination results.'

A record of achievement can include success outside school as well as within; it will refer to all the four achievement aspects mentioned above. It may also embody a record of experience compiled by the student, a kind of personal log of what she has attempted and achieved at school.

In 1984 the DES set the objective of having Records of Achievement for all school leavers by 1990. There has already been considerable experiment. A number of LEAs have set up programmes to see how such a wide assessment could be made. The Manpower Services Commission has used similar methods on its YTS courses. Some of the newer examinations embody such Records of Achievement or 'Profile' — for example, the CPVE and TVEI mentioned in chapter 5.

2. Negotiated assessment. CPVE and TVEI go further than simply including a wide range of qualities, skills and achievements. They involve the pupils in the assessment process. Tutor and student work together filling in the various parts of the 'profile', putting an agreed comment. This makes assessment a valuable part of teaching as the pupil faces the truth about himself and discusses ways forward. Two jargon words must be distinguished — 'formative' assessment is the regular reporting of progress which helps the pupil develop; 'summative' assessment is the final report that goes with him when he leaves.

All this is fairly new and is met with a few cautions from the teacher's point of view: can standards be set so that Records of Achievement have universal value, and not all be different? Some teachers are reluctant to pass firm judgment on pupils' motivation and character. They see this as 'subjective' and 'not their job' — though they have always made judgments of the 'lazy, could do better' kind on school reports.

All teachers agree this is a demanding and time-consuming business. It will be very expensive. One authority made a rough calculation of over £500 a leaver by the time all the extras in curriculum and assessment were taken into account.

There are also pluses and minuses from the pupils' point of view:

'At worst, the effect will be even more devastating than the worst excesses of public examinations. Subject to continuous, comprehensive scrutiny of every aspect of their life and work, pupils will be subject to an even more pervasive destruction of their self-image than they may be at present. Other pupils, who, as they do now, early learn to play the system, will quickly realise the values teachers espouse and will seek to present the appropriate front for such assessment. Still others will retreat from this nightmare of benign surveillance.'

On the positive side:

'The promise of profiling is that of an assessment which can make a reality of the aims of education which we set for ourselves. It offers a vision of education which is characterized by democratic teacher-pupil relations; in which pupils have a sense of self-worth; in which they may voluntarily negotiate their own curriculum path; in which they develop the ability to be self-critical and thus to take responsibility for their own learning, and in which the competition is primarily with themselves and their own previous performance rather than with others.'

The 1988 Act says nothing about all this. It is to be hoped it does nothing to stop the development. Results of the tests prescribed by the Act will be part of the achievement shown on the Records of Achievement.

CHAPTER 8

Standards

and how to raise them

The Secretary of State has repeatedly said the 1988 Education Act is to raise standards. The discussion documents said the National Curriculum would do this by:

● A broad curriculum for all, so pupils will not drop vital subjects too early;

● Clear objectives that are 'realistic but challenging';

● Key content, skills and processes for all pupils;

● Regular checking on progress.

The subject of standards is closely connected with that of assessment dealt with in the previous chapter. There is sufficient difference, however, to deserve a short chapter looking at what standards are and how they might be improved. It will, inevitably, contain some statistics, but I hope not too many or too incomprehensible.

Every month or two the national press gives news of a report saying standards are falling in education. These are usually followed by a medley of letters, some from educationalists saying standards are, in fact, going up, and others by parents and employers giving a variety of stories, good and bad, about youngsters. It is hard to avoid the conclusion that editors find bad news about schools good news for them. They may have a shrewd idea that their readers feel comprehensive schools are 'failing the nation' and like to be given illustrations of this assumption. The trade press — such as the *Times Educational Supplement* — ploughs a steady and sober furrow, giving good and bad reports impartially and prosaically and attracting a similar-style medley of letters. Three questions clearly need answering: what are 'standards'? Can they be measured? Are they rising, falling, or staying steady?

WHAT ARE 'STANDARDS'?
Most people (and most newspapers) assume that standards are

measured in examination scores. If the average score on an English test in 1914 was 100 (to quote one example) and in the same test today's youngsters average 96, then standards in English have fallen. If 85% of Japanese school leavers get a particular sum right against 49% of UK leavers, then Japanese standards are higher. The standard, then, is a level of achievement, taken overall.

Everyone agrees individual pupils do well, and have always done well — so well that we used to have a 'brain drain' as other countries were anxious to pay our doctors, scientists and research workers more than we did. But 'standards' is used of education as a whole — the overall performance of a year group, or oddly enough, the performance of a random sample. This odd reaction appears when letters saying, for example, that reading standards are rising, are answered by employers writing to say that three out of the last five applicants could not read the application form correctly. Similarly, people comment about girls on supermarket checkouts who seem surprised when the customer works out three at 89p in their head as quickly as the machine does it. 'My mother worked in a grocer's,' they say, 'and her mental arithmetic was brilliant. Standards aren't what they were.' In fact, it is doubtful if that mother would be working on a checkout today. She would be more likely to have stayed at school and qualified for a different job. One writer on youth employment says:

> 'It is true that the quality of 16-year-olds available for work has declined in the recent past. This has happened because more and more able students have either stayed on at school or have gone on to further or higher education. Employers who have stuck with recruiting this age group are thus recruiting from a significantly different range of ability.'

Mention of further and higher education may draw stories from university and college lecturers who are convinced their students are not as good as they used to be. Therefore, schools aren't what they were. In fact, the number of university full-time students increased from 173,000 to 305,000 in the 20 years to 1985 and numbers in polytechnics and other colleges went from 133,000 to 284,000. Nearly doubled in all. Schools did wonders to motivate and prepare so many — a major change in the country's educational pattern. Comparing 1985 with 1965 is misleading. The best 173,000 today may well be quite as good as the whole 173,000 was in 1965.

So, what can we mean by 'standards'?

1. It can be 'a standard', like spelling 100 words correctly, or playing ten scales on the piano correctly or swimming 100m — an objective performance. Everybody knows what it requires.

2. It can be the percentage of a year group which reaches the 'standard' in sense 1.

3. It can be the percentage of a group I meet who can reach the standard in sense 1.

4. It can be the level of achievement of a random individual I happen to meet.

The 1988 Education Act uses 'attainment targets' to mean 'standards' in sense 1. It proposes to lay down for each subject a series of skills, concepts and knowledge which an average child should have by age 7, 11 or 14. As mentioned in the last chapter, the usefulness of this will depend upon what items are chosen. It will, however, be objective in sense 1 — the same for everyone, clearly stated. *What* should be included will be contested — for example, it is as important to have an attainment target for spoken English as for written; for problem-solving using arithmetic as for arithmetic sums on their own.

The Secretary of State has repeatedly said that children will differ in attainment. The 'target' is what an average 7-, 11- or 14-year-old should know. Some may get there earlier, some later. The 'target' simply fixes a mark to measure them by.

CAN STANDARDS BE MEASURED?

As mentioned in the last chapter, we are better at measuring some things than others. Recent examinations test the recall of information that has been memorized. They are less good at testing whether the candidate can use the information, and still less whether she can find information in a library or workplace. Factual knowledge is easier to measure than a practical skill like dressmaking or model-making.

Another difficulty is that the testing situation distorts the picture. Everyone knows someone who has 'examination nerves' or a learner driver who usually drives perfectly but failed the test. On the other hand some candidates may be coached hard for the examination to the exclusion of all else. An HMI report commented:

> 'In mathematics, exams were one factor in encouraging narrow, repetitive practice and standard routines divorced

175

from application to the situations.'

Some people are lucky in exams when 'the right questions come up'. Others get a swimming certificate 'on a good day'. The exam nerves, good luck and the repetitive practice, of course, don't alter the standard. They simply add to the problem of interpreting candidates' performance on the day.

The testing industry — and Examination Boards in particular — is very jealous of its standards. There is a 'special difficulty' procedure. For example, if you were ill during one paper, you might get a grade awarded on the other paper in that subject. But if you were ill for both papers, they won't give you a grade just because your teacher says you were well up to the standard.

Those who set the tests try to make them fair for everyone, but I once knew a Chinese student who was stumped by a mathematics question which referred to a 'circular race-track'. Her mathematics was well up to it, but her English vocabulary was limited.

Finally, what do tests tell you when they are published? They tell you about the people who attempted them — that is, the standard in sense 3 above. Sixty per cent pass a driving test the first time. Maybe you could find out that, say, 45% of the population have passed the driving test. That doesn't say anything about the ability of the rest of the population — maybe many of them could reach the standard but they haven't applied for the test. People take driving tests at all ages. What makes GCSE and A-levels different is that they are mostly taken at 16 or 18 and it is assumed that everyone who is capable will be entered. Certainly the 7, 11, 14 age-tests will be of that sort. So the results should give us an overall picture of achievement — in other words, the standard in sense 2 above. For GCSE and A-level this is not quite true, because people do take these exams — certainly A-level — at different ages, some at evening class, some at 19 after failing the first time.

So 'standard' in sense 1 — an attainment target — can in many cases be measured. But it leaves questions about what the measure means.

ARE STANDARDS RISING OR FALLING?

This is the bone of contention. Usually 'standards' is being used in the discussion in sense 2 or 3 — the rate of achievement of the year-group or a particular set of people. In that sense the Director of the CBI put his foot in it when he complained:

'In spite of Industry year, the nation's secondary schools are in urgent need of reform. Around half of all school leavers do not have a single GCE O-level pass or CSE equivalent.'

He was answered by a headteacher who wrote:

'The fact is true but the interpretation is false. The now defunct GCE O-level and its CSE equivalent were designed for the top 20% of pupils. That State schools have repeatedly exceeded that limit is surely proof of success.'

Percentages are thrown around, almost all showing apparent improvement. For example:

● The percentage of school leavers achieving five or more higher grade (A-C) O-level/CSE passes has risen from 20% in 1965 to 27% in 1984;

● The percentage of leavers with no graded results has fallen from 50% in 1965 to 11.7% in 1984;

● The percentage of leavers with one A-level rose from 16.6% in 1971 to 18.1% in 1985;

● The percentage of leavers with three A-levels rose from 5.5% in 1966 to 9.8% in 1984.

The Assessment of Performance Unit (APU) mathematics survey showed a 'small but statistically significant improvement in the performance of 11- and 15-year-olds between 1978 and 1982.' And that in English language there was 'no evidence of widespread illiteracy . . . no collapse of standards was discovered . . . Over the five years of the surveys, improvement in the performance of primary pupils was evidenced, while secondary performance remained stable.'

Research in Scotland on 40,000 pupils in 1976, 1980 and 1984 showed that attainment had increased for all social classes and most sharply among children from manual occupation families.

The critics are unmoved. More people are reaching the target, they say, because the targets are being lowered. It is easier to get an A-level than it was in our day. Teachers sourly comment that this does not stop the critics wanting their own children to get all the devalued certificates they can. More seriously, the criticism fails to account for the APU surveys. In the case of GCE examinations it is harder to decide, since (as explained in the last chapter) the examinations are 'norm-referenced'. However, an attempt was made in 1973:

> 'In this study, which was instigated by Margaret Thatcher, the then Education Secretary, senior examiners compared A-level English literature, Maths and Chemistry scripts from 1963 and 1973. After re-marking the 1963 papers, provided by the Joint Matriculation Board, they concluded that "by and large . . . improvements had been effected" during the period.'

A-level teachers would heartily agree. Syllabuses get fuller not thinner. Questions are certainly no easier.

Reading tests consistently show improvement. Mean scores at age 11 have risen from 28.2 in 1954 to 31 in 1982. In 1977 the headline said 'Reading standards highest since the war'. That left the critics cold — 'Of course, the war was a low point; children evacuated; teachers called up into the services'. They dug up a test from 1914 which showed (slightly) higher scores. Sir Alec Clegg, doyen of Chief Education Officers, made the whimsical comment 'I understand that it implies that we can no longer teach children how to read, though if this is so I am puzzled by the fact that Puffin books increased their sales from 600,000 in 1961 to six million in 1975.'

It all looks like a futile battle in the dark with statistics as the ammunition. Can we get some sense into it?

Dividing the topic into three areas may show how misunderstandings arise and may even cast a little light on the main question of whether standards are falling. Let's look at the difficulties in: comparing different groups; the selective/comprehensive argument; and the performance of non-white pupils. All of these illustrate the complexity of the problem.

1. False comparison. The search for a single figure that will tell you all about a group is hopeless. There are always other things to be said. For example, in 1983-84 independent schools turned out 46% of their leavers with three A-levels and 74% with five O-levels. For grammar schools the figures were 35% with three A-levels and 77% with five O-levels. For comprehensives there were 7% with three A-levels and 23% with five O-levels. This gives a fair statement of the probability of a pupil in the various schools getting the given results. But comparison is impossible. The grammar schools are a tiny minority — only 170 of them altogether in 1983-84, increasingly selective, catering for pupils of whom three-quarters had strong educational background. The independent schools were a much larger group, even more highly selective and more likely to have professional parents. These able pupils were taken out of the system before the 4,000 or so comprehensive schools got started.

The question for an individual parent is 'If Mary could pass the entrance exam to St Ethelreda's, will she be in the 46%? If she went to Bloggs Comprehensive up the road, will she be in the 7%?' You need, of course, to be sure that St Ethelreda's is up to the national average (Harrow gets a lot more than 46% so some schools must be doing much worse) and that Bloggs Comprehensive is up to the national 7% standard. The answer to both questions is very likely 'Yes'. That leaves several other questions about the schools which have little to do with examination results.

One major attempt at comparison was made by the National Child Development Study (NCDS). The Study followed the development of the 16,000 children born in a particular week in 1958. The sample therefore is likely to be a fair cross-section of the British population. When the children were 16, they were tested in Maths and English and the scores compared with those obtained at age 11. The results showed that children of high ability (their scores were in the top 20% when they were tested at 11) made, on average, the same amount of progress in reading and Maths over the five years of secondary education regardless of whether they went to grammar or comprehensive schools. (There were plenty of grammar schools about in the period 1969-74 when these children were in secondary education.) These claims were vigorously attacked. A full report of the children's later examination performance was published later (1983) and the following conclusions drawn:

● Grammar schools give O-level pupils an advantage equivalent to two-thirds of a pass over comprehensive pupils of similar ability and background;

● Grammar school pupils are more likely to get five or more O-levels than comprehensive pupils of similar ability and background;

● The exam results of comprehensives are no better or worse than secondary moderns and grammar schools taken together, even though;

● The comprehensives were virtually secondary moderns in their ability and social class ranges;

● Grammar schools are not better than comprehensives for bright

179

working-class children;

• There is no conclusive evidence that bright children do worse in comprehensives.

The very detailed report gave a mass of information from which debaters could choose what suited them, but the overall impression was that the type of school a child attended was less important than other factors in their development.

2. The selective/comprehensive argument. The National Child Development Study survey is an example of the debate over the type-of-school issue. So much has been written about this that one suspects that people are defending personal positions rather than seeking the truth — or else that the truth is that schools of all sorts vary and children in the schools vary so much that not a lot can be said decisively. Dr Davie of the National Childrens Bureau summed up his report as 'dispelling a few myths at the extremes, for example that comprehensives are a complete disaster or alternatively that the sun shines out of them.'

Other reports and features give rise to conflicting headlines: 'Where comprehensives score'; 'The verdict is still "not proven"'; 'Why comprehensives fail'. The argument was hottest in the late 1960s and 70s. Some in the profession will remember the *Black Papers* of 1969 which kept the debate boiling, as politicians and academics wondered what the educational world was coming to. It is a rather more academic issue now, since Britain is 90% comprehensive. But still rearguard actions keep suggesting we should undo it all. Two contributions are given to show how the debate proceeds.

First, statistics need watching, as has been said many times. A particularly glaring misuse comes from 1979 when the Chairman of Governors of Manchester Grammar School entered the fray claiming that selective schools gave 42.46% A-level passes as a percentage of leavers in 1977 while comprehensives scored only 27.71%. Diagram 21 shows how it was done: the 'selective' system contained 42,000 grammar school leavers and 103,000 secondary modern with 61,500 A-level passes between them. This made 42.46%. The comprehensive leavers totalled 650,000, with 180,000 A-levels between them. This made 27.71%.

But when the boffins got to work on it they pointed out that since the grammar schools were supposed to take only 20% of the ability range, the secondary moderns should have

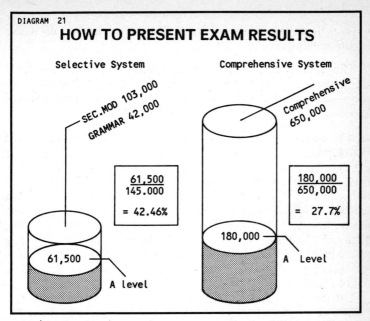

DIAGRAM 21

HOW TO PRESENT EXAM RESULTS

Selective System   Comprehensive System

SEC.MOD 103,000
GRAMMAR 42,000

Comprehensive 650,000

$$\frac{61,500}{145.000}$$

= 42.46%

$$\frac{180,000}{650,000}$$

= 27.7%

61,500

A level

180,000

A Level

been taking 80%, i.e. four times as many, which would make 168,000, not 103,000. Where had the 65,000 gone? Obviously into the comprehensives. The comprehensives were not true comprehensives. Some of the more able had been creamed off into the grammar schools. These 65,000 should be added to the 'selective' pile. They would take a few A-level passes with them, but not many as they were all in the lower 80% (say 1,000 passes). The revised figures should be 29.8% and 30.6% — about the same, as diagram 22 shows.

Second, in a more recent book *The Comprehensive Experiment*, by Reynold, Sullivan and Murgatroyd (1987), three researchers look at the change from selective to comprehensive system more widely. It is not just a matter of examination passes, but the preparation for life and developing whatever skills and personal qualities children have. Have standards of such care increased? The writers think not. They see comprehensives as being too anxious to copy the old grammar schools and trying to give 'grammar school education for all' while failing to carry on the good traditions of good secondary modern schools.

'Secondary modern schools and their traditions were

181

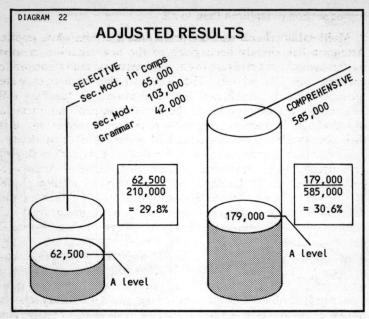

DIAGRAM 22

ADJUSTED RESULTS

SELECTIVE
Sec.Mod. in Comps 65,000
Sec.Mod. 103,000
Grammar 42,000

COMPREHENSIVE
585,000

$\dfrac{62,500}{210,000}$ = 29.8%

$\dfrac{179,000}{585,000}$ = 30.6%

62,500

179,000

A level

A level

unwisely resisted as the new schools were formed, and it is time their strengths were rediscovered and blended with some of the existing grammar school traditions to generate authentic comprehensives for children . . . Shift attention away from the top one-third of the ability range who have proved more than able to cope, and care more, socially and academically, for the lower two-thirds.

To argue that schools should become more concerned with all their children and to argue that social goals are as important as academic goals in modern society may be currently unfashionable in many quarters. But unless the schools manage to give all children the social development that parts of the education system have managed in the past, together with intellectual development that other parts of the education system have delivered, the future of British society will in our view be bleak.'

This tries to broaden the question of standards. It raises social questions of its own, but is a welcome break from continual discussion of statistics that reflect only one aspect of development — and an aspect that is of far more relevance to one section of children than to all.

3. Multi-racial schools and the performance of non-white pupils.

Attention has already been given to the new situation created by the arrival over the last twenty-five years of many non-white children into UK schools. The administrative challenges were mentioned in chapter 2 and the implications for teachers will be dealt with in chapter 10. In the present context, the question of 'standards' is relevant. Are these pupils under-achieving, or is their potential being developed as well as that of other children?

The Swann Report (known as Rampton in its earlier stages) gave figures which appeared to show that pupils of Asian origin achieved much the same as white pupils but that pupils of Caribbean origin achieved significantly worse. Much of the difference was said to be accounted for by home educational and occupational background. Further research into this was proposed but not carried out. For some LEAs it was not a live issue — only 3% of pupils in Cheshire or the Isle of Wight were non-white. But in Brent the figure was 53% and in Haringey 50%. In ILEA as a whole it was 35% and a major study of fifth-year pupils was conducted in 1985 and 1986. One hundred out of 144 secondary schools took part in the review with a total of over 15,000 pupils. The detailed statistics were summarized in an 'average performance' score, obtained by counting O-level grade A = 7, B = 6, down to CSE grade 5 = 1 point. The full summary was as in the tabulation.

DIAGRAM   23

RESULTS BY ETHNIC GROUP

1976	1985		1986 No.	Actual	sub-group comparison		Diffce
					Actual	Predicted	
	16.9	African	386	17.6	19.4	16.2	3.2 +
	14.0	Arab	123	14.1	15.1	13.1	2.0 +
	8.7	Bangladeshi	535	9.3	14.5	11.2	3.3 +
(10.3)	13.6	Caribbean	2629	13.5	13.8	14.2	0.4 -
(14.0)	14.9	Eng/Scot/Welsh	7985	14.7	15.0	16.4	1.4 -
	17.6	Greek	170	19.5	20.0	15.0	5.0 +
	24.5	Indian	387	22.0	22.9	15.6	7.3 +
	16.6	Irish	1037	16.6	16.9	16.7	0.2 +
	21.3	Pakistani	255	20.9	21.6	15.0	6.6 +
(18.4)	19.1	SE Asian	326	19.5	25.1	16.1	9.0 +
	11.9	Turkish	285	12.2	12.7	12.0	0.7 +
		Other Black	135	14.7	14.9	14.8	0.1 +
	19.6	Other European	649	21.0	21.2	16.2	5.0 +
		Other White	120	17.5	18.8	16.8	2.0 +
(13.7)	15.6	All	15042	15.2	15.7 (12631)	15.7	

The figures on the right were obtained from a sub-group for which performance scores were available based on predictions made when the pupils were aged 11. The figures in brackets on the left are for a comparable test in 1976 — the 14.0 covers Irish as well as English, Scots and Welsh, and the 18.4 covers all Asian (Bangladeshi, Indian, Pakistani and SE Asian.)

Girls did better for all ethnic groups. Overall their performance score was 17.7 against the boys' 13.7. Also significant is that the proportion of non-white pupils, in the schools surveyed, rose from 18% to 37% between 1976 and 1985.

In the discussion of these figures, the ILEA report draws attention particularly to the differences in the actual and predicted scores. Most pupils did better than expected. The main, and surprising, decrease is for English/Scots/Welsh pupils. The report suggests this is due to the fact that the 11-year-old prediction was based partly on a test and partly on headteacher's report. Either the headteachers were too hopeful of white British pupils, or the others made better use of their time in secondary school.

This report is summarized at some length to show the complexity of the issue. It raises a lot more questions about background, motivation, teacher expectation, and all those already given in the last chapter about the reliability of GCE/CSE examinations in general. But it is a serious attempt to relate a large sample of pupils to an objective standard. The fact that it shows improvement almost everywhere may give ILEA some satisfaction. It is also, incidentally, an example of the good use of figures broken down by ethnic origin. At various times this has been resisted (not least by the ethnic minorities themselves) for fear the figures might be used prejudicially. But if you don't know what is happening, you are even more at the mercy of prejudice.

Under the 1988 Act ILEA is due to be disbanded and its duties spread about among the constituent boroughs. It is doubtful whether any of these boroughs will be able to mount such an extensive statistical exercise. It is also sadly doubtful whether some will either want or be able to give such a well-supported programme of help to the many ethnic groups in the authority.

But what of other, less measurable, standards? Statistics deal almost exclusively in examination results. Standards of behaviour, care, tidiness are much harder to catch in figures. Stories about these matters are local; each has a story to tell of his own experience. Questions like 'Are you satisfied/dissatisfied/don't know with standards of behaviour in secondary schools?' may feature in a pollster's list but answers are not very informative. Questions about quality of teaching reflect parents' interpretation of their children's experience and such answers merit attention. Schools are accountable to the public. Examination figures tend to make this a *national* accountability, lumping the whole service together. It would be better if schools could make their case locally, one by one, by close relationship with parents and the community. This means finding some way of publicizing all that goes on. It may be impossible, since a lot that goes on is between teacher and individual children a thousand times a day. That builds up a relationship of trust, care, respect and sometimes rebellion, which defies neat measurement and communication. Particularly in the case of primary schools this unmeasurable quality is what is most important. As testing at 7 and 11 creeps down to primary schools, let us hope it does not take over. Some of the signs are good and when the first 7-year test comes, probably in 1991, let us hope we shall have developed such good communication of all the school does that the publication of a few figures about subject tests will not overshadow more important items.

WHOSE FAULT?

As hinted above, it is one thing (and a difficult thing) to say *if* standards have changed. It is quite a different thing to say why. The knee-jerk reaction of the media is to blame the school for any drop in educational standards, parents for rise in juvenile crime and the Government or the churches for most else. There are, however, many factors involved. Teachers are not the only people to influence children. Children spend longer in front of a television screen than in front of a teacher. A few factors are noted.

● **Population changes.** Everyone knows the birth rate went down sharply in the 70s. What is less well known is that this decrease was sharper among manual workers than professional and managerial classes. Diagram 24 shows the change. Social classes I and II accounted for 17% of births in 1964 and 28% in 1977. These families are more likely to have a tradition of staying into sixth form or further education, followed by university. They are more likely to encourage their children in this way, so we should expect the number staying on to increase, and the number of A-level passes to continue to increase as a proportion of the age group.

● **More girls are staying on at school.** Social trends have made it more likely and more acceptable for girls to spend longer in education. The increase in A-level passes is partly due to the

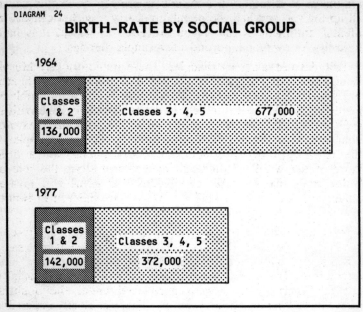

DIAGRAM 24

BIRTH-RATE BY SOCIAL GROUP

1964

Classes 1 & 2
136,000

Classes 3, 4, 5   677,000

1977

Classes 1 & 2
142,000

Classes 3, 4, 5
372,000

great increase over the last twenty-five years in the number of girls staying at school. At university and polytechnic the change is even more marked. The rapid expansion of higher education was partly due to the increasing number of girls entering — girls now account for over 40% of new entrants — so that the total numbers are much nearer balance than they were.

● **We are an increasingly visual society.** Television has accustomed us to rapidly changing pictures in highly professional presentations. It seems almost a miracle that reading scores have increased. Teaching styles have changed, too. Chalk-and-talk does not get across to today's TV-generation. This also means that the art of *listening* may be in decline. Some examinations are introducing 'comprehension' — listening to a taped statement and answering questions about it.

● **Changes in society have made older standards less relevant.** The 1914 English test, for example, was given in a society where writing was a main form of communication. Nowadays children communicate mostly by phone, at parents' expense; they go to work in offices where communication is by forms that are filled in, or word-processors. Copper-plate writing in ledgers has given place to anaemic computer printouts. Mental arithmetic is less vital in a society where the checkouts add it all up for you and half the population carry a pocket calculator. Mental arithmetic is fun if you are good at it, but it is hard to justify for everyone, beyond a few simple routines.

● **Attitudes and values are changing.** These are notoriously difficult to measure. Are standards of honesty decreasing? Certainly attitudes to marriage have changed and concern for world-problems increased. Society seems to be gripped as a whole by materialistic goals of wealth, success and the good life. Schools have not done much to foster this, except perhaps for the example of the teachers' own campaign, often very public, for a little more of the wealth. Home and media must share the role of 'value transmitters'. Research suggests that home is a greater influence than school — so if you want your children in twenty years' time to be like you are now, take heart.

Why have 'standards' dominated educational discussion recently? Perhaps because there has been genuine disquiet that some schools, or some authorities have been paying less than due attention to 'basics'. Perhaps because parents' expectations have grown. Comprehensives were introduced under the doubtful sales-line of 'grammar schools for all'. That was clearly impossible from the start. Standards (in our sense 1) stay put. Some children will reach them quickly, some will not get there at all. If parents are told everyone can get there, they are being misled as much as the man who said he wanted *everyone* to have more than average wages. So perhaps parents are looking for someone to blame — or maybe politicians are looking for a reason why we have not arrived at the ideal humane society they promised us. So we go in for the welter of statistics, finding out where our child comes in the pile, how she compares with everyone else. In the quaint language of King James' day, 'they, measuring themselves by themselves and comparing themselves among themselves, are not wise'.

Let children be the children they are, not striving to be some average or above-average model. And let them be happy as they develop into the young people they can be, and not feel guilty because they can't reach the 'standards' their parents or even teachers wish for them. What society needs is the will to change its values to match what children are, in all their variety, rather than to attempt to process all children to match its misguided values.

CHAPTER 9

Life after School

careers

Some of the most significant changes in education in recent years have been due to the collapse of the job market for the 16-year-old leaver. Several factors combined to bring this about. World recession; the growing pace of automation, making many unskilled jobs obsolete; larger numbers in the age groups; swathes of basic industry — coal, steel, shipbuilding, all full-time, male, skilled and semi-skilled jobs — disappeared. Unskilled labour needs plummeted.

A NEW WORLD OF WORK

The government response to this was not spearheaded by the Department of Education and Science but by the Department of Employment. The newly formed, heavily funded Manpower Services Commission (MSC), now the Training Commission, set up the Youth Training Scheme (YTS — successor to YOP) to give training and one year's work to as many as possible. The scheme was extended to two years with promises of a place for everyone and has become a major feature of the 16+ post-school scene. Diagram 25 shows the scope of the change. 'Normal' employment fell from 60% of the age-group to 20% in ten years. Unemployment trebled. Pupils stayed on in full-time education a little more — 37% to 45% over the ten years. YTS plugged the gap. Some YTS schemes are very good and the overall average for employment after the scheme averages 60% or more. But it is doubtful if it has really replaced the apprenticeship schemes of the past. In 1979 100,000 apprentices were taken into industry; in 1983 it was 40,000. Employers had almost withdrawn from training, though some areas (like automotive engineering — garage mechanics) have been incorporated in the YTS programme. By comparison, West Germany trains 600,000 apprentices a year. Charges were made that the education system was letting the nation down:

- By age 18 a high proportion of British young people had

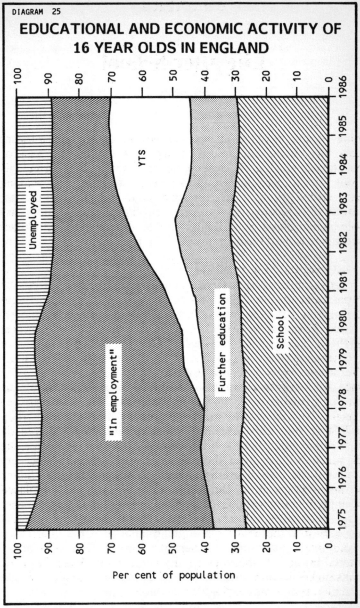

DIAGRAM 25

EDUCATIONAL AND ECONOMIC ACTIVITY OF 16 YEAR OLDS IN ENGLAND

Per cent of population

Taken from Statistical Bulletin 2/87 DES

189

no formal qualification or very limited vocational or academic attainment;

● Because of the collapse of the apprenticeship schemes, industry and commerce had no sustained flow of technically and occupationally trained new blood;

● There was no tradition of continuing education for half the age group — compare Japan where 95% stayed in education till 18.

All this took place against more than usually fierce political wrangling, so it is little wonder that no smooth, clear solution was found immediately. Nothing as powerful as this had ever hit education before. The whole legitimacy of State education was called in question, at least in the eyes of the pupils and many parents. For years pupils had been told 'If you work well and get your qualifications, you'll get a job.' That quite clearly wasn't true any more. School teachers manned the traditional barricades and said they were there to give general education, making rounded people, not to give job training to fill employers' factories.

Further education colleges were quicker to change but still found it hard to realize that decades-old skills were no longer required and that the new YTS trainees needed very different attention on their days at college. Even some of the good ideas had bad side-effects. For example, the excellent TVEI programme (see chapter 5) raised shouts of 'Unfair'. It was well funded (for the few schools involved) and so served to point out the relative underfunding of the rest of schools. Teachers (and politicians) who wanted *Education* to do the job, resented the MSC coming in and sloshing Department of Employment money about — much as the back-street kids dislike the rich kid coming into their patch on his smart new bike. There may have been a twinge of conscience as the swashbuckling, new-broom MSC contrasted with the cautious, fearful tradition of the DES. At least it got things done.

The split between Government Departments is a running sore. In 1980 the National Association of Headteachers proposed a single 'Department of Education and Training' to bring all needs and resources in the area under one roof. It hasn't happened yet. It could be the best thing ever for young people.

The upshot of these sadly unco-ordinated moves has been nearly ten years of uncertainty; gloom and dismay for many pupils; low morale for many teachers; but some chinks of light here and there which give hope that schools are regaining the initiative.

Four main areas need to be looked at: continuing at

school — the academic route; leaving full-time education and working — with or without some training; leaving full-time education and joining the unemployed, and what the 1988 Act has to do with all this.

FURTHER AND HIGHER EDUCATION
It's not easy to get into higher education, but at least schools know all about it. Most teachers climbed those ladders. A few regard them as the only decent ladders there are. All will help pupils get as far as they can. At age 16, students who want more of the same have a number of options. They also face a bewildering lot of letters, so pause a minute to note the umpteen qualifications on offer:

GCSE (General Certificate of Education) already explained in chapter 7;

CPVE (Certificate of Pre-Vocational Education) see chapter 5;

RSA (Royal Society of Arts) courses in typing, shorthand, book-keeping that will be remembered by some of today's parents who did them at night-school;

CGLI (City & Guilds) — a huge range of technical skills, from catering to telecommunications; many of today's parents took such exams in their own apprenticeship days;

BTEC (Business and Technician Education Council) the successor to the older Ordinary and Higher National Certificate or Diploma which many of today's parents worked for on day-release and at night-school;

GCE Advanced Level (A-level) and the new **Advanced Supplementary Level** (AS-level) which is taken to be about 'half an A-level';

and many others — so many in fact that the Government has a National Vocational Qualifications Committee working on a programme to drag all these together in some sort of order and comparability.

So, how does a student get some of these qualifications?
1. Go into the **school sixth form** — for a one-year course to improve GCSE results or to follow a CPVE course; or for a two-year A-level course.

2. Transfer to the **sixth-form college** which combines sixth-form provision for a whole area and so offers wider course possibilities.

Again — one-year courses, probably wider scope than most sixth forms — RSA, CGLI, BTEC General, as well as CPVE and GCSE; or two-year courses leading to A-level; or, one plus two years, getting to the A-level goal a bit later.

3. Go to **college of further education** — a very wide range of one-year introductory vocational courses, including CGLI, GCSE, RSA, CPVE — one- and two-year A-level courses; two-year BTEC diploma courses in everything from Accountancy to Youth Leadership.

4. Go to **tertiary college** — provided in some Authorities, bringing all sixth-form and further education courses together in one institution, so providing the widest possible choice of courses.

The first two options account for about 30% of the year group and the last two for a further 15%. At 16 there are more girls than boys, but since more girls than boys take only a one-year course, by age 17 the proportion is about the same.

The FE colleges will also be providing courses for part-time day and evening students, day- and block-release students, YTS students and adult education, but for the moment we consider just the 45% who stay on into further full-time study.

Let's look at some imaginary examples:

Jane has six GCSEs and always wanted to be a nurse. She is staying at her school into the sixth form to do a two-year A-level course in English, Biology and Music. She hopes to do a community service placement in a hospital or institution.

Surjit wants to improve her GCSE performance and is going to the sixth form college to repeat English and add Typing, Art and Economics. Then she hopes to go on to the FE college and do a BTEC qualification in Community Care.

Anthony is a musician. He is going to the sixth-form college to do a double Music A-level course and two AS courses (Italian and German). He hopes then to go on to a Music college for a performing degree.

Ahmad is going to the further education college to do a BTEC Diploma in Business Studies. He will combine this with A-level courses in Economics and Computing.

Charmaine is going to the tertiary college hoping to go on to a polytechnic Engineering course. She will do A-levels in Physics and Maths and some practical courses in Control Technology and Computer Graphics.

Gregory is also going to the tertiary college for a retailing course for one year after which he is promised a job in his uncle's clothes store — with hope of further day-release training.

These are mostly academic people, good at the sort of things examinations test, good at studying theoretical subjects. The system is well set up to give them what they need and they enjoy the process and the success it brings. About one-third will leave education after a year and the rest will press on to take A-level or BTEC at 18 or 19. About half these will then go into employment. The other half will press on to higher education (about 15% of the year group). The majority will be full-time students on three-year degree courses. Some will be 'sandwich' students, sandwiching years of study between years of employment. In the last ten years the number of students on degree courses have increased steadily — see diagram 26. There are 47 universities, from Exeter to Aberdeen. The 1988 Act alters their manner of funding a little but they still have considerable autonomy, and determine their own admission policies.

About sixty polytechnics and colleges of higher education will be funded under the 1988 Act through a new Polytechnics and Colleges Funding Council. Previously they were controlled by LEAs. A number remain under LEA control or administered by private trustees. They all have considerable control over their student admissions.

Entry into university is a well-worn trail. Careers teachers and counsellors know every crucial date and step. The university trail starts in September/October with the application to the Universities' Central Council for Admissions (UCCA). Students will have gone over this in the previous term and possibly visited a university or two. If they think this is the right route for them, they select up to five university courses, arranging them in an order of preference; they fill in their own claim to fame, why they want the universities and why they think the universities should want them; the school or college fills in the reference page and it goes off on a wing and a prayer to the Central Admissions Office in Cheltenham. Fortunate students get called for interviews and get provisional acceptance offers based on required A-level, AS-level or other examination grades.

All then awaits the middle of August when A-level results are published. If the grades are right, places are confirmed. If not,

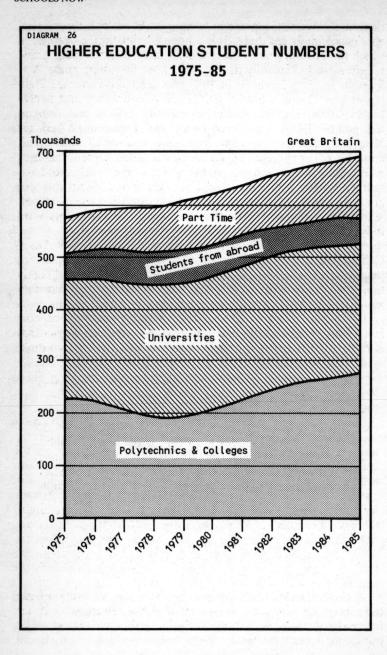

DIAGRAM 26

HIGHER EDUCATION STUDENT NUMBERS
1975-85

Thousands   Great Britain

Part Time

Students from abroad

Universities

Polytechnics & Colleges

there is a chance of a place in 'clearing'. About half the original applicants finally get there. It is a huge administrative exercise in which the A-level grades are a crucial factor. The average grade requirement has steadily risen (worked out by calling grade A = 5 points to E = 1 point): in 1975 you needed on average eight points (for example grades CCD) for Accountancy and twelve points (BBB) for Veterinary Science. By 1986 it had risen to ten points (BCC) for Accountancy and fourteen (AAB) for Veterinary Science. The universities of course said it wasn't their fault, because firstly, the Government has raised degree standards without lengthening courses, so universities have to rely more and more on what has been taught in sixth forms (their cost per graduate is low by international standards) and secondly, whatever Vice-chancellors say, entrants are convinced that selectors want high grades, so entrants are competing among themselves.

Entry to polytechnics is by a similar system (called Polytechnics' Central Admission System, PCAS) with a similar form. It can be used as the only application, or alongside UCCA. Again there is a wide range of courses (everything except Medicine) and offers are made conditional on A-level or BTEC results.

It is a little ironic that the A-level industry gets such support from these admission procedures, since the research shows that A-level is not a good predictor of degree result. One study (about experience at Oxford Polytechnic) commented:

> ' . . . a student with two grade Es could have considered that he had the same chance of a good degree as one with two B grades. One can also argue that the entry policy of offering places conditional on the achievement of certain A-level grades has been, perhaps unwittingly, educationally irrational. Nevertheless this policy continues possibly because in those subject areas where the demand for places exceeds the supply some method of selection must be employed, and no other suitable method has yet been devised. The findings of this paper highlight the fact that the conditional A-level method of selection is simply an administrative convenience to obtain the target number of students rather than a scientific method of selecting those students most likely to obtain good degrees.'

A third system, the Colleges' Register and Clearing House (CRCH) deals with entry to **colleges of higher education** — either for **teacher training** or for other degree or diploma courses. The procedure is much the same.

One way or another 15% of the year group will end up, at age 18 or 19, on a higher education degree course, taking them along the road to management, teaching or some other profession, or research. Few fail to find a job and the rewards are high. On the whole, schools and colleges can claim to be good at helping those who go this way. They are overwhelmingly middle-class — social class I and II (29% of the population) took 73% of university places. That may be due largely to parental expectation and pressure. Schools — certainly maintained schools — are conscious of the disparity and can fairly claim to help all aspirants.

Those who do not clear the higher education hurdle usually end up with one or two A-levels and go directly into employment, sometimes continuing study part-time. Some wanted this from the beginning. In some schools this 'higher education' group of students get comparatively little careers teaching apart from information about filling in the UCCA, PCAS or CRCH forms, and often a lot of personal advice from individual staff about particular degree courses. After all, they are going to study, not work in industry yet.

Things are changing, not least among the perceptions of students. Some teachers pioneering 'life-skills' courses for non-examination fifth formers were surprised to get the following 'petition' signed by nearly a hundred 'exam' pupils:

> 'We the undersigned think that a lot of the work being done by the "leavers" on their Contemporary Studies Course is very important, very educational and prepares them for life after school. We, in the exam. group think the work is equally important for us and we ought to be doing the same.'

Unfortunately they had to be told there wasn't time for them to do a similar course as they had to get on with their examination subjects. In many schools similar Careers and Life Skills courses are now given to all fifth-year pupils, and included in many sixth-form courses as well.

Finally, in this section, mention must be made of the facilities available for students with **special needs**. The problems of 'getting on' which all students face are increased by problems of coping with physical handicap. All colleges have made strides in accommodating students with many handicaps, enabling them to live 'normally' in the college and study along with other students. For those with more serious handicap there are a few specially designed colleges such as Hereward College, Coventry. Nicholas Drew, a student, writes of his experience:

196

'Possibly the aspect of the College which has surprised me most is the optimism and friendliness. It strikes you as soon as you enter the building. In a place full of severely handicapped people, it would be all too easy for there to be a depressed, quiet and sullen atmosphere. Some of the students face the prospect of early death or unemployment, and certainly the fact that their lives will be harder than a physically "normal" person's. Yet people — both students and staff — are genuinely cheerful and have a very real vitality and willingness to get on with the job.

'There is a formidable job to do, as well. As in any college there are courses to follow and exams to be taken. But here the range of courses and ability has to be wider than ever. Many students have had to spend a large part of their childhood in hospital and so have missed whole chunks of school education. Foundation Courses are provided to help these students catch up on basic education and get to the starting line for other courses, such as O-level, Certificate of Office Studies, A-level and Diploma in Business Studies. This last is the course I am doing and I enjoy it very much. The work is interesting and closely connected with business skills I hope to use later on. Also it is run in conjunction with the Tile Hill College, a "normal" FE college, next door. We go over there some mornings and students from Tile Hill come to us in the afternoons. This overlap of "normal" and "special" education is valuable experience for both groups of students and has given us a wider range of friends.'

TO WORK — WITH OR WITHOUT TRAINING

The 45% who stay in full-time education — and in particular the 15% who go on at 18 or 19 to higher education — are the most familiar customers of the schools. Teachers — and many parents — used to regard these as 'normal' pupils. The rest (55% of them) slid quietly out into the world of work at 15 or 16 and teachers saw them no more.

The changes of the last ten years have meant they no longer disappear so cheerfully and confidently. The Youth Training Scheme (YTS) has taken on a major training role. The proportions will vary from area to area. A North Yorkshire survey of pupils leaving in summer 1986 showed that by January 1987, 5% were still unemployed; 50% were in YTS schemes, mostly for two years, and the remaining 45% had jobs outside the

YTS, some with part-time education or training.

Preparing pupils for this transition to work is now seen as part of the schools' job. The DES publication *Better Schools* said:

> 'It is vital that schools should always remember that preparation for working life is one of their principal functions . . . All the elements of a broad 5-16 curriculum are vocational in the sense that they encourage qualities, attitudes, knowledge, understanding and competencies which are the necessary foundation for employment.'

The DES also provide a Careers Service — a full-time service of Careers Officers administered by LEAs and working with schools. This usually involves an individual careers interview for all fifth-form pupils who are likely to leave. In some cases the Careers Officer is seen as an associate member of the teaching staff of the school, spending considerable time there, knowing staff well and understanding staff attitudes and career programmes. Ideally the Careers Officer will be present with school careers staff when career-related decisions are made about 'options' at the third-form stage. A lot will depend upon how much time can be spared and how many schools have to be covered by one Careers Officer.

There is still residual distrust among teachers. Are Careers Officers recruiting agents for employers, filling their labour requirements? Is it all part of the Government's aim to get everybody into 'wealth creation'? Careers Officers have one foot in each camp — the teachers' camp, where all is supposed to be in the interest of the pupils; and the employers' camp, where profit is the key. They are usually very well informed on local job vacancies and the qualifications needed and are a valuable support to school careers staff. One teacher response suggests a common goal: 'to help individuals to achieve a work role which they will find personally rewarding and fulfilling and which enables them to make a contribution to the creation of the nation's wealth, and/or the well-being of society.'

This is far removed from traditional 'subjects' traditionally taught. A more modular approach is needed — dividing subjects up; picking out common skills and concepts; teaching some parts separately as specialist units and some as general abilities, as mentioned in chapter 5. The requirements of the workplace have been summarized as:

1. Adaptability — flexibility of attitude and ability to cope with changes in future technology, career and lifestyle;

2. Transition to adult role — it is very different being a young adult in employment from being a pupil at school;

3. Skills
— physical: manipulative skills for various vocational needs;
— science/technology; an understanding of the nature and discipline of science and its relationship to technology in design and production;
— communication and numeracy to meet the basic demands of the workplace and give basis for further learning;
—learning: confidence and competence to use information sources and learning opportunities;
— interpersonal; being sensitive and tolerant to others, and being able to develop good personal relationships;
— information technology: an understanding of the application of such technology to society, and ability to learn procedures in a particular workplace;
— problem-solving: capacity to approach various kinds of problems methodically and effectively, to decide strategies, evaluate and modify;
— coping skills: meeting everyday situations, co-operating with others, dealing with unexpected demands.

4. Health, environment, social values: an understanding of factors affecting health and personal well-being; awareness of the physical and technological environment and its relation to social and community values; a knowledge of the workings of modern society, and the development of a reasoned set of social and moral values related to this.

5. Creativity — cultivating imagination and developing powers of appreciation and critical judgment for vocational and leisure purposes.

Some of these have always featured in schools programmes. Current careers education makes the whole pattern more explicit. At 16+ level these requirements are the main substance of the Certificate of Pre-vocational Education (CPVE) mentioned in chapter 5.

UNEMPLOYMENT
Not everyone is fortunate enough to get a job. Not everyone who does a YTS programme will get a job at the end of it. Should schools be preparing pupils for unemployment? Teachers don't like being too closely involved with employment — too

'vocational' for some. They have even less desire to give pupils 'unemployment' skills. Yet if unemployment is to be a long-term feature of our society, something must be said about it.

Schools will be giving pupils 'employability skills' — job-search skills; job-getting skills (filling in application forms, interview technique, etc.) but if these fail, pupils may also need a lot more:

1. Understanding unemployment
— its reasons nationally and locally;
— its alienating and debilitating effect on people, especially those for whom 'working' is a major factor in self-esteem;
— its effect on social behaviour, friendship groups and psychological health;
— the particular difficulties of black young people and their experience of discrimination.

2. Alternative employment
— the opportunities for self-employment, new business, legal and financial implications;
— unusual jobs, breaking down gender stereotypes (male home-helps; women on building sites) increase in service industries; finding new wants to satisfy;
— job-sharing possibilities;
— voluntary service opportunities.

3. Surviving unemployment
— how to claim benefit, fill forms in; agencies that can help;
— where to find out your rights; redundancy or unfair dismissal;
— how to live on limited income.

4. Attitude to unemployment. Most importantly, young people need to develop a view of the world and work. The so-called 'work ethic' is a very powerful part of our society, so that people not in paid work feel guilty. The harder they try to get paid work, and fail, the worse they feel. Seventy-five per cent of young people in one survey showed very high commitment to employment. 'I'm looking for jobs as hard as ever, after six months' unemployment.' 'I'd still want a job even if I won the pools.' In some areas, especially for the less academically qualified, there simply are very few jobs. To blame the victims is cruel and unfair. They are likely to be underprivileged in other ways, too. Unemployment is an additional burden. Rather, they need a wider philosophy of 'work' to include unpaid work as equally valuable and praiseworthy. Household duties, voluntary work, community service can be encouraged. Young people can contribute in many ways while drawing unemployment benefit with cheerful heart and clear conscience. Leisure skills can be cultivated too. Young people, it seems, are better than older folk at using leisure facilities while unemployed, with resulting better psychological health.

Some of all this can be taught in Careers and Life Skills lessons, without suggesting failure for any. It is, in fact, an important part of Personal and Social Education to challenge the very high value given to paid employment, as if it were somehow a personal virtue. It has gone along with a conspiracy to undervalue household work or family care, so that some mothers feel they have to apologize for being 'just a housewife'. We need to keep alive the idea of personal responsibility to contribute to the community and to value the contributions of others. If this is in paid employment, a fair day's work for a fair day's pay is a worthy ideal. If unpaid, it can still be personally rewarding and valuable to others.

Teachers with above-national-average salaries may not be the best people to get the message across, but there are not many other people trying at the moment. In the early 1990s there will be many fewer young people leaving school for the labour market, because of the lower birth rates in the 70s. The problem of youth unemployment will ease a little, but there will still be some at the bottom of the academic pile who will need the help suggested here.

GOVERNMENT ACTION ON SCHOOL AND WORK — THE 1988 ACT

The response from successive Secretaries of State for Education to the alleged skilled labour shortage has been to make the schools more involved. Comparisons with overseas keep hammering the message home that our competitors have much better training arrangements. Some of the hype may be overdone, but Ministers and their officials who fly round the world looking at show schools from New York to Hamburg are convinced we could do more. The YTS scheme is already doing a lot but that is the Department of Employment and outside school. The Department of Education has chipped in a Report or two and now a major Act. Everyone keeps saying that many schools are excellent, but not enough are good enough. The Act makes two main provisions: the City Technology Colleges, and the National Curriculum.

The **CTCs** were described briefly in chapter 1. These new institutions are to be set up in twenty inner-city locations. They are to be examples of excellence to inspire others. They hope to do this in two ways. First, by harnessing local business interest — and plenty of local business cash. They will have very strong local roots in the industry and commerce around them. This will give opportunity for realistic work experience and also highly informed advice on equipment and processes for which pupils will be training. Second, by specializing in technological education they will attract pupils with such an interest and cultivate it. In some schools, the option schemes at 14 are said to make it hard for pupils to stick with engineering goals. It is hoped that the enthusiasm and ethos of the college will encourage more pupils to stay on into the sixth form and that more will go on to do technology degrees in higher education.

Against the predictable criticism that this is all an undignified grovel to big business, the Chairman of the CTC Trust argues that:

> 'Old-fashioned educationalists with their roots in the Sixties sometimes criticize technical education, claiming it doesn't educate children. They are wrong. For older pupils, courses in robotics, automation, control of manufacturing, programming machine tools and robots, data processing and computing, biochemistry, microbiology and enzymology, even hotel management marketing and retailing, not only help them to learn marketable skills but encourage them to think clearly and to solve problems.'

Other criticisms have already been raised. *If* the colleges take a genuinely wide cross-section of pupils from the inner-city area; *if* they don't milk the rest of the area for good teachers in shortage subjects; then they may well deserve a cautious welcome. The output of three or four thousand technologists a year from 1995 will not turn the UK round overnight, but could help, and might inspire modest emulation elsewhere.

The other main emphasis in the Act is the **National Curriculum**. The Secretary of State puts great store by this for raising standards and giving skills. This is to be achieved by ensuring that pupils study a broad and balanced range of subjects throughout their compulsory schooling and do not drop subjects too early (Britain is the only leading industrial country in which the choice against Mathematics or Physics can be made at 15 or younger), giving clear objectives for what children over the whole range of ability should be able to achieve, to give a 'realistic but challenging level' for each child. At present pupils and teachers are said to have too low expectations for too many children. The *National* Curriculum will also help to check on progress so that the able can be stretched and the weaker can get necessary help.

Exactly how the new proposals will achieve these fine aims is not clear from the Act or the consultative papers. But the main hints are in the core subjects — Mathematics, English and Science will ensure vital things are not dropped prematurely; and in the foundation subjects, which include Technology. Everyone will have a chance to meet this new area and become more aware of the technological basis of modern society. Testing, certainly at 11 and 14, will ensure that the subjects actually do get taught and will, it is hoped, act as a spur to teachers and pupils alike. The advent of GCSE, the Inspectors say, has already improved teaching. Perhaps these new tests will be equally encouraging.

The last point — testing — is the crucial one. Certainly teachers' and pupils' expectations can do with raising a bit; but not unreasonably. Many pupils already struggle under a sense of failure, partly because they are being set tasks that are impossible for them. Much depends on the nature of the tests.

Professor Black and his Task Group (see chapter 7) have made a bold start. It will not be only abstract knowledge or verbal-reasoning ability that will be tested. If this can be carried over into the subject test schemes a real leap forward could be obtained. Children could be set broad targets that cover more than abstract learning. It is all very well for the pundits to say we are changing to a 'thinking' society from a 'manual' society. Thirty per cent 'think' and seventy per cent 'do' in 1900 must give way to seventy per cent 'think' and thirty per cent 'do' by the year 2000. But that can't be done by Act of Parliament. The normal distribution of intelligence (see discussion of IQ in chapter 3) is probably a 'given'. Some improvements in performance can be made here and there. But the wholesale redesigning of the human species is not on. We must take account of what children *are* and use the capacities they *have*, and design our society to fit the people who make up the society. It is no good trying to redesign people to fit a super-theoretical society.

In 1900 Elvaston Castle near Derby employed ninety gardeners and groundsmen. The three or four lads who joined each year were not all academically clever. They all learned to tend the beautiful grounds, and probably to appreciate them too. Today half a dozen people keep the grounds tidy for Derbyshire County Council, and there may be pressure to put even that reduced job out to private tender to save money.

203

Mr Baker has given us his Act. He seems genuinely concerned about the least able, but his Act cannot develop skills they do not have. No Act can. Maybe he should ask his fellow Ministers to create areas where tomorrow's young people can use the skills they *do* have with dignity and pleasure.

CHAPTER 10

Teachers

and how to make the best of them

Education is among the most labour-intensive of activities. It is essentially about people serving people. From the tiny village school where one teacher looks after ten children, to the large comprehensive school where 125 teachers have nearly 2,000 pupils, the teacher in the classroom is the key to the whole process. All the equipment, buildings and management are only the setting for the teacher to get on with the job. Who are these teachers? How do they prepare for such a job? What is it like to be a teacher? And how do they cope with all the changes?

TEACHERS' TRAINING

In 1950 there were three miners for every teacher. Now there are three teachers per miner. This shows how mining has declined, but also the huge growth in education. This is partly because of the increased number of children; the higher leaving age; and also the improved teacher-pupil ratio. In 1946 the average primary class was thirty-two and secondary twenty-one; by 1986 it was primary twenty-one and secondary sixteen — these are, of course, averages over the whole country and also take no account of the 'free' time in the school day when teachers are marking or preparing work. The actual class sizes will vary, but the figures do show the dramatic reduction over the years. There are about 400,000 teachers altogether in England and Wales. The average primary school has about eight teachers; the average secondary school has about fifty teachers.

In the selective days of the 50s and 60s, secondary grammar school staff were mostly graduates of British universities who had done a three-year degree course in some specialist subject. This was followed by a one-year Post-Graduate Certificate in Education (PGCE) — one year of training which included one term of practice teaching. Not everybody did the training year, though most did and by 1973 it was compulsory for everyone — except teachers of 'shortage' subjects, mathematics and physics. Many of today's parents will remember grammar school speech days, with staff resplendent in gown and hood, from which the experts could tell which university they had attended — all except the PE staff who had usually trained at PE colleges and did not count as graduates.

The staff of secondary modern schools included some graduates but were mostly trained in teacher training colleges. Some did a one-year 'emergency' course after the war, but usually a three-year course with some specialism and often more direct classroom experience than the PGCE. The primary school teachers also came mainly (95%) from the training colleges. Colleges were linked with a university, whose name graced the resulting Certificate of Education.

Entry to graduate courses was the usual university hurdle of two A-levels minimum. Entry to the colleges was about two-thirds A-level (one to three subjects) and one-third O-level (five to eight subjects). Women outnumbered men three to one in 1970, but many left teaching on marriage or when starting a family. More than half the college students came from manual occupational family background. Teaching was a major way of social class improvement.

In the 1970s the entry requirements were raised considerably. The O-level entry was stopped — in some ways a pity as many excellent primary teachers came that way. The minimum entry was two A-levels plus three other subjects at O-level which had to include English and Mathematics. Previously Mathematics was not compulsory. A new degree was set up — the Bachelor of Education (BEd) which comes in Pass (three years) or Honours (four years) versions. The profession is now about 40% graduate. The percentage of graduates in primary schools has risen from 4% in 1960 to 21% in 1985, and in secondary from 37% to 57%.

A few teachers with 'alternative qualification' are approved every year by the DES through a variety of regulations. Proposals to simplify this route, and have a class of 'licensed teachers', have been met with suspicion by the unions. They see it as a short-cut to fill gaps, and likely to threaten their members' jobs and to lower the standard of teaching.

The statisticians' famous mistake in 1972 caused chaos. A projection that the birth rate would continue to rise led to a *Programme for Expansion* — larger colleges, more teachers. It didn't happen. Births declined so colleges had to be closed — a tragedy, as many of the smaller colleges had been excellent centres of training and built up a strong ethos and tradition. Many colleges were sold off to other uses. Others were swallowed up by the education departments of polytechnics, where students mixed with all sorts of other students. This could have been a useful experience in some ways, but it meant that the close community, centred on education, was merged in the amorphous mass of students-in-general. The output of teachers collapsed, while the number of pupils went down and down. By the early 1980s the birth rate had begun to climb again, so the teacher training industry is back in hesitant business. According to DES forecasts (now received with some caution) we shall be needing a lot more teachers by the 1990s. By 1995 one in five of suitably qualified school leavers should go into teacher training.

TEACHER EMPLOYMENT

During their last two terms of training, teachers are looking for jobs. They usually start work in September and commence a probationary year. During this time they are supposed to have a slightly lighter timetable, get support from senior staff in the school and visits from LEA inspectors. If all goes well, they complete this year with good reports and are registered as fully qualified teachers. If things don't go all that well, the probationary period can be extended.

In the 1960s and 70s finding a job was fairly easy. Pupil numbers were rising, especially in sixth forms. Promotion was rapid, so teachers moved from their first school very soon. Teacher turnover was too rapid for the good of the schools, but it meant new teachers were welcome. Some secondary schools jokingly referred to 'getting a new cricket team every year'. Many LEAs had a 'pool' of primary teachers and advertised in the spring, recruiting 100 or more new teachers to make up for expected losses and moves, Teachers would then be told in July exactly which school they would be working in in September.

By the late 70s all this had changed. Pupil numbers in primary schools had begun to decline. The glow of an expanding service was over. Very good teachers applied for dozens of jobs. One headteacher told me he had such a good shortlist for a Scale 1 English post that he would cheerfully have swapped his entire English department for the shortlist if he could have done.

Teachers have to decide what type of school to look for, and also which part of the service to try. They will have had some idea about this during training, and may have been allocated to a teaching practice school with this in mind. For example, a teacher thinking of the independent sector may well have done a teaching practice in such a school. The independent sector recruits mainly from the senior universities, usually starting at national salary levels, adjusted for additional duties (for example, boarding). The school trustees are the employers and make their own conditions of service, notice, and so on.

LEAs are employers of all other teachers, according to salary scales and conditions of service laid down nationally. Appointment is to the LEA, but usually to a designated school. If that school becomes overstaffed, the teacher can be moved to another school in the LEA under a redeployment policy. Usually the teacher has some say and can turn down at least two 'offers' of transfer. So if John Smith was appointed by Blimpshire LEA in 1979 to teach Geography at Bloggs Comprehensive School (then 1,200 pupils) he may find himself in 1988 on the redeployment list since the school now has only 800 pupils and does not need three geographers. He may be offered a lower school Humanities job at Burks Comprehensive School, turn it down, hoping for something nearer his present job, and eventually end up on a one-year job at Nerks Comprehensive similar to his own, covering for a teacher going on a year's course. In some cases LEAs have introduced early retirement schemes — especially where schools have been amalgamated and it is difficult to absorb all the teachers involved. Some LEAs have given very generous terms and teachers have 'retired' as early as fifty with 'enhancement' which gives them increased pension and lump sum payment.

CONDITIONS OF SERVICE

The 1965 Remuneration of Teachers Act set up the Burnham Committee through which LEAs and teachers associations negotiated salaries. Unbelievably, this Committee did not discuss conditions of service, which were dealt with by a separate Committee. This must be one of the few cases where pay and conditions were not negotiated together; almost a recipe for trouble. Also, Burnham was committed to *national* basic scales, the same for primary as secondary, for all parts of the country — except for a 'London allowance'. This may be an ideal of 'equality' or 'fairness' but is hard to justify commercially in terms of recruitment. One critic writes:

> 'National uniformity is the first piece of blatant nonsense. No one in their right mind could possibly suppose that the pay required to attract a given quality of teacher to a nice rural grammar school would be anything like the same as the amount needed to attract the same quality of teacher to a run-down and dangerous inner-city comprehensive surrounded by flats and high-priced private housing.'

There used to be SPA (Social Priority Area) allowances, but

these were not generous. Teachers who work in difficult areas need above-average dedication, even a vocation. The alternative of a 'free-market' in teachers' pay is not very attractive either. Unions fear the Grant Maintained Schools may be the thin end of this wedge. Many independent schools already pay well over national scales, though teachers there may have additional responsibilities. Local financial management at present ties governors to national scales, but some would like this restriction removed. If society wants a *national* system of education, in which inner-city schools get the same quality of teacher as the leafy suburbs, some compromise will be needed between 'equality' and free-market anarchy.

In the placid days of 1965 things went quite well, but soon Burnham became a battleground and most parents' memories will be of impassioned teachers' representatives appearing on television to say why the current offer was derisory, and employers saying how unreasonable the teachers were. Parents meanwhile had to arrange for neighbours to give John and Mary lunch when teachers were 'withdrawing goodwill' and not supervising school dinners. Patience finally ran out in 1986 when long and bitter negotiations failed to produce a workable pay *and* conditions formula. Whether they were 'nearly there' is a matter of dispute. The Secretary of State imposed a solution. The Teachers Pay and Conditions Act 1987 repealed the 1965 Act, and Burnham went to unlamented burial. The Education (School Teachers' Pay and Conditions of Employment) Order, 1987, laid down salary scales and conditions of service. For the first time, regulations attempted to say what teachers are contracted to do. A pity, as a profession ought to be trusted to do what is needed, but the experience of the last five years had soured everyone, and a 'contract' mentality had developed.

The new regulations provide that:

● Schools are open for children for 190 days per year;

● Teachers attend a further five days — 'Baker days' — for training and such other duties as the Head directs;

● Teachers may work at the Head's direction for up to 1,265 hours per year and in addition do whatever is necessary by way of preparation and marking to ensure the job of teaching is properly done;

● Lunch-time supervision is no longer part of teachers' duties.

This budgeting of time (including staff meetings and parents' evenings) will produce teething problems and be a point of friction, but it will still be better than the chaos of recent years.

All this was imposed with little consultation, and no negotiating body has yet been set up to replace Burnham. Something is promised by 1990. Teachers' associations were very angry, but the mood may be changing slightly. The more militant NAS/UWT (National Association of Schoolmasters and Union of Women Teachers) and the NUT (National Union of Teachers) lost members during the various disputes to the more moderate AMMA (Assistant Masters and Mistresses Association) and the new PAT (Professional Association of Teachers) which scored a dramatic rise to 50,000 members. PAT members are pledged not to strike, to the dismay and contempt of NAS/UWT and NUT who refuse to recognize PAT as a 'proper' union and at one stage tried to avoid sitting at a negotiating table with them. Perhaps a new mood will develop. The NUT at its 1988 conference tried to adopt a softer style — the executive fighting off the more militant fringe. A less militant stance may win them more respect from parents and public. It is just possible that teachers will agree to a 'no-strike' formula in return for an independent review body like the police or the nurses. It will be some time coming, and teachers will not sell their negotiating rights (whenever they get them back) easily.

THE 1988 ACT

Under the new Act the governors of a school will have more say in teacher employment. They were nearly always consulted or represented in secondary appointments, but the LEA was always represented, and had considerable influence, for example, through redeployment policies. In future LEAs will continue to:

- Fix staffing for primary schools with less than 200 pupils;

- Administer the payment of salaries for all maintained schools;

- Be responsible for the inspection of maintained schools;

- Supervise probationary teachers in maintained schools;

- Provide in-service training as required;

- Give professional advice.

All other maintained schools — in other words, those with more than 200 pupils — will have local financial management (see chapter 2 for details). This enables governors to decide how many teaching and non-teaching staff they can afford within their budget. Existing staff will carry on, but any vacancy will be at the governors' discretion. The governors must notify the LEA of the vacancy. The LEA may 'nominate for consideration for appointment to the post' any person who is an employee of the LEA and appears to be qualified. This would be similar to the present redeployment policy but governors do not have to appoint, or even to say why they are not appointing, the LEA's nominee. This will severely weaken the LEA's present redeployment policies, in fact redressing the balance between the interest of the school and the interest of teachers.

Governors advertise vacancies and interview applicants. The Chief Education Officer (or delegate) is entitled to attend and give advice at interviews for headteachers and deputies, and may be asked by governors to attend and give advice for other appointments. After interviews, governors recommend an appointment to the LEA who can refuse only if there are 'staff qualification requirements' not met (for example, an applicant has not completed an approved training qualification or passed a medical examination).

Governors and headteachers have authority to suspend teachers (on full pay) where in their opinion the 'exclusion from the school is required'. LEA must be informed. Such cases are rare and usually arise out of a crisis, affecting a teacher, that needs time to arrive at a final decision. Power of dismissal also lies with governors who may notify the LEA that 'any person employed to work at the school should cease to work there'. The LEA must then 'give him notice terminating his contract of employment with the Authority'. Costs of dismissal are not to be charged to the school budget without 'good reason'. An LEA policy of 'no redundancy' is not a 'good reason'. The person to be dismissed has 'opportunity to make representation with respect to the action they propose to take' which usually involves the right to be accompanied by a 'friend' such as a union representative.

All this adds up to a considerable shift of power to governors. Over the last ten years the education service has been almost unique in having no compulsory redundancies. LEAs have operated a 'ring fence' policy, not advertising vacancies nationally until all possibilities of transfer within the LEA had been exhausted. Redeployment (with retraining) has filled many vacancies, often less than ideally. Heads and governors have been frustrated that they could not advertise and get newly trained people, or the new expertise they would like. Even so, some 'surplus' teachers could not be absorbed and several hung on, extra to establishment in their old school, being found jobs to do — not very good for them or for the morale of other teachers. The Senior Chief HMI in a report on the ILEA commented:

> ' . . . there is a surplus of secondary teachers to requirements that has resulted in large numbers of teachers remaining in schools as supernumeraries without a job to do. That situation has caused serious problems for some Heads, not least because quite a number of the supernumerary teachers become a source of discontent and trouble.'

It is a moral dilemma. Authorities want to be 'good employers', looking after their teachers. Unions have negotiated very favourable 'no redundancy' agreements. But schools have suffered through delays and having eventually to accept staff who were less than ideal. The balance now seems to be corrected a little, but the sadness for 'surplus' teachers will remain.

The other main change is the advent of **Grant Maintained Schools** (see chapters 1 and 4 for details). All staff working at the school before transfer will have their contracts transferred to the new governing body, along with all their former 'rights, powers, duties and liabilities'. If the job in the new school is very different from the old one they can terminate contract and expect compensation but not if the job is much the same. The fact that teachers don't want to work in a Grant Maintained School is not adequate reason, and if they resign on that ground they are not eligible for compensation. The consultative papers leading up to the Act also provided that salaries and conditions of service should be in line with national agreements, but governors could pay extra in some cases; also they can appoint teachers who have not completed normal teacher training provided they have 'relevant qualifications' (they have to get DES approval — LEAs can do this now). Governors are responsible for teacher appraisal and in-service training. Statutory probationary requirements will not be required — senior staff will be expected to supervise new teachers.

Considerable misgivings are expressed about all this:

● Teachers are losing the security of being employed by a large authority, where redeployment has in the past ironed out fluctuations in numbers between schools;

● The option of paying higher salaries will enable Grant Maintained Schools to compete unfairly for 'shortage' subject teachers;

● Teacher appraisal will lack cohesion. Few governors will have expertise to do this and there will be no standard of comparison between schools;

● Governors are responsible for in-service training, which they will have to buy in. They may be tempted to reduce this to cut costs;

● Probationers' supervision will no longer be the steady, experienced work of LEA inspectors. It may be hard for such a teacher to move to an LEA school later, as the governors' approval may carry little weight.

IN-SERVICE TRAINING AND APPRAISAL

Teaching changes; so must teachers. New examinations like GCSE need a lot of preparation. So do new courses like TVEI or CPVE. In-service training (INSET) is a major concern of government and LEAs. The fall in pupil numbers enabled LEAs to spare some teachers on secondment for full-time courses of retraining — often in shortage subjects like Mathematics, Craft Design and Technology and Computing. Many more were given places on short courses, or one-day-a-week courses to update skills or learn new jobs. An increasing proportion of educational budgets has been directed to INSET — from courses organized nationally by the DES, to 'Baker days' organized by LEAs or the school itself. In many LEAs money is placed at the disposal of the headteacher to spend on the training needs of the staff of a particular school. There is a danger that the 1988 Act — with its local financial management and its Grant Maintained Schools — may tempt governors to save in this direction. It would be a false economy.

Teachers keep up to date with their specialist subjects and teaching methods by a multitude of professional associations — The Historical Association; the National Association for the Teaching of English; the Association of Mathematics Teachers; the National Anti-Racist Movement in Education, and many others. The Christian Education Movement provides material and an annual conference for RE teachers. The Association of Christian Teachers covers teachers in all subjects and its Education Centre at Stapleford, Nottinghamshire, offers courses in most subject and administrative areas. In addition, the teachers' unions publish journals and run courses on all manner of educational topics. All this welter of support — for which teachers themselves pay cash and time — is a mark of their commitment to their trade.

Another recent development is Staff Appraisal. This was picked on by the media as 'weeding out the bad teachers'. In fact at one stage there was a suggestion that appraisal would be linked with salary increments. This was however dropped, which helped the unions abandon their initial, predictably defensive, reaction and to contribute. The NUT published their own proposals in *A Fair Way Forward*. No one wants to admit their members are inadequate. Everybody agrees privately that there are a few passengers. The ideal is to strengthen the weak and enthuse the ill-motivated and this does often happen by good in-service training. The main emphasis of appraisal is for *all* teachers, to assist them in their personal and career development. The new conditions of service make it obligatory for all teachers to take part in arrangements 'within an agreed national framework for the appraisal of his performance and that of other teachers'. There is no agreed national framework yet but several LEAs have pilot schemes which are well developed and well received by teachers. The schemes aim to review teachers' performance in the context of their school and to:

● Improve learning opportunities for all pupils in a school, and the management of the learning process;

● Recognize and support individual teachers' effective practice and identify both their potential and areas for their development and improvement;

● Help teachers in their career development and also help to identify those whose performance falls below par so that matters may be rectified and, in the extreme, employment terminated.

Seven stages in the process of appraisal are distinguished: preparation, classroom observation, the appraisal interview, results, monitoring, moderation and evaluation.

This will require a variety of skills. ' . . . ascertaining someone's potential for a future role, possibly a much changed one, requires techniques different from those for identifying training needs for the present job. Identifying leadership potential may sometimes be deceptively difficult.' It will be expensive too. Those doing the appraisal will need training. Each appraisal will take eight to twelve hours in all, requiring cover to be provided for the teacher's classes. It will be worth it if all teachers are encouraged, developed, redirected and used to maximum benefit. The public may be reassured that performance is being reviewed, even if the more bloodthirsty headlines about 'weeding out the worst' are not satisfied, and there are no public hangings in the playground.

All this emphasis on training and teachers' adapting to new roles and methods makes sad reading for some. They were trained to a high level as honours graduates in a specialist subject and got their main fulfilment from teaching able children in A-level subjects. Now, in many areas, A-level is being concentrated in sixth-form colleges or tertiary colleges, leaving schools to cater for ll- to 16-year-olds. One English specialist feelingly expresses her response to the situation:

'For many teachers, A-level classes are their life-blood, making much of the lower-form hassle, with possibly big classes and little motivation, bearable. I cannot be the only teacher who has toiled through a second form lesson on punctuation with a lighter heart for the knowledge that next lesson the sixth form and I will be wrestling with Lear or with Satan himself in Milton's epic verse . . . So change we must . . . My intentions, interests, aspirations and needs are all in the direction of my subject . . . I have studied to Master's level not educational theory or philosophy, but English, its language and literature. I am there to do that because that's what I do . . . So adapt I will, but I am not a Jill of all trades, and my one-year postgraduate certificate, despite double distinctions in both educational theory and teaching practice, did not train me for her job. I'm not qualified to teach sex education or sociology or the best way to manipulate the welfare benefits system . . . If I'm in the classroom at all, I'm there because I have a subject to teach. For me, and I swear for many honours graduates like me, I'm a subject teacher first, and a teacher of children second.'

For such a teacher, appraisal will be a demoralizing experience, though perhaps we could hope it would be a renewing experience. In all kindness it has to be said that children must be protected against anyone who puts them second. Teachers must 'teach Johnny English' with as much interest in Johnny as in the subject. Perhaps appraisal, even with anguish, may show the teacher she can, after all, do both well.

THE CHANGING JOB

From this it is clear that the teacher's job is a changing one. In the last twenty years major changes in the structure and philosophy of education have altered the scene out of all recognition. Twenty years is only half a teacher's life in school. Some older teachers are glad to be leaving. They are too old to change now. Others welcome change, even if they are not among the avid band of initiators, who thrive on conferences and write to each other in the journals — or are disrespectfully referred to by colleagues as 'course junkies'.

Parents need to change, too. Schools are not as they remember, except perhaps some independent schools — and even there things may be subtly different for Alastair from what they were for his Dad. In one way, this book is an invitation to parents to update themselves. More detail can be obtained by spending time in the local primary school; or sifting out the anecdotes of life in secondary school from teenage children and their friends.

In addition to those already mentioned, three areas may be considered: primary practice; comprehensive schooling and multi-cultural schools.

1. Primary practice has moved from the class as the major unit to the child or small group as the unit. The teacher no longer teaches the whole class for long periods and then helps each child, marking, explaining — a situation in which all pupils do much the same work. Children now work much of the time individually or in small groups. The teacher has to gain skills of administration, keeping careful record of what each child is doing and how far they have got. More subtly, there is a psychological change from being in charge with a beady eye on everyone in the class, to being in charge because everyone is usefully working while you concentrate attention on one child or small group. Reduction in class size over the years has helped, but it is still a different challenge that demands different skills and self-confidence. Something has already been said about this in chapter 2.

2. Comprehensive reorganization is now virtually complete. More than 90% of secondary pupils now attend comprehensive schools of various sorts. For teachers who never met the most able 20% of pupils this was a stretching, not to say testing, experience. The danger was that their expectations would be too low and the more able children would not be pushed hard enough. For those who had never met the other 80% it was traumatic. They had to learn how difficult it is for the average child to respond to methods and material the cleverest 20% can cope with. Much, though not all, indiscipline is the result of inappropriate curriculum. Nowadays a few teachers in comprehensive schools went to comprehensive schools themselves. It is home from home and they don't know what the fuss is about. But the majority went to grammar schools and only met the rest of their age-group socially, if at all. The whole ethos and quality of life and behaviour is different. So there is a double temptation — either to assume that nothing can be done and that this is the way people behave in the new scene; or to try and keep the old line and standards for everyone. Both are bad for teacher morale and self-confidence as well as bad for the school. Comprehensive schools have gone to considerable trouble to devise systems and standards suitable to their clientele, but it has not been an easy task.

3. Multi-cultural schools were discussed in chapter 2 from the point of view of administration. They raise issues for teachers, too, which need consideration. We teachers are white — most of us anyway — and went to schools where almost everyone was white. Playgrounds and classrooms were white. Now the children in many playgrounds and classrooms are of all colours, but the teachers are still mostly white. At County Hall, almost exclusively white officers decide about resources, catchment areas and school structure. Attempts to recruit black teachers have not been very successful. Only 2.6% of students in training were from ethnic minorities in 1988. Maybe successful black students note the difficulty white teachers have in multi-ethnic classrooms and decide teaching is not for them. Discrimination in staff-rooms and in promotion prospects is well enough documented to be off-putting, too.

Most white teachers will claim that 'colour of skin makes no difference' and this is an honest intention. But we are heirs of a long tradition in which skin-colour did matter, a tradition of white-supremacy. The media, and our school textbooks, brought us pictures and stories of black people in poverty and backwardness. Perhaps Oxfam posters still do the same. Our knowledge of other cultures came from the occasional film, or tales from travellers, servicemen or missionaries. Few of today's teachers ever sat beside a black child at school. Only a few of us live next door to an Indian or Caribbean family in our street.

It is the teachers (and possibly the Health Service and police) who face this change in our society most sharply. Everybody goes to school, from the well-to-do Pakistani doctor's children to the frightened children of the Bangladeshi families whose tower-block homes are the targets of racial attack. Teachers are expected to know all about them, their culture, family customs, language difficulty. The Swann Report tried to be fair to good work done by some teachers, but accused teachers at large of 'unintentional racism'. Not surprising, as attitudes grow slowly and change even more slowly. Teachers are a cross-section of (more educated) society and so are likely to have prejudices and expectations similar to that section of society. One Gallup Poll survey asked: 'Do you agree or disagree to your child being sent to a school of a predominantly different ethnic background in the interest of racial integration?' The answers were 'Agree 4%, disagree 88%, Don't know 8%.' Teachers are going to have to work hard to distance themselves from that background and provide a welcome for all children.

Teacher training used to pay little attention to this. Even now, very few institutions make multi-cultural teaching a compulsory part of the training. 'There aren't any ethnic minorities in 70% of the schools,' is a poor excuse. It is precisely in the all-white schools that attitudes are formed. All-white schools in all-white areas provide the bulk of the future leaders who will decide the policy of a pluralist multi-cultural society. Teachers need to know a lot about it. As it is, they 'learn on the job' — in the staff room, in the classroom and playground. They pick up the folk wisdom and myth — 'Asian children are serious enough but West Indian children are bouncy' . . . 'they have unrealistic ambitions for their children.' Add to this the depressing comment 'what can you expect from a neighbourhood like this?' and you have the 'low-expectation' syndrome which is all too often self-fulfilling. Schools have come a long way to meet these changes and many teachers have spent many hours and tears developing new teaching skills and reviewing their own attitudes and prejudices. It is not easy and they deserve all the help and understanding they can get.

STRESS

These and other changes combine to make teaching a stressful occupation. The 1983/84 retirement figures showed:

- On grounds of 'infirmity' — 2,069;

- Normal age retirements — 4,548;

- 'Premature' retirements — 9,285.

Some of the 'premature' were probably due to stress, too. A number of studies have shown how teachers experience stress and respond to it.

There is 'role-tension' in which different people want different things from you. The school policy has to be observed; some pupils demand extra attention and others say they are neglected; some parents want 'firmer discipline' while others like things as they are; visiting inspectors are often helpful, but may add to the pile of conflicting advice.

Few jobs are as continuously demanding in terms of personal contact. If a teacher cannot control up to thirty adolescents for thirty hours a week everyone assumes that the teacher is incompetent. If a policeman has trouble with six of the same youngsters for an hour on a Saturday he can't be blamed.

Teaching is open-ended; the job is never 'done'. So teachers have to settle for some standard as 'enough'. Many feel they can't do everything well enough; there isn't time for preparation; there isn't enough adrenalin to keep up the energy to deal with so many lively pupils. So 'the individual feels unable to deal with the demands of the situation, while at the same time he feels that he must.' There may be frustration that the Head and senior staff are not definite enough, or don't do enough, or don't care. Heads may be frustrated by inadequate staff, or delays in getting staff cover, or the apparent bureaucracy at County Hall. The worst part of this is that teachers feel very alone in their stress and even guilty. So they don't readily talk about it or seek help, though 'talking it through' shows up over and over again as a way of coping with stress. Less helpful ways include alcohol (seven per cent of headteachers saw this as a short-term remedy) over-eating, chewing gum and tobacco. Golden rules for dealing with stress start with:

● Don't isolate yourself — work as part of a staff team;

● Accept that you are not always infallible;

● Do not over-react — keep things in perspective;

● Talk to friends outside school who experience real pressure;

● Accept that some things can be changed, others modified and some things cannot be changed at all.

Uncertainty adds to all this. There was a time when honest service, loyalty and patience guaranteed a long and secure life at a school with good possibility of promotion. Now all hangs on pupil numbers and LEA policy.

One way of coping with stress is 'If you can't beat 'em, leave 'em.' Not packing up teaching altogether, though there is a society that exists specifically to help teachers to get out into other fields of employment. Some teachers who feel ill-trained, or temperamentally unsuited to comprehensive schools have made good in the more selective ethos of the independent sector. Some who feel overwhelmed or affronted by the whole secularist philosophy of the State system have opted for the new

Christian schools, though those schools could do with pioneers and enthusiasts rather than refugees.

Stress is being identified more and more as a risk in many occupations. More is being done to give 'coping skills' and to help people to rearrange their circumstances and get necessary support. The teacher appraisal schemes will include some attention to this and could point a way forward to the identifying of problems and solving some of them.

TEACHERS' PERSONALITY

Parents have memories of the teachers who taught them. They see a few teachers at parents' evenings. For the rest they get their image of teachers from the media — usually colourful images of delegates at conferences or marchers carrying placards. What sort of people are they? Who is teaching our children?

The overwhelming picture that comes from research is of well-meaning, conscientious people. In spite of the 'short days, long holidays' image, the National Foundation for Educational Research found that teachers on average put in the equivalent of thirty-eight hours a week for a forty-eight-week year. Some work much more; some do less.

There are some political activists — often in inner-city schools where deprivation and the inequality of the system is most obvious. But this is a tiny minority. The TES poll of teachers' voting intentions in the 1987 general election showed primary 52% for the Alliance and secondary 41%. That was, admittedly, a surge from the 23% and 31% respectively in 1983 (and the 1979 picture of 59% primary and 45% secondary for Conservatives). So teachers may be naive idealists but they are not, in general, revolutionaries.

Equal opportunity is nearer in education than in some occupations, though still not by any means complete. The difficulty of attracting black teachers has been mentioned, and they are under-represented in the profession. Women fare a little better. They form 79% of the primary teaching force (but hold less than half the headteacher and deputy-head posts) and 45% of secondary (where they have about 25% of the head and deputy-head posts). The NUT first campaigned for equal pay in 1919 — a move which prompted the breakaway of the National Association of Schoolmasters (NAS) in 1920. In 1936 the NAS opposed equal pay as 'unjust to the schoolmasters, the boy in the school, the taxpayer and the ratepayer.' In those days, secondary school boys were taught mainly in single-sex schools. Women taught in primary and girls' secondary schools. The advent of mixed education made a different situation. For one glorious day it looked as if equal pay had come. An amendment to that effect was passed — by 117 votes to 116 — in the debate on the 1944 Education Act. Alas! Mr Churchill got the House of Commons to repeal it next day. Equal pay finally came in 1961.

The change in the status of women in society is vividly illustrated by the reminiscence that in 1927 the House of Commons *rejected* the Married Women (Employment) Bill, designed to allow women teachers to keep their jobs after marriage. Now the profession depends on married women — many returning to teach when their families are old enough. Teachers are very conscious — perhaps even self-conscious — of their relative isolation from the world of work. Very many went from school to university or college and straight back to teach at school. A very few who did their National Service in the early 50s are still teaching, and an increasing number have come into the profession from industry or commerce. The government hopes to get more of these to teach in the new City Technology Colleges. The old jibe, 'man among boys, boy among men' is rarely heard but teachers may feel that they are a cloistered group. They are successes of the system. Many are first-generation graduates who have come up from manual employment backgrounds. It is natural, therefore, that they value education highly and urge all their charges to profit by it and climb the same ladders.

TEACHERS' DILEMMA

Some teachers just love their subject — like the English teacher mentioned in an earlier section. They don't mind children as long as they want to learn that subject. Most teachers like children and this poses a dilemma. Whom do they serve?

Teachers in maintained schools are paid by the LEA and financed by taxes and rates. Does this make them agents of the State? They distrust the State 'use' of education to ensure the right kind of employee for industry and the right kind of elite filtered out for administration. The 1988 Act raised cries of 'Centralization'. Teachers feel their professional judgment is being eroded or overridden by edicts from on high about National Curriculum and the like. The Manpower Services Commission (now Training Commission) seems to enjoy more government confidence than the Department of Education and Science.

In law, teachers are *in loco parentis* doing what a reasonable parent would do. The wags have said that few parents have thirty children and certainly not all the same age. So, which

221

parents? Parents' views often conflict and teachers sometimes feel they are almost protecting a child from over-ambitious parents. Sadly, the school is sometimes a haven of rest for a child from a warring household. In most cases, teachers and parents meet cheerfully enough and find themselves happily at one over Leroy's good progress or Pauline's infuriating absent-mindedness. The 1986 and 1988 Acts give parents more say. Teachers will want to be sure it is well-informed 'say' and on behalf of all children.

Then there are the children. Do teachers serve them? In some ways the relationship is near that of social worker to client. Teachers are often entrusted with confidences which embarrass them. Increasingly they advise pupils about courses and careers, and often about personal matters too. Not all pupils relish the teacher's care and concern. But, especially in primary schools where the teacher sees fewer children for a much longer time, the sense of serving them and 'doing the best for them' is very strong. Tutors and Year Heads in secondary schools feel the same about their flocks.

Another tension, mentioned in chapter 7, arises from assessment. The new GCSE requires the teacher to assess the pupil's course-work. The 1988 Act with its 7, 11 and 14 tests will again cast the teacher in the role of assessor. In many cases testing is good for you. Pupils can be helped better if their strengths and weaknesses are known. But teachers fear test results will be wanted for other reasons. Parents may use the test results for their own child sensibly, or may use them as a whip. If the school's results are to be published, then all manner of pressures will be let loose to ensure the picture is a good one. The school must compete in the market place where parents want 'results' and test scores are all there are to satisfy this demand. Teachers are caught in the middle again, trying to do tests for everyone and every purpose.

So the question remains for teachers. To whom am I responsible? In some societies the State does come top. This may be modified by appeal to law. The law may enshrine some broad principle or ideal or right to which parents can appeal. Others would claim that there is a Western European tradition of learning, care and responsibility against which current practice can be judged and by which the rival claims of different groups must be weighed. This could be rephrased in religious language to say that God is judge of all and pre-eminently the guardian of children. However the question is stated, teachers think very seriously about their profession. It is more than a job. It is a responsibility and, for many, a calling.

The last word in the chapter on teachers comes from a much younger writer:

'Our school is not very nice but my teacher is nice. When it rains it rains indoors and it is smeily. Mrs Richards looks after us all the time. She is not always good-tempered though. Sometimes she is not good-tempered when it is something else that has upset her that is not what we have done. But we understand and do not mind too much because she is nice really. She is kind to us, I think and we all think, because she is kind inside. When I grow up I want to be like Mrs Richards.'

CHAPTER 11

Governors

and their task

In many ways, society is kept going by the voluntary work of people of goodwill. Education is one such area. Governors contribute time and expertise to support the headteacher and staff in the running of the school.

The Education Act 1944 required governing bodies for all maintained and voluntary schools and subsequent Education Acts have enlarged and clarified their powers and duties. The 1986 Education Act in particular made very wide changes, some of which will not be fully implemented until September 1989. The details given below include this Act as far as its effect is known at present.

GOVERNING BODIES AND THE 1986 EDUCATION ACT

Governors' appointment, powers and duties are laid down in the Instrument and Articles of Government. This used to be partly the responsibility of LEAs and partly of the Secretary of State. Under the 1986 Act the Secretary of State will issue new model Instrument and Articles of Government, and LEAs will be responsible to adapt these for all county, voluntary and maintained special schools in their area. In the course of this the LEA must consult with the governors and headteacher of each school, and must secure the agreement of the foundation governors of any voluntary school.

The Instrument of Government lays down the basic **constitution** of the governing body; who may be appointed, how they are to be appointed, provisions for election where appropriate, disqualification of governors, the procedure for meetings, quorum, declaration of interest, sub-committees, and so on. The Articles of Government lay down the functions of LEA, governors and headteacher in the administration of the school.

TYPES OF SCHOOLS

The nature, powers and duties of the governing body will vary according to the type of school. The number of governors and groups from which they are drawn vary with the size of the school.

Before the 1986 Act the LEA usually appointed the majority of governors. The Taylor Committee (1977) said, 'No one interest should have all the power in running schools', and though its divisions of governors were not followed in detail, this basic idea has worked through in legislation. The principal points are as follows:

1. County school — i.e. completely maintained by the LEA. LEA is responsible for everything: school buildings, maintenance, running costs. The LEA is the employer of all staff. The 'act of worship' required by the 1944 Act must be undenominational. RE must be taught according to the LEA's Agreed Syllabus. The number and source of governors is laid down for various sizes of school, for example a primary school of between 100 and 299 pupils would have three parent governors, three LEA governors, one teacher governor, the headteacher and four co-opted governors. For a secondary school of more than 600 pupils, the numbers are: five parents, five LEA, two teachers, headteacher and six co-opted. The Clerk to the governors is appointed by the LEA.

2. Voluntary Controlled School — i.e. the Trust (usually a denominational body) owns the buildings, the LEA pays all maintenance and running expenses. The LEA is the employer of all staff. The 'act of worship' can be denominational. RE must be taught in accordance with the LEA Agreed Syllabus, except that if parents request religious instruction in accordance with the Trust denomination, this must be provided, and governors may appoint staff for this purpose. The number of governors is the same as for county schools, except that three of the co-opted governors (four, for secondary) must be appointed by the Trust and are known as 'foundation governors'. The method of appointment of the Clerk to the governors will be laid down for each case in the Articles of Government. Governors of a Controlled School can apply to the Secretary of State to change their status to Voluntary Aided School in accordance with regulations to be published.

3. Voluntary Aided School — i.e. the Trust owns the building and contributes 15% of the cost of alteration and external maintenance; the DES pays all other maintenance and running costs. The governors are responsible for appointment and dismissal of all staff (before the 1988 Act, of teaching staff only). The 'act of worship' can be denominational. The teaching of RE must be in accordance with the Trust denomination. The governing body is made up of two LEA, one parent, the headteacher and one teacher (for primary schools) or two teachers (for secondary schools). Primary schools have one governor representing the 'Minor Authority' (e.g. the district council in an English shire county). In addition there will be foundation governors appointed by the Trust. One of these must be a parent, and in total they must outnumber the 'others' by two where there are less than eighteen governors in all, and by three where there are more than eighteen in all. The Clerk to the governors is appointed by the governors.

4. Grant Maintained Schools created by the 1988 Act are dealt with below.

TYPES OF GOVERNORS

No one under 18 years of age can be a governor. It is not clear whether an 18-year-old student can now be a governor. Before the 1986 Act many schools had 'pupil observers' who gave governors direct access to pupil opinion. These are discontinued, which is a pity.

LEA governors are appointed by the Local Authority Education Committee. Members of that Committee will usually have a governorship themselves, so that the Committee has plenty of first-hand experience of the needs and opportunities in schools. There will be far more schools than Councillors, so the Committee looks for local people of experience and usually, though not always, sympathy with the political stance of the Committee. The Articles of Government say that the governors are to act 'in conformity with the general policy of the Authority', and LEA governors see that this happens.

Parent governors are normally to be elected — the LEA and headteacher to arrange a suitable procedure for a secret ballot. 'Pupil-post' may be used. Parents must be notified of any vacancy for parent-governor. The only requirement for nomination is to have a child at the school at the time of election. A nominated parent may submit a short personal biographical statement which will be sent out with the voting papers. If there are insufficient nominations the other governors may fill any vacancies by themselves appointing a parent. They may do this also in special circumstances, such as a school where 50% of pupils are boarders and an election is impracticable. If governors appoint parent-governors, they may not appoint an elected member of the LEA or an employee of the authority or anyone who is already a governor of another of the LEA's schools. These restrictions do not apply to parents offering themselves for election.

Teacher governors are elected by secret ballot of the teaching staff. The previous provisions for a member of the non-teaching staff to be elected as governor no longer apply. Such a person could be one of the 'co-opted' governors, but it is a pity to see this recognition of the importance of ancillary staff no longer recognized officially.

The headteacher can choose whether to be a governor or not — some feel they have greater freedom to fulfil their responsibility as Head if they are not governors. The headteacher will, of course, attend all governors' meetings in any case.

Co-opted governors are appointed by the other governors. In their choice, the governors must have regard to the connection with the local business community. If this is not well represented among existing governors, then at least one of the co-opted governors must be from that community. Otherwise the power to co-opt should be used to 'strengthen the links between the school and the community it serves.' A county or voluntary-controlled primary school must allow one of the 'co-opted' governors to be appointed by the 'Minor Authority' where this exists.

Governors are appointed in various ways but not as 'representatives' of any group. A parent-governor is a 'representative parent', not a 'parent representative'. That is, they contribute to discussion and vote as they think best for the school, without having to refer back to parents, or stick to any agreed 'parent line'. Governors are appointed for four years, though they may resign at any time.

Even in this simplified version, these provisions for the constitution of governing bodies are detailed and complex. They are a considerable change from previous arrangements and give much greater representation to parents. LEAs can easily be painted as power-hungry bodies who know what's good for everybody and impose it by using committee majorities. In fact the number of cases where this happened in governors' meetings is probably tiny, if any at all. The new arrangements have been labelled a 'charter for extremists' who can get themselves in as parents or co-opted members even if they are not LEA appointees. Certainly it will be the most forceful parents who offer themselves for election, but enthusiasms differ so they are unlikely always to work together, though they may enliven proceedings. The new pattern offers an opportunity for more people to prepare and present themselves as governors. If the challenge is taken up by those of genuine goodwill and concern, the management of schools may benefit. On the other hand, it may result in giving far more power to headteachers. The LEA control will be reduced and if the governors come to rely even more on the headteacher's advice, her wild or brilliant schemes may be easier to get through. Years ago I was told by a distinguished Head of an independent school that the first thing is 'to get the governors where you want them'. Such benevolent dictatorship is fine if the dictator really is benevolent — and knows everything. The new Acts are designed to ensure that governors are not so easily tamed.

GOVERNORS' DUTIES

The 1986 Act also placed specific duties upon governors. First, there is the question of curriculum. Governors of Voluntary Aided Schools are responsible for the whole curriculum, taking account of the LEA's policy and also representations made by members of the community or the Chief of Police. Governors of other schools must consider the LEA's policy on the secular curriculum (that is, other than RE) and decide, in consultation with the headteacher, if (and how) it should be modified for their school. Their curriculum statement must be available for inspection at the school. The headteacher is responsible to determine and organize the curriculum in a way compatible with the policy of the governing body.

This has been modified by the 1988 Act which places upon LEA, governors, and headteacher alike the duty of ensuring that the requirements of the National Curriculum are satisfied.

The provision of **sex education** in the curriculum is now entirely at the discretion of the governors. They must decide whether to provide it and, if so, how sex education should be taught. Where provided, it must 'encourage pupils to have due regard to moral considerations and the value of family life'. A statement of their decision must be available for inspection at the school.

The governors must ensure there is **no 'partisan political activity'** in primary schools, and that political matters arising in school lessons are dealt with in a 'balanced' way.

As part of the plan to involve parents more in schools, the 1986 Act lays down that governors must make an *Annual Report to Parents* and to send this to all parents. They must arrange an Annual Parents' Meeting at which this report will be discussed. If the arents attending number more than 20% of pupils on roll, they may pass resolutions addressed to LEA, governors or headteacher.

The Articles of Government require governors to 'inspect and keep the Authority informed as to the adequacy, condition and state of repair and decoration of the school premises'. The Health and Safety at Work Act 1974 requires **regular inspections** of premises to ensure they are properly and safely maintained and free from hazard, and it is usual for governors to be involved in this, by appointing two or three of their number to join the headteacher or deputy on one of these inspections each year. In Voluntary Aided and Grant Maintained Schools where the governors are the employers, they are, of course, totally responsible for meeting the Health and Safety requirements.

Governors also have responsibility for the times of **school sessions** (within the Acts) and also for fixing the **dates of school holidays** within LEA limits. In practice LEAs fix dates for the whole Authority, after discussion, and governors rubber-stamp this for their school. They usually have an occasional day or two to authorize. In the case of Voluntary Schools this may be used for religious purposes like Ascension Day.

GOVERNORS AND THE 1988 ACT
The 1988 Act has still further extended the powers and duties of governors. Four main areas are affected: finance; admissions; Grant Maintained Schools and Voluntary Aided Schools.

1. Finance. As mentioned in chapter 2 (on management), the Act introduces a scheme of local financial management. This is again designed to give more control of the school to governors, or to take more of the LEA's power away. The LEA must make part of the general schools' budget of the Authority available for allocation to individual schools (except primary schools of fewer than 200 pupils), on the basis of the number and ages of pupils in the schools. The LEA will retain funds sufficient to meet capital building and debt charges, administration of government funds given for specific purposes, and 'other items' which will include the cost of processing teachers' salaries, maintaining inspector and advisor services and various welfare provisions. The governors may then use their share 'as they think fit for the purposes of the school' and may delegate this matter to the headteacher. The governors will not incur any liability for anything done in good faith under this section. The governors are responsible to produce audited accounts for their spending, and the LEA must give them an account of its spending on the school. Both must be included in the Annual Report sent to parents.

The LEA must discuss with all governing bodies and submit a scheme to the Secretary of State showing how it will calculate the amount to be divided, and how it will be divided. If the LEA thinks a governing body shows 'gross incompetence', it can 'suspend' the delegated finance and inform the Secretary of State. The financial management then returns to the LEA until the governors show they can manage properly. These provisions will give governors much wider powers — for example, in staff appointment within the budget given by LEA (see chapter 10); or the ability to use money underspent in one direction (due to a staff vacancy, for example) for some other purpose. This transfer is known as 'virement' and was not allowed before. They will also have many duties at present carried out by LEA departments, such as repairs and maintenance of buildings.

This all amounts to a great addition to governors' responsibility. For a small primary school it may be £100,000; for a large secondary more than one million pounds. Even if an adequate bursar is provided, governors will still be dealing with much larger amounts than most of them are likely to be used to.

The *Times Educational Supplement* gave a sample budget for a primary and a secondary school, with notes to explain the various items. This is given as an appendix to this book and shows the size of the task governors will now be facing.

There will also be initial problems — for example, if the buildings are in very poor repair, the governors may want a guarantee that this will be allowed for in fixing their share.

2. Admissions. Until the 1988 Act, governors of county and controlled schools had admission limits fixed for them by the LEA. This has been on a basis of spreading pupils around to ensure that schools have viable numbers. The new provisions (as mentioned in chapter 4) are designed to promote 'competition'. The LEA may not now fix an admission limit which is less than 'the relevant standard number' — in general this is the number of pupils admitted to a school in the year 1979/80. There are provisions for all sorts of factors that may have happened since then, such as alterations to buildings, and possibly the need for more space by some courses such as GCSE and TVEI. Proposals to reduce the standard number must be submitted to the Secretary of State, with reasons. Admission has always been at the discretion of governors, subject to admission limits set by LEAs. Now governors must take, up to the new 'relevant number', any child whose parent wishes them to come to the school. Governors of county and controlled schools have no power to reduce this number (because they like having more room free, for example) without the approval of the Secretary of State. They can increase the number, after consultation with the LEA. Governors of Voluntary Aided Schools have a little more latitude. LEAs must negotiate admission arrangements with them and consider the ethos of the school — for example, admitting many more non-Catholics to an RC aided school might change its overall ethos.

3. Grant-maintained Schools. This new type of school is introduced by the 1988 Act, again to give parents more choice and spread 'competition'. Some details have already been given in chapters 1 and 4. Here the provisions affecting governors of the school 'opting out' are given:

Grant Maintained status can be achieved at the initiative of either governors or parents of all secondary schools and primary schools with more than 300 pupils.

Governors can resolve by a simple majority to hold a ballot of parents. This decision must be confirmed at a second meeting of governors held twenty-eight days later. Alternatively, a group of parents (a minimum number equal to 20% of the pupils on roll) can give a written request to the governors. The governors must then tell the LEA (and 'consult' with the Trustees of a Voluntary School) and organize a secret postal ballot. Details are given as to how the ballot is to be conducted — at government expense, and giving parents full details of the proposal. If a simple majority of those voting supports the proposal, then the governors must, within six months, publish detailed plans for the Grant Maintained School and submit them to the Secretary of State. Objections may be lodged with the Secretary of State by any ten or more local government electors, by the LEA, by the Trustees or governing body of any school concerned.

If the plan is approved, an instrument of government will be made by the Secretary of State, giving the constitution of the governing body. There must be five parent-governors, one or two teachers, the headteacher, a number of 'first governors' or 'foundation governors' sufficient to ensure they have a majority (two of these must be parents). The term of office will be not less than five nor more than seven years. The Act gives details of how these various groups of governors are to be elected or appointed.

Once the governing body is appointed, all the property, rights and liabilities of the former LEA are transferred to the governing body, along with any rights and liabilities of the former governing body. The LEA is not allowed to dispose of any of the property while the proposals are under consideration.

The staff of the school are transferred to the new Grant Maintained School by regarding their contracts with the former LEA as having been made with the new school on the 'transfer date'. They have no rights of termination of contract 'by reason only of the change in employer' but could have if their job was seriously changed. Governors, as employers, are totally responsible for staff — welfare, in-service training and support, discipline, appointment and dismissal. They can pay over national scales for individual teachers, and this raises anxieties about the provision for shortage subjects in other schools.

The whole of the finance of the school becomes the responsibility of the governing body. It will be financed by the Secretary of State at a rate per pupil equal to that being paid by the LEA for similar schools in the area. The governors may also raise funds themselves and 'accept gifts of money, land or other property.'

Admission must be to an 'approved admission number' calculated like the 'relevant standard' for other schools. Governors cannot admit fewer than this, though they can apply to the Secretary of State to vary the number. This would presumably be intended to stop the governors immediately following a severely selective policy.

There are provisions for ceasing to be Grant Maintained — it requires five years' notice — and regulations for winding up and disposing of property.

This is a far-reaching change of policy in education, based on the belief that there are people prepared to take on this very great responsibility, and also able to run the school better than the LEA and existing governors can do it. The Secretary of State clearly recognizes the crucial importance of governors in the scheme. The Act allows him to appoint two governors if he thinks those appointed are 'not adequately carrying out their responsibilities'.

It is not known how the Secretary of State will assess applications. The discussion documents said he would take account of any reorganization plans in the neighbourhood and that a school would not change its type or character on becoming Grant Maintained. Similar assurances were given in the Parliamentary debate. The Act gives no specific provisions to avoid selection on grounds of race, ability or religion. In some ways it is a return to the Direct Grant School system which was wound up by the Government in 1975. Those schools had a strong link with LEAs, taking at least a quarter of their intake every year by LEA scholarship from among the more able pupils. They also received a (relatively small) grant from the DES. After 1975 many of them chose to go fully independent rather than be absorbed into an LEA system.

The present situation is not exactly parallel, as most of the Direct Grant Schools were of very long standing, with governing bodies of some experience and often considerable financial backing. These schools also had very high academic standing, having catered for able pupils for many years, and being able to 'pick the thoroughbreds'. The new Grant Maintained Schools will have no such base to work from and will have to build up expertise, reputation and capital. There will be restrictions on the governors' ability to make a selective admission policy. They will, of course, have the advantage of a 100% grant which will give some financial security. No doubt it can be done, but it is, like marriage according to the Prayer Book, 'not to be enterprized nor taken in hand unadvisedly, lightly or wantonly . . . but reverently, discreetly, advisedly, soberly and in the fear of God.'

4. Voluntary Aided Schools. Governors are now responsible as employers for all staff, teaching and non-teaching. Previously non-teaching staff were employed by the LEA. Their isolation from the LEA is slightly tempered by the provisions regarding the appointment of headteacher and deputies. The governors must invite the LEA's Chief Education Officer or representative to attend and advise governors at all meetings, including interviews, in connection with these appointments. The Secretary of State can direct that the Chief Education Officer attend where he thinks this is appropriate.

GOVERNOR POWER?

The 1986 and 1988 Acts represent a major transfer of influence to governing bodies, away from LEAs to parents and other members of the community. This rests partly on dislike of a few well-publicized LEAs; partly on distrust of LEA administration — everyone has a horror story of bureaucratic nonsense — and partly on the strongly held political commitment to choice and competition. The argument between supporters and critics of the changes will spring ultimately from views of human society.

The new Acts see the future in individuals taking a hand in their own destiny (and their children's destiny); standing on their own feet; deciding what they want and doing something about it. It suggests that such participation has been stifled by local politicians deciding for everyone what is good for their children. Opponents see the change as a 'devil take the hindmost' policy in which powerful parents look after their own children, and may even get that wrong — instead of showing compassion and care for all.

LEAs have tried to keep a balance and look after the weak as well as the strong. The new policy will set school against school. Governors will compete for the best staff, following the hire-and-fire policies of industry, and will tout for the best pupils. LEAs have tried to see that all schools have a fair share of resources, all teachers have a firm career structure, and all pupils a good education. Also, governors may be here today and gone tomorrow. The LEA stays put.

Most LEAs will admit there is the occasional delay and even the very occasional poor decision. Educational Administration is a profession with its own career structure, so the Building Surveyor dealing with your school may have got a promotion and move just when you thought you had finally tied him down to seeing about the drains. Now you start from square one again. But that could happen anyway, and, besides, will the governors be wizards at getting drains fixed?

Things are rarely as good or as bad as opposing 'sides' make them. For better or worse we have this transfer of power. How can governors make a significant use of it?

WHAT CAN GOVERNORS BRING TO THE JOB?

Some bring **expertise**. Especially with the vastly increased financial responsibility, a person with sound experience of interpreting accounts will be valuable. Someone with wide interviewing and personnel experience will be a godsend. Someone from local industry or commerce will be a useful link and counsellor. A strong chairman is essential, so we hope one governor will be used to making a committee face choices and set priorities. Teacher-governors and headteacher contribute solid knowledge of educational practice and possibility. They are not there just to safeguard sectional interest.

All governors contribute the particular value of lay people — **common sense and concern for children**. It is good for headteachers to have to explain their policies and practices in layman's language. The education industry is weighed down with jargon, some of which is self-justifying. Simply having to write a report and present figures makes a headteacher think whether it makes sense or is just the result of convention. Involving governors in staff selection and interview ensures procedures that are clear and open. Having to present a case for staff discipline for governors' judgment makes for fairer and more balanced consideration.

All governors can be **links with the community**. Parents should feel able to ring them up in praise, blame or question. Employers should know a governor or two. Staff welcome governors visiting the school — it may be embarrassing to be watched, but nice that someone wants to know. One big problem is getting this genuine community link. My student body was about 15% non-white. I never had a non-white governor.

Headteachers value governors' advice, interest and support. Many meet regularly with the chairman, sometimes to clear decisions, sometimes to air questions, always to feel less alone.

Another question which is often asked is, what do governors *need*?

1. Knowledge and skills. Education is a bubbling cauldron of conflicting needs, interests, ideals and philosophies. Teachers and their associations have wrestled with it all for years. Governors need some guide to the debate. Perhaps a book such as this might help them appreciate the terms of discussion, see the conflicts in perspective and make some judgment in particular cases. Knowledge of the particular school is invaluable, too, so that discussion can be on the basis of the real situation. Such knowledge is obtained by visits to the school and taking every opportunity to meet parents and staff. This needs tact. Schools have been closed institutions for a long time and questions are often seen as criticism. Parent-governors will also get a pupil-tinted version of events from their own children.

Governors also need the skills of committee procedure, how to use the formal structure to good effect; what information is needed and how to get it.

2. Commitment. There is a great need for people of large enough vision and heart to take a whole view of the school and community. The Minister of State has appealed to industry to allow its 'best people' to become school governors. More than 20,000 will be needed, she said. Our social structures too often push people into representational roles, speaking for one group, making sure 'we' are not squeezed out. To think widely of all children and staff in the school requires a different view of the world. Governors need to see their appointment as a major commitment, not just a three-times-a-year attendance at a routine meeting.

3. Continuity. One unhappy effect of the increasing political involvement in education has been the lack of continuity on governing bodies. Local authorities can change 'colour' every four years and the new party ensures it is well represented on governing bodies. Sometimes this means appointing people with little time to spare for the job. The new regulations may bring more non-political folk in from the community as co-opted members, prepared to stay a long time. Grant Maintained Schools in particular will need strong people prepared to put in their seven years to get them established.

4. Realism. It is naive to suppose that LEAs have always been niggardly, bungling bureaucracies. They have budgets and bottlenecks and have to make priorities. Now governors will have to set priorities. They will have local financial management — and will say it is inadequate, no doubt. They will no longer have an LEA to kick. Certainly they can get the drains fixed quickly, at a price — and pay for it somewhere else. The wording of the Act is bland: 'spend any sum available . . . as they think fit for the purposes of the school.' Good fund-raisers will be welcome, but they will already know it is hard enough to raise money even for a swimming-pool, and that has to be the only thing you are pushing for the time. The school can easily use the cost of a dozen pools. Hard thinking about priorities will be needed. The carrot is that any economies made in routine running expense will go back to the school. The temptation will be to prune the less obviously vital support for staff and pupils.

5. Training. With all these things to do, governors clearly need training. The Taylor Report saw the size of the job ' . . . the biggest adult education programme this country has ever seen, since, to do the job, governors will need to be familiar with the aims and conduct of learning as never before.' Skill and understanding gives confidence. Legal requirements need careful explaining; possible problems need thought before they arise — for example in role-play; the framework in which the particular school operates must be made clear. LEAs have done a certain amount of training for governors. Other voluntary groups (addresses at the end of the book) have produced material: the Advisory Centre for Education (a booklet); the National Association of Headteachers (a training pack); the National Association of Governors and Managers welcomes members and publishes papers on various aspects of governors' duties. Diocesan Education Boards arrange some courses for governors of voluntary schools in their denomination, and Christians in Education arranges non-denominational training for governors of all types of school. The Open University has a course.

If this new lease of life for governing bodies is met with serious participation and flanked by adequate training, then a new pool of talent will be tapped. This could be a substantial raising of expertise and concern, a large voluntary input into the whole system. Whether it will be as startlingly better than present LEA and governors as the Secretary of State suggests, we shall see. Certainly it could involve more people more intelligently in the local school, and that can't be bad.

BOOKS AND REPORTS

Chapter 1
DES Statistics
Times Educational Supplement
Curriculum 11-16, HMI, DES, 1977
Education for All (Swann Report), HMSO, 1985
Education Observed (series of pamphlets), HMI
DES *Half our Future* (Newsom Report), HMSO, 1963
Education Reform Bill, Brief No.1, NAHT, 1987
Higher Education (Robbins Report), HMSO, 1963
Improving Primary Schools (Thomas Report), ILEA, 1985
Teaching in a Multi-Racial Society, M.E.J. Hobbs, Paternoster, 1987
The Education Act 1944, Dent, ULP, 1957
The Fourth R (Durham Report on Religious Education), SPCK, 1970

Chapter 2
The Uses of Literacy, R. Hoggart, Pelican, 1958
Education and the Working Class, B. Jackson & D. Marsden, RKP, 1962
Towards Better Management of Secondary Education, Audit Commission/Industrial Society, 1987
Mixed Ability Work in Comprehensive Schools, HMI, HMSO, 1978

Chapter 3
Dilemmas of the Curriculum, G.H. Bantock, Robertson, 1980

Chapter 4
Is the School Around the Corner Just the Same? J. McCarroll, Brandsma Books, Dublin, 1987
Opting Out, S. Lawlor, Centre for Policy Studies, 1988

Chapter 6
Action Plan: A Policy 14-18, NAHT, 1986
A Framework for the School Curriculum, DES, 1980
An Alternative Approach to the Curriculum 14-16, SE Regional Examination Board, 1986
Aspects of Secondary Education in England, HMI, HMSO
The National Curriculum 5-16 — a consultation document, DES, 1987

Chapter 7
Commitment & Neutrality in Religious Education, E. Hulmes, Chapman, 1979

Education and Belief, B. Watson, Blackwell, 1987
Parental Attitudes to Religion in State Schools, P.R. May and O.R. Johnston, in Durham Research Review, V:18, April 1967
RI and Surveys, Maurice Hill, National Secular Society, 1968

Chapter 8
General Certificate of Education — A General Introduction; National Criteria, DES, HMSO, 1985
Improving Secondary Schools (Hargreaves Report), ILEA, 1984
National Curriculum: Task Group on Assessment and Testing, DES, 1988

Chapter 9
Ethnic Background & Examination Results, 1985 & 1986, ILEA, 1987
The Sunday Times, 9 December 1979

Chapter 10
A-levels, Age and Degree Performance, D. Rees, (in *Higher Education Review* 13:3 1981)
Education, Unemployment and the Future of Work, A.G. Watts, Open University 1983
Entry Qualifications and Degree Performance, T. Bournier and M. Hamed, CNAA 1987
Higher Education, Meeting the Challenge, DES, HMSO, 1987
Lifeskills Teaching, B. Hopson and M. Scally, McGraw-Hill, 1981

Chapter 11
Conditions of Employment, J. Sutton, SHA, 1987

Chapter 12
Schools for the Future, NAGM/London Diocesan Board for Schools, 1987

ABBREVIATIONS OFTEN USED

IN EDUCATION

ACE	Advisory Centre for Education
ACT	Association of Christian Teachers
AMMA	Assistant Masters and Mistresses Association
APU	Assessment of Performance Unit
AS	Advanced Supplementary Level (GCE)
BTEC	Business and Technician Education Council
CBI	Confederation of British Industry
CEM	Christian Education Movement
CGLI	City and Guilds of London Institute
CHE	College of Higher Education
CIE	Christians in Education
CSE	Certificate of Secondary Education
CTC	City Technology College
CPVE	Certificate of Pre-Vocational Education
CRAC	Careers Research and Advisory Centre
CRCH	Central Register and Clearing House
DES	Department of Education and Science
ESN	Educationally Sub-Normal
FTE	Full-Time-Equivalent
GCE	General Certificate of Education
GCSE	General Certificate of Secondary Education
GDP	Gross Domestic Product
GMS	Grant Maintained School
HMI	Her Majesty's Inspectorate
INSET	In-Service Training
IQ	Intelligence Quotient
LEA	Local Education Authority
MSC	Manpower Services Commission (now Training Commission)
NAHT	National Association of Headteachers
NAME	National Anti-racist Movement in Education

NAS/UWT	National Association of Schoolmasters and Union of Women Teachers
NUT	National Union of Teachers
PAT	Professional Association of Teachers
PCAS	Polytechnics Central Admissions System
PGCE	Post-Graduate Certificate of Education
PNEU	Parents National Education Union
PSE	Personal and Social Education
RSA	Royal Society of Arts
SACRE	Standing Advisory Council for RE
SEC	Secondary Examinations Council
SHA	Secondary Heads Association
TC	Training Commission (formerly MSC)
TVEI	Technical and Vocational Education Initiative
UCCA	Universities Central Council for Admissions
YOP	Youth Opportunities Programme
YTS	Youth Training Scheme

ADDRESSES

Action for Governors' Information and Training (AGIT), c/o Community Education Development Centre, Briton Road, Coventry

Advisory Centre for Education, 18 Victoria Park Square, London E2 9PB

Assistant Masters and Mistresses Association (AMMA), 7 Northumberland Street, London WC2

Association of Christian Teachers, 2 Romelands Hill, St Albans, AL3 4ET

Association of County Councils, Eaton House, 66a Eaton Square, London SW1W 9BH

Association of Metropolitan Authorities, 35 Great Smith Street, Westminster, London SW1P 3BJ

Business and Technician Education Council (BTEC), Central House, Upper Woburn Place, London WC1H OHH

Campaign for the Advancement of State Education (CASE), The Grove, High Street, Sawston, Cambridge.

Careers & Occupational Information Centre (COIC), Rufford Road, Cross Ends, Southport PR9 8LA

Careers Research and Advisory Centre (CRAC), Sheraton House, Castle Park, Cambridge CB3 OAX

Central Register and Clearing House (CRCH), 3 Crawford Place, London W1H 2BN

Centre for the Study of Comprehensive Schools (CSCS), Wentworth College, University of York, Heslington, York YO1 5DD

Christian Education Movement, Lancaster House, Borough Road, Isleworth, Middx TW7 5DU

Christians in Education (CIE), 16 Maids Causeway, Cambridge CB5 8DA

City and Guilds of London Institute (CGLI), 47 Britannia Street, London WC1X 9RG

Commission for Racial Equality, Elliott House, 10 Allington Street, London SW1E 5EA

Council for National Academic Awards (CNAA), 344-54 Grays Inn Road, London WC1X 8PB

Department of Education and Science, Publications Despatch Centre, Canons Park, Honeypot Lane, Stanmore, Middx HA7 1AZ

Education (Journal), 5 Bentinck Street, London W1M 5RN

Library Association, 7 Ridgmount Street, London WC1E 7AE

Manpower Services Commission (MSC), Moorfoot, Sheffield S1 4PQ

National Anti-racist Movement in Education (NAME), PO Box 9, Walsall WS1 3SF

National Association of Governors and Managers (NAGM), 8l Rustlings Road, Sheffield

National Association of Headteachers (NAHT), 1 Heath Square, Boltro Road, Haywards Heath, West Sussex RH16 1BL

National Association of Schoolmasters/Union of Women Teachers (NAS/UWT), Hillscourt, Rose Hill, Rednal, Birmingham B45 8RS

National Association of Teachers in Further and Higher Education (NATFHE), Hamilton House, Mabledon Place, London WC1H 9BH

National Confederation of Parent-Teacher Associations (NCPTA), 43 Stonebridge Road, Northfleet, Gravesend, Kent

National Foundation for Educational Research (NFER), The Mere, Upton Park, Slough SL1 2DQ

National Union of Teachers (NUT), Hamilton House, Mabledon Place, London WC1H 9BD

Open University, Walton Hall, Milton Keynes, Bucks.

Polytechnics Central Admissions System (PCAS), PO Box 67, Cheltenham, Glos. GL50 3AP

Professional Association of Teachers (PAT), 99 Friar Gate, Derby DE1 9BR

School Library Association, 29/31 George Street, Oxford, OX1 2AY

Royal Society of Arts (RSA), Murray Road, Orpington, Kent BR5 HRB

Scripture Union in Schools, 130 City Road, London EC1V 2NJ

Secondary Examinations Council (SEC), [and **School Curriculum Development Committee (SCDC)**] Newcombe House, 45 Notting Hill Gate, London W11 3JB

Secondary Heads Association (SHA), 107 St Paul's Road, Islington, London N1 2NB

Times Educational Supplement, Priory House, St Johns Lane, London EC1M 4BX

Training Commission (formerly Manpower Services Commission), Moorfoot, Sheffield, S1 4PQ

Universities Central Council on Admissions (UCCA), PO Box 28, Cheltenham, Glos. GL50 1HY

SCHOOL EXPENDITURE

AVERAGE, 1986-87

	Primary			Secondary		
	Per pupil	Per school of 200 pupils	% of total	Per pupil	Per school of 800 pupils	% of total
	£	£	%	£	£	%
Teaching & establishment						
(a) Teaching salaries	532.7	106,540	55.8	796.6	637,280	54.7
(b) Educational support	33.0	6,600	3.4	29.7	23,760	2.0
Administration & clerical	13.9	2,780	1.5	24.4	19,520	1.7
(c) Other employee expenses	4.7	9400	0.5	6.6	5,280	0.5
(d) Books, stationery equipment and materials	26.6	5,320	2.8	50.8	40,640	3.5
(e) Other supplies and services	2.4	480	0.3	16.1	12,880	1.1
(f) Establishment expenses	5.9	1,180	0.6	10.5	8,400	0.7
	619.2	123,840	64.8	934.7	747,760	64.2
Premises						
(g) Staff salaries (excluding grounds)	49.1	9,820	5.1	61.0	48,800	4.2
(h) Repairs, alterations, maintenance and grounds	49.0	9,800	5.1	61.8	49,440	4.2
(i) Fuel, light, cleaning materials and water	35.5	7,100	3.7	51.2	40,960	3.5
(j) Furniture and fittings	2.2	440	0.2	3.4	2,720	0.2
(k) Rent, rates etc.	22.8	4,560	2.4	48.2	38,560	3.3
(l) Debt charges	47.7	9,540	5.0	81.4	65,120	5.6
	206.3	41,260	21.6	307.0	245,600	21.0
(m) School meals * all costs less income, but excluding value of pupil free meals	44.2	8,840	4.6	44.2	35,360	3.0
Transport						
(n) Home to school	7.8	1,560	0.8	33.1	26,480	2.3
(o) Other	3.1	620	0.3	4.8	3,480	0.3
	10.9	2,180	1.1	37.9	30,320	2.6
(p) Aid to pupils * (mainly free meals)	19.8	3,960	2.1	25.1	20,080	1.7
(q) Community Education l.e.a. overheads *						
(r) Administration, inspection, psychological and careers services	41.6	8,320	4.4	88.9	71,120	6.1
(s) In-service training (INSET)	12.5	2,500	1.3	17.3	13,840	1.2
	54.1	10,820	5.7	106.2	84,960	7.3
(t) TOTAL EXPENDITURE	954.5	190,900	100.0	1455.1	1,164.280	100.0

Taken from the *Times Educational Supplement* 1988, 'Governors and Governing', Barry Knighton

Index

A

Accountability 71

Achievement 47, 122, 155, 170–71, 174, 175, 176

Act of worship 8, 127, 137, 140–44, 225; withdrawal from 133, 141, 143

Admission policy 8, 17, 19, 31, 47, 85–86, 89, 193, 230–31, 232, 233

Agreed Syllabus 126, 137, 225

Agreed Syllabus Conference 103, 127

Annual General Meeting 48, 228

Annual Report 48, 144, 228, 229

Appointment of staff 8, 15, 17, 34, 40, 57, 89, 207–208, 210–13, 232

Areas of learning 66, 110–14

Assembly *see* Act of worship

Assessment 9, 20, 45, 103, 104, 105, 106–107, 121, 124, 148–72, 173, 175–85, 203, 222

Assessment of Performance Unit (APU) 177

Assistant Masters and Mistresses Association (AMMA) 210

Assisted places scheme 30, 34, 84

Association of Christian Teachers 213

Association of Mathematics Teachers 213

Avon County Resources Centre 132

B

Bachelor of Education (BEd) 206

Baker, Kenneth 7–10, 12, 25, 103, 204, 209

Bantock, G.H. 70

Barking 166

Barnet 166

Beloe Report *see* Educational reports

Bennett, Neville 44

Birth rate 23, 102, 185, 201, 206–207

Black Papers 180

Black, Professor 159, 203

Boarding schools 20, 91–93

Brent 183

Brighouse, Tim 58

British Humanist Association 129

BTEC (Business and Technician Education Council) *see* Examinations

Burnham Committee 208–209

Bursars 33, 57, 230

Butler, R.A. 10, 126

C

Callaghan, James 99, 103

Cambridge University 84

Capitation *see* General Allowance

Careers, preparation for 37, 66, 82, 104, 116, 120, 121, 122, 139, 188–204, 222

Careers Service 198

Cattell 166

CBI 176

Centre for Policy Studies 90

Certificate of Education 206

Certificate of Office Studies 197

CGLI (City and Guilds) *see* Examinations

Cheshire 183

Christian Action Research and Education 134

Christian Education Movement (CEM) 128, 213

Church of England 12, 91, 126, 144

Churches 10, 127–28, 143; schools 11–12, 85–86, 91, 126

Churchill, Winston 126, 221

City Technology Colleges (CTCs) 9, 13, 17–18, 24, 201–202, 221

Clegg, Alec 178
Colleges' Register and Clearing House (CRCH) 195, 196
Community 18, 25, 47–51, 56, 82, 119, 185, 227, 228
 service 201
Community colleges 50–51
Community homes 93
Competition 69, 82, 91, 93, 161, 231
The Comprehensive Experiment 181
Comprehensive schools 20–21, 23, 31, 42–43, 45, 46, 49, 51, 53–54, 98, 106, 138, 173, 178–182, 187, 216, 219
Concepts 62–63, 104, 112, 113, 117, 118, 132, 138, 154, 175, 198
Conditions of service 17, 35, 103, 208–210, 212, 214
Conservative Party 9, 21, 24–25, 129, 149
Corporal punishment 34
Counselling 34, 37, 40, 124
County Careers Officer 37
County schools 15, 18, 19, 47, 86, 126, 132, 140, 225, 227, 230
CPVE (Certificate of Pre-Vocational Education) *see* Examinations
Criteria 153–54, 155, 159
Crowther Report *see* Educational reports
Culture 48–55, 217
Curriculum 9, 17, 37, 43, 48, 49, 51, 52–53, 78, 79–80, 81, 82, 86, 89, 91, 97–125, 126, 127, 129, 152, 159, 164, 198, 216, 228
see also National Curriculum

D
Daily Herald 148
Davie, Dr 180
Dawson, Peter 76
Department of Education and Science (DES) 8, 15, 18, 26, 70, 109, 114, 144, 163, 164, 171, 190, 198, 201, 206, 207, 212, 221, 225, 232
Department of Employment 188, 190, 201
Deputy heads 33, 34, 229
Devlin, Lord Justice 77, 131, 139
Dewsbury 95

Diploma in Business Studies 197
Direct grant schools 232–33
Discovery method 68
Discrimination 52–55, 200, 217
Discipline 31, 33–34, 48, 50, 52, 76, 89, 94, 216
Drew, Nicholas 196–97
Dual-system education 15
Durham Report *see* Educational reports

E
Edinburgh Review 81
Education Acts (1870) 11–12, 15, 127–28; (1902) 12, 13; (1944) 7, 8, 10, 20, 22, 65, 77, 97, 126, 127, 130, 138, 140, 141, 142, 221, 224, 225; (1976) 24; (1980) 9, 86; (1981) 9; (1986) 9, 34, 48, 75, 111, 139, 222, 224, 226, 228; (1988) 7–10, 13, 17–18, 22, 31, 32, 34, 40, 56, 57, 59, 69, 72–73, 86–87, 89, 93, 94, 97, 103–105, 110, 111, 113, 126–27, 129, 137, 138, 140, 142, 143, 144, 152, 158, 163, 172, 173, 175, 184, 193, 201–204, 210–213, 213, 221, 225, 228, 229–33
Education Otherwise 22
Education vouchers 93–94
Educational psychology 19, 61–63
Educational reports
 Beloe 148;
 Crowther 128;
 Durham 72, 126, 135, 140;
 Hadow 95;
 Hargreaves 170–71;
 Newsom 29, 98, 128;
 Norwood 65, 148;
 Nottingham 52, 63;
 Plowden 29, 44, 128;
 Robbins 29, 98;
 Spens 128;
 Swann 25, 52, 58, 64–65, 183, 217;
 Thomas 55, 111
Educationally sub-normal (ESN) 65
Eleven Plus *see* Examinations
Elvaston Castle 203
Employers 107, 114, 148 164, 170, 174, 188, 198
Employment skills 37, 107, 122, 199

England 13, 22
Etchells, Ruth 169
Evolution 59–60
Examinations 30, 37, 44, 45–46, 48, 50, 83, 89, 107, 121, 124, 148–72, 175–85;
  Eleven Plus 44, 45, 63–64, 98–99, 149;
  School Certificate 148, 149;
  Higher School Certificate 148;
  GCE 45, 148, 153, 155, 177, 184;
  O-level 106, 114, 122, 148, 149, 153, 155, 156, 158, 166, 167, 168, 177, 178, 179, 183, 197, 206;
  A-level 48, 51, 84, 91, 106, 120, 121, 122, 123, 149, 152, 156, 167, 168, 176, 177, 178, 180–81, 185, 191, 192, 193–95, 196, 197, 206, 215;
  CSE 45, 106, 114, 148, 149, 153, 177, 183–84;
  GCSE 48, 51, 83, 91, 118–19, 121, 122, 123, 148, 149, 153–58, 160, 168, 176, 191–92, 203, 213, 222, 230;
  AS-level 152, 191, 193;
  CPVE 66, 122–23, 140, 171, 191, 192, 199, 213;
  RSA 191, 192;
  CGLI 191, 192;
  BTEC 191, 192, 193, 195
Eysneck, H. 65

F

'Family' groups 32
Farmington Institute for Christian Studies 136
Further education 15, 22, 36–37, 97, 174, 185
Further education colleges 9, 21, 22, 26, 120, 121, 122, 123, 190, 192

G

General Allowance 55, 57
General education 32, 40, 120
Governing bodies 8, 9, 13, 15, 18, 75, 76, 224–28, 229, 231–33
Governors 9, 15, 17, 18, 31, 32, 33, 34, 35, 41, 47–48, 55–57, 75, 76, 77, 85, 87, 88, 89–90, 103, 127, 138, 139, 142, 143, 145, 147, 159, 210–12, 213, 224–37

Grammar schools 20, 21, 24, 40, 45, 50, 53–54, 63, 97–98, 106, 128, 129, 138, 142, 148, 149, 178–82, 205, 216
Grant Maintained Schools 8, 13, 18, 24, 30, 34, 88–91, 127, 161, 209, 212–13, 226, 229, 231–33

H

Hadow Report *see* Educational reports
Handicapped children *see* Special needs
Hargreaves Report *see* Educational reports
Haringey 183
Harrow 179
Heads of department 35, 137
Headteachers 17, 31–35, 37, 42, 45, 48, 55, 58, 71, 74, 75, 76, 78, 81, 89, 90, 96, 103, 105, 127, 137, 138, 142, 143, 145, 147, 161, 170, 184, 209, 211, 219, 224, 226, 227, 228, 229, 231
Health and Safety at Work Act (1974) 34, 228–29
Health education 80, 110, 112, 139–40
Her Majesty's Inspectors (HMI) 9, 15, 32, 42, 46, 76, 107, 109, 110, 138, 158, 175, 203, 212
Hereward College 196–97
Hidden curriculum 58, 92, 109
Higginson Committee 152
Higher education 9, 35, 36, 37, 106, 107, 120, 123, 174, 186, 191, 193–96, 202
Higher Education Corporation 9
Historical Association 213
Hoggart, Richard 49
Home, education at 22, 78
House head/tutor 31, 34, 36, 42
Huddersfield Grammar School 50
Hulmes, Edward 136

I

In loco parentis 27, 78, 80, 221
Incentive allowances 34, 41
Independent schools 13, 22, 26, 27, 30, 34, 83–85, 90–91, 93, 94, 98, 102, 106, 128, 129, 142, 148, 178, 207, 209, 216, 219, 232;
  Christian-run 79, 220
Indoctrination 85, 135–36, 137, 140

Industry 17, 35, 99, 107, 113, 120, 123, 169, 176–77, 188–89, 202, 221
Information technology 99, 105, 121, 122, 124, 199
Inner London Education Authority (ILEA) 9, 13, 30, 52, 55, 183–84, 212
In-service training (INSET) 19, 30, 35, 40, 53, 54, 90, 121, 139, 144, 158, 209, 210, 213, 232
Instrument and Articles of Government 31, 34, 224, 225, 226, 228
Intelligence 50, 55, 63–65, 166, 203
Intelligence quotient (IQ) 44, 45, 63–65, 106, 149
Inter-School Christian Fellowship (ISCF) 128–29
Isle of Wight 183

J
Jackson, D. 50
Jensen, Arthur 64, 65
Johnson, President 70
Joint Matriculation Board 156, 178
Joseph, Keith 9, 158, 167

K
Ken, Bishop 69
Kent Education Authority 94

L
Labour Party 24, 84, 129, 149
Lancaster University 44
Leaving age 11, 99, 138, 149, 205
Leisure 107, 114, 201
Lewis, C.S. 60
Libraries 37, 53, 56
Life skills 37, 51, 99, 107, 110, 116, 118, 196, 201
Liverpool, Archbishop of 126
Local Education Authorities (LEAs) 8, 12–17, 18, 19, 20, 22–24, 25, 26, 27–30, 31, 32, 33, 34, 41, 48, 51, 55–58, 64, 76, 78, 82, 85, 86–87, 88–89, 90–91, 93, 95, 103, 105, 120–21, 126, 127, 137, 139, 144, 149, 159, 166, 171, 183, 193, 198, 207, 208, 210–13, 214, 219, 224, 225, 226, 227, 228, 229–37

Local financial management 8, 17, 32–33, 55–58, 89, 90, 209, 210, 213, 229–30
Local Government Act (1988) 139
London, Bishop of 144
London School Board 128

M
Machiavelli 125
MacInnes, Colin 49
Management 21, 31–58, 70–71, 227
Manchester Grammar School 180
Manpower Services Commission 120, 171, 188, 190, 221
Marsden, B. 50
Mason, Charlotte 22
Matrix system 40–41
Mitchell, Basil 135
Mixed ability 32, 46–47, 80
Moral education 59, 67, 110, 112, 123, 129, 130–31
Motivation 68, 89, 118–19, 122, 123, 124, 170, 184
Mowrer, Herbert 67–68
Multi-cultural education 52–55, 58, 64–65, 136–37, 141, 142, 143, 183–84, 217–18
Murgatroyd 181

N
National Anti-Racist Movement in Education 213
National Association for the Teaching of English 213
National Association of Headteachers (NAHT) 22, 30, 123–24, 190
National Association of Schoolmasters and Union of Women Teachers (NAS/UWT) 210, 220
National Child Development Study (NCDS) 179–80
National Children's Bureau 180
National Curriculum 8, 9, 18–19, 91, 97, 103–106, 109–114, 161, 167–70, 173, 201, 202, 221, 228
National Curriculum Council (NCC) 8, 103
National Curriculum Testing 159–64, 167–68, 185, 203, 222–23

248

National Foundation for Educational
    Research 220
National School Students Union 74
National Secular Society 129, 134
National Union of Teachers (NUT)
    210, 214, 220
National Vocational Qualifications
    Committee 191
Negotiated assessment 171–72
Neutrality 136, 138
Newcastle Commission 11, 27
Newsom Report *see* Educational
    reports
Norm-referencing 155, 178
Northampton 20
Northern Ireland 13
Norwood Report *see* Educational
    reports
Nottingham Report *see* Educational
    reports
Nursery schools 22

O

Open evenings 48, 82; *see also* Parents
Open plan 44
'Opting out' 8, 18–19, 24, 76, 88–91,
    231
Oxford Polytechnic 195
Oxford University 84

P

Parents 25, 27, 34, 42, 43, 47–48, 51, 52,
    70, 74–96, 98, 129, 149, 159, 163,
    216, 221–22;
  choice of schools 15, 22, 83–93;
  governors 18–19, 75, 77, 224–37
  involvement 9, 54–55, 56, 75–76, 79–
    80, 94, 147, 185, 228;
  meetings 32, 36, 37, 48, 75, 209, 220;
  rights 17, 18, 24, 78–79, 86, 88, 95,
    105, 127, 138, 143, 145, 222, 228,
    230, 231
Parents National Educational Union
    (PNEU) 22
Parent-Teacher Associations 48, 75, 94
PCAS (Polytechnics' Central
    Admission System) 36, 195, 196
Personal and Social Education (PSE)
    99, 104, 124, 139–40, 201; *see also*

Social education, Life skills
Piaget, Jean 61–62, 117
Pipes, Michael 30
Plato 64
Plowden Report *see* Educational
    reports
Policy Study Unit 30
Political education 111, 228
Polytechnics 9, 22, 27, 36, 37, 98, 120,
    174, 186, 193, 195, 206
Polytechnics and Colleges Funding
    Council 193
Post-Graduate Certificate in Education
    (PGCE) 205–206
Preparatory schools 102
Pre–school education 22
Primary schools 18, 27–28, 32, 33, 34,
    36, 41–42, 43, 45, 46, 47, 50, 53, 55,
    56, 68, 85, 87, 88, 99, 102, 110–11,
    117, 118, 128, 137, 141, 158, 159–60,
    177, 185, 205, 206, 207, 210, 216,
    220, 222, 225, 226, 227, 228, 229,
    230, 231
Problem–solving 68, 107, 112, 113, 114,
    116, 121, 122, 154, 155, 158, 170,
    175, 199, 202
Professional Association of Teachers
    (PAT) 76, 210
Profile 160
Public schools *see* Independent schools

R

Racism 25, 52, 53, 54, 55, 130, 217
Records of achievement 170–72
Redeployment 89, 208, 210, 212
Religious education (RE) 12, 15, 18–
    19, 48, 72, 89, 103, 104, 110, 112–13,
    117, 118, 119, 126–147, 154–55, 225;
  withdrawal from 127, 141
Remuneration of Teachers Act (1965)
    208, 209
Reynold 181
Robbins Report *see* Educational
    reports
Roman Catholic Church 12, 87, 91, 126
RSA (Royal Society of Acts) *see*
    Examinations

249

S

Salaries 17, 29, 34, 41, 56–57, 103, 137, 201, 208–209, 210, 212, 220–21, 232

School Certificate *see* Examinations

School Examination and Assessment Council 8

School leavers 36–37, 66, 102, 121–122, 170–71, 177, 188–204, 207

School Leaving Certificate 170

Schools Council for Curriculum and Examinations 98, 149

Scotland 13, 177

Scripture Union in Schools 128–29

Secondary Examinations Council (SEC) 153

Secondary Heads Association (SHA) 85, 124–25

Secondary modern schools 20, 50, 53, 97, 148, 149, 179–80, 181–82, 206

Secondary School Examinations Council 148

Secondary schools 12, 20, 27–29, 33, 34, 36, 37, 41, 45, 48, 50, 56, 83, 99, 106, 117, 118, 138, 141, 176, 177, 183, 205, 207, 216, 220, 222, 225, 230, 231

Secretary of State for Education and Science 7, 9, 13–15, 17, 18–19, 22, 35, 56, 57, 60, 66, 75–76, 87, 90, 91, 93, 95, 103,.104, 105, 127, 134, 135, 139, 143, 149, 152, 158, 173, 175, 201, 202, 209, 224, 225, 228, 230, 231, 232, 233, 237

Selective system 20–21, 23, 31, 45–46, 63, 65, 94, 97–98, 149, 178–79, 205–206

Self-esteem 61, 107, 172

Setting 32, 46

Sex Discrimination Act (1975) 120

Sex education 27, 48, 75, 89, 111, 112, 114, 139, 228

Sixth-form colleges 21, 41, 191–92, 215

Skills 44, 51, 61, 66, 103, 104, 110, 112, 113, 115–16, 118, 119, 120, 122, 123, 125, 131–32, 140, 152, 154, 155, 158, 161, 167, 170, 175, 181, 197, 199, 200, 202;
  see also Life skills

Skinner, B.F. 61, 63

Social education 25, 48–50, 58, 62, 67, 99, 111, 122, 123, 170;
  see also Personal and Social Education

Special needs 19–20, 32, 87–88, 91–92, 93, 114, 161, 196

Special schools 15, 18, 19, 56, 87–88, 93

Spens Report *see* Educational reports

Staff appraisal 213–15, 220

Staffing ratios 20, 41, 205

Standards 7–8, 46, 49, 55, 161–64, 173–87, 195, 217

Standing Advisory Council for Religious Education (SACRE) 143, 144

Standing Conference of Regional Examination Boards 119

Stapleford 213

State 78–79; *see also* Department of Education and Science, Education Acts, Secretary of State for Education and Science

Stereotypes 46, 53–54, 64–65, 70, 218

Streaming 32, 45–47, 50, 106

Stress 218–20

Sullivan 181–82

Sunday Times 21

Swallow, John 125

Swann Commissions 64–65

Swann Report *see* Educational reports

T

Tameside 25

Taylor Commission 9, 75, 225

Teacher training colleges 128, 195, 205–206

Teachers' associations (unions) 89, 90, 103, 104, 126, 206, 210, 212, 213;
  see also individual entries

Teachers' Pay and Conditions Act (1987) 209–210

Teachers' training 40, 205–206, 218;
  see also In-service training

Teaching style 43–45, 68, 98, 186

Technical colleges 99

Technical schools 20, 97

Technological change 70, 99

Technological education 9, 17, 113–114, 202, 203

Tertiary colleges 21, 41, 192, 215

Thatcher, Margaret 178
Thomas Report *see* Educational reports
Thring, Dr 42
Tile Hill College 197
Times Educational Supplement 44–45, 49, 53, 102–103, 145, 159, 175, 220, 230
Tower Hamlets 52
Trades Union Congress 23
Training Commission 120, 188, 221; *see also* Manpower Services Commission
Travel 13, 85, 93
Truancy 76
TVEI (Technical and Vocational Educational Initiative) 121–22, 123, 140, 171, 190, 213, 230

U
UCCA (Universities' Central Council for Admissions) 36, 193–94, 195
Understanding 103, 111, 113, 117, 132, 155, 158, 161
Unemployment 102, 114, 166, 188, 199–201
Uniforms 33, 94
Universities 9, 15, 22, 30, 36, 37, 84, 98, 106, 120, 152, 174, 185, 193–94, 196, 206, 207
Uppingham School 42
Utilitarianism 67

V
Vaizey, John 29
Vandalism 51, 67
Voluntary Aided Schools 12, 13, 15–16, 18–19, 31, 83, 85–86, 91, 126, 132, 140, 224, 225–26, 228, 229, 230–31
Voluntary Controlled Schools 12, 15, 18–19, 31, 85, 126, 132, 140, 224, 225–26, 227, 229

W
Wales 13, 22
Warnock Committee (1978) 19, 87–88
Wensleydale 104
Work experience 17, 37, 116, 120, 124, 202
Wragg, E.C. 44

Y
Year head/tutor 31, 34, 35, 36, 42, 52, 222
YTS (Youth Training Scheme) 35, 37, 125, 171, 188, 190, 192, 197, 199, 201

SINGLE PARENT

Maggie Durran

'When I left school I was pregnant and soon married.' So begins Maggie Durran's story. Six weeks after the baby was born, the marriage broke down. *Single Parent* is about the next twenty years — the pain, the heartache, and the hope.

This book offers real encouragement to parents who are struggling. With warmth and honesty Maggie Durran looks at the problems of single parenthood and shares her own experience of how a single parent family found its own identity.

Single Parent also gives pratical advice on how and where to find help. It's a book for any lone parent, and for anyone concerned to help and understand an increasing number of families in society today.

ISBN 0 85648 848 8

BELIEF IN A MIXED SOCIETY

Christopher Lamb

Western society is now irretrievably mixed and
pluralist. In Bradford, a third of babies born are of
Asian origin. Thirty schools in the inner city have
more than 50 per cent Asian Muslim children. A
councillor told a BBC Panorama team: 'We're
sitting on a time-bomb here. You've only got to
look at the figures to see what the risks are.'

What happens to religious conviction in such a
society? Many from Muslim and Hindu
backgrounds see the West as bankrupt of moral and
spiritual values. Those from a traditional Christian
background may be deeply suspicious of the
'threat' of non-Christian cultures.

How far are schools a battleground, how far are
they a unifying influence in society? What is the
place of religion in schools? How far should we
respect different attitudes to women in society, to
marriage and the family? Food, health, morality
and the law, attitudes to work, to freedom and
truth in the media, to wealth and power, all these
are areas in which people have to come to terms
with those of other faiths or none.

Christopher Lamb writes from personal experience
of living in an Asian culture, academic study of
Islam and from constant contact with the most
pluralist parts of Britain. From 1979 he has been
co-ordinator of the Other Faiths Theological
Project, run jointly by two Anglican missionary
societies. He and his family live in Birmingham,
where his wife teaches English to children newly-
arrived in Britain.

ISBN 0 85648 210 2

CHARNWOOD

Grace Wyatt with Clive Langmead

Charnwood is the name of a very remarkable
nursery centre which gives handicapped and normal
children the opportunity to play, learn and grow
together. Today the experts readily acknowledge
the all-round benefits of this kind of integrated
learning. In the 1960s, when Grace Wyatt's pioneer
work began, it was a very different matter and there
were many battles to fight.

This is a story of handicapped children and their
families, the agonies and the triumphs. It carries a
strong message of hope for all who are in any way
involved with handicap, and for the 'normal' too.
There is joy in loving a child purely for who he is,
and great reward in seeing children with very
different abilites play together in a child-world
untouched by lables and restrictions.

ISBN 0 7459 1137 4

A selection of top titles from LION PUBLISHING

SOCIAL CONCERN

BELIEF IN A MIXED SOCIETY
Dr Christopher Lamb   £3.95 ☐
MAKING UNEMPLOYMENT WORK
Dr Michael Moynagh   £3.95 ☐
SOCIAL WORK: A Christian Perspective
Terry Philpot   £4.95 ☐
CHARNWOOD
Grace Wyatt with Clive Langmead   £2.50 ☐
CHRISTIANITY ON TRIAL Colin Chapman   £4.95 ☐
WHOSE PROMISED LAND Colin Chapman   £3.50 ☐
THE STRESS MYTH Richard Ecker   £3.95 ☐
SINGLE PARENT Maggie Durran   £1.95 ☐

All Lion paperbacks are available from your local bookshop or newsagent, or can be ordered direct from the address below. Just tick the titles you want and fill in the form.

Name (Block letters) ....

Address ....

....

Write to Lion Publishing, Cash Sales Department, PO Box 11, Falmouth, Cornwall TR10 9EN, England.

Please enclose a cheque or postal order to the value of the cover price plus:

UK: 60p for the first book, 25p for the second book and 15p for each additional book ordered to a maximum charge of £1.90.

OVERSEAS: £1.25 for the first book, 75p for the second book plus 28p per copy for each additional book.

BFPO: 60p for the first book, 25p for the second book plus 15p per copy for the next seven books, thereafter 9p per book.

Lion publishing reserves the right to show on covers and charge retail prices which may differ from those previously advertised in the text or elsewhere, and to increase postal rates in accordance with the Post Office.